THE GROUND BELOW ZERO

9/11 to Burning Man, New Orleans to Darfur,
Haiti to Occupy Wall Street

NICHOLAS POWERS

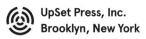

UpSet Press, Inc.
Brooklyn, New York

UpSet Press, Inc.
P.O. Box 200340
Brooklyn, NY 11220
www.upsetpress.org

Cover photograph by Jason Florio
Cover and text design by Aaron Kenedi

Library of Congress Control Number: 2013938666

UPSET PRESS is an independent press based in Brooklyn. The original impetus of the press was to upset the status quo through literature. The press has expanded its mission to promote new work by new authors; the first works, or complete works, of established authors, including restoring to print new editions of important texts; and first time translations of works into English. Overall, the Press endeavors to advance authors' innovative visions and bodies of work that engender new directions in literature.

Established in 2000, UpSet Press organized readings and ran writing workshops until 2005, when it published its first book, *Theater of War*, by Nicholas Powers. The Press has increased its publishing efforts in recent years and has multiple titles forthcoming in 2014. The University of Arkansas Press became the official distributor of UpSet Press in 2011. For more information, visit upsetpress.org.

First printing, Fall 2013
ISBN 9781937357993
Printed in the USA
10 9 8 7 6 5 4 3 2 1

Reader, this book straddles genres of memoir, fantasy, journalism and myth. I have condensed scenes, changed dialogue and at times just made things up. The pieces that were published as journalism are exactly that – names, places and actions are reported as happened. Everything else is more than true.

ACKNOWLEDGMENTS

Mom, thank you for this vision. You gave me your experience before I knew the world. When I entered it, I discovered so much of what you said was true.

Chris, thank you for sharing with me your life, your humor, your courage worn like snug, broken-in leather. You freed yourself from a bigotry that could have killed you by the strength of your mind. I learned how to dance around bombs from you.

Rob, thank you for believing in me, for gambling to make money to publish our dreams, and for the long talks, where we unraveled our confusion.

And Dawn, thank you for being my muse and best friend, my adversary and my sunrise.

My brother Brad, our epic adventures opened new worlds for me and I love you for being the brave one.

Jason, thank you for sharing with us the photo that became the cover. You took it at one of the most harrowing moments of your life.

Big up to my students, you have inspired me over the years. Wayne Koestenbaum, you encouraged me to play with my voice and to be wary of microwavable rhetoric. Barbara Webb and James de Jongh, you guided my dissertation to clarity. DJ Lee Mayjahs, I thank you for giving me a soundtrack for my many transformations. Arun Gupta, our long-ass arguments, debates and hilarity deepened me. John Tartleton, you have been a constant friend and editor over the years. Thanks to everyone at the Indypendent (Frank, Liz) who gave me the space to write many of these articles.

CONTENTS

FOREWORD

The Ground Below Zero introduces a new and important voice, one with a trajectory reaching from New York's left and alternative cultures to the present world's vistas of death. It is a voice partly urban-hip and partly epic and tragic. The story it tells is part journalism, part memoir, and part prophetic-apocalyptic vision.

The journalism, about a third of the whole, responds to the apocalypses of the past dozen years. The chapters cover flood-hit New Orleans, genocide in Darfur, the police murder of Sean Bell and the daily disasters of Nicholas Powers' Brooklyn community. They take us to Burning Man, the half laughable, half sublime alternative world built and destroyed yearly in the Nevada desert, and its satellite festivals. They touch on New Age idiocy and the machinelike pounding of leftist orthodoxy.

Journalism, an ephemeral genre, can live again only if written with a poet's sensibility, one in tune with an era's inner pulse, its horror and silliness, its intermittent prophetic fires. And that is exactly Powers' sensibility. The journalism here is joined seamlessly to the autobiographical narrative of a young man arriving in New York for graduate study just before 9/11.

We learn of his family background, with its own all too common terrors; of the small and ultimately failed harbors of love and sex; of the commitment to first-hand witness that takes him on his journeys. Irony, honesty, and empathy both sustain and torment him on these journeys and on his return. If the journalistic voice is sometimes constrained by the requirement for closure within a set word limit, the memoirist's voice is open, questing, and unsure of itself or its place in the bubble of privileged life atop the long mudslide of contemporary history.

The book moves along a steel spine reaching from the largest events to one's mental states. It witnesses the immense violence piercing downward into everyday life. It exposes the hatred mirrored in self-hate and replicated in exploitation. We see in the text Haitian police stealing and selling relief supplies, leftists and humanitarians profiting psychically as well as politically from social disasters. And we experience the answering moments of love, in the bedroom or beneath tarps at Occupy Wall Street, in the street on the night of Barack Obama's election victory, in vision at Burning Man.

The style in turn moves from factual narrative through counterfactual fantasy to phantasmagoric vision. So an early chapter, "Notes from the Underground," encompasses in a relationship's beginning the end that has already occurred, from which only a possible future may free us. Balancing this, near the end of the book, "The Last Horizon" moves forward and backward in time to a relationship's start that prefigures one of its possible endings. So, too, the drowning seas and possible rebirth of the Middle Passage, evoked in a chapter near the beginning, sound again in the universal vortex and possible renewal of its apocalyptic conclusion.

The Ground Below Zero, which starts in factual destruction, ends in prophetic vision. It is a vision in which Powers dares to rewrite Greek myth, one that reminds us of the dry bones reviving in Ezekiel and the seas yielding up their dead in Revelation. It is a vision—Powers' imagination suggests—whose realization lies within our power but only if we can bear to face what they are doing to us, what we are partly doing to ourselves, only if we can make with him the journey from 9/11 to Burning Man, New Orleans to Darfur, Haiti to Occupy Wall Street and beyond.

– Christopher Z. Hobson
April 2013

PREFACE

After 9/11 we asked, "Why do they hate us?" The question itself is telling. American amnesia is like a fog that is cleared by reading history. The War on Terror began sixty years ago when the United States and Soviet Union stood over the rubble of World War Two and fought to own the future. One capitalist, the other communist – both peered over the Iron Wall and saw an enemy half-imagined, half-real. They paid foreign leaders, created client states to encircle each other and then armed, in turn, the political opposition of their mutual enemies. They built tens of thousands of nuclear missiles and aimed the arsenals at us, the people, trapped between them. I remember having childhood nightmares of bright rising mushroom clouds.

Our government was in a blind rush to defeat the U.S.S.R. and when they invaded Afghanistan, we funded Islamic rebels to fight them. Our reckless arming of religious fundamentalists set the region on fire. "You're creating a Frankenstein," Pakistan's Prime Minister Benazir Bhutto warned President George H. W. Bush. He of course didn't care and two decades later, his son, elected president in 2001, listened in dumb terror as an aid told him that al-Qaeda rammed jets into the Twin Towers.

In New York, we staggered home in a blizzard of ash. Panicked that bombs would explode in subways, our rage filled the city like a mist of gasoline. Another attack would ignite hate mobs to hunt Muslims. It was terrible. We swallowed questions as politicians on TV banged the drums of war. Osama bin Laden's face was on "Wanted Dead or Alive" posters in stores. On TV, our military marched into Kabul.

A year later, I was on the far side of the nation in a seemingly endless desert. Friends told me of a wild neo-pagan ritual in the Nevada badlands. In August 2002 we drove into a carnival city of tents in a vast dried out lakebed. It was Burning Man, a seven day festival in which we burned, on the last night, a nearly

100ft tall effigy called The Man. It symbolized, for me, the nation state that drove the planet to war. After The Man crashed into an orange blaze, I danced around the bright heat and felt the terror of 9/11 flying out of me. The tall flames made us into shadows leaping in and out of the light. Staring at the reddish blaze, I imagined it was Dresden, Hiroshima, Ground Zero and Kabul; soon, I knew it would be Baghdad.

After Burning Man, I returned to New York with a need to feel history. When a crisis hit, I ran to the epicenter to read its truth with my senses. Like the War on Terror, I learned each disaster was the past becoming present that was pushed by the ruling class back into the silent masses. Once there, it was kept from view, building pressure.

The lessons were painful. I helped families wade through black water in a drowned New Orleans and interviewed Darfur refugees in aid camps. History was a nightmare but it was also the euphoria of freedom like hugging strangers on Obama's first election night, singing at anti-war marches or camping at Occupy Wall Street. I was a human pendulum swinging between terror and ecstasy. And with each stroke, I cut further beneath the ever present "now" and felt the building pressure of earlier decades erupting in our lives in the form of war, flood and revolt.

The Spiral of History

In the 1980s, if mom and I missed the bus, we walked home and her voice lit the night like a movie projector. I saw her childhood was a single cold wind blowing between her parents. Grandpa was old when he married Grandma and did not see her resentment at being his crutch. He also gambled, not seeing how others judged it reckless. He lent money not realizing it could not buy respect. At his life's end, glaucoma clouded his eyes and those last years of blindness symbolized his life.

Grandma never forgave mom for being born dark or the child of a husband she hated. They lived in a Puerto Rican enclave in 1950s Brooklyn, an island of Spanish in an English speaking New York. Mom stayed in that tiny world until a college teacher gave her the *New York Times* to read and soon the outside became clearer, more navigable and she walked into an America fighting loudly over the Vietnam War.

At the rallies, the ideas of the New Left boomed over megaphones and settled like a healing mist into her eyes. She saw her darkness as beauty and raised her fist. She opened a community center. She hosted parties where Black Panthers and Young Lords boasted of the impending fire. One night, a nationalist who used bombs came into the room and the air electrified with danger and promise. She worked for The People but it was still work and when tired of politics she hung out with hippies, tonguing LSD, dancing under lights that circled her outstretched hands like comets.

When the fun became aimless she returned to The Struggle. But after '68 she saw comrades stumbling in the street with glazed eyes and deep inward stares. "I swear," she said during a walk home, "the government let drugs into the city to destroy our politics." The 1970s came, passion ebbed. Her friends floated in the debris of the Movement. And she moved on to carve a life in reactionary America.

In the 1990s she felt safe enough to tell me more. I learned that she squirmed into cracks left open by The Movement, after college she became a secretary at high-end offices. One night she met a man named Joe Rivera. They had a night of haphazard sex and I was the accidental consequence. She didn't love him but she loved the idea of me. Mom kept me like a grain of sand around which she planned to create a translucent, pearled life.

Method Writing

I became a Leftist to play a role in the fiery drama of my mother's youth. By middle-school it was instinctive reflex. When President Reagan was shot, I stared in disbelief at teachers openly weeping. By college, Leftism was a mask of militancy to scare people or a sign of commitment to shame them. I walked around with an open book, reciting what were for me beautiful myths. They gave me the innocence of other people's suffering and the nobility of sacrifice but not an answer to my personal questions.

In 2001, I was accepted to the Graduate Center in Manhattan. I moved to New York in August and it was there, shaken by the collapse of the Towers, swept in the anti-war marches, that I began to write. I took ideas from my classes to the street. Roland Barthes' book *Mythologies* and Freud's *The Psychoanalysis of Everyday Life* were models. It is possible, if not endurable, to see the invisible architecture of ideas that gives our actions meaning; the challenge is to remain in that line of vision. I thought it would change the reader by showing how each object and act was embedded in a constellation of ideology.

It was my way of keeping sane during the crisis years after 9/11 when the Terror Alert System injected spasms of fear into us. After class, I'd walk out of the 34th street Graduate Center into the shadow of the Empire State Building, the tallest skyscraper left in New York, and wondered if one day a terrorist attack would collapse it and I would be crushed when it fell.

Even though it was a new war and a new generation, I was walking in my mother's footsteps. She had been here before and we stood superimposed upon each other, a Nuyorican woman of the 1960s and me, in the New Millennium, both of us living in a nation at war over "The War." Her voice was once my destiny, it resurrected me from the flux and flow of change but in New York, breathing the funeral ash, I realized our innate fragility, how easily the body is pulped and mashed and silenced. What did it have to say about history? What was the body's voice?

Instead of exposing the invisible ideas we live within, I searched for that moment when the temperature of words rise. I looked for language that risked my self-image to excavate what was inside. It was more instinctive writing and I learned quickly I did not have the strength to do it. What I lacked, history provided.

In 2005, New Orleans was flooded by Hurricane Katrina. I flew there to report, hand out food and clothes. When I got back, the memory of the panicked people poured through and emptied my secrets on the page. Surrounded by death, danger and dire need, one's feelings and acts are fused into sinuous motion. Words came out of an unknown interior, caught in the flood that lifted the past into the present.

After it ebbed, I felt how much had been buried. The emotional force of history, when not locked in facts, can flow through and transform us. I called it Method Writing, in which writers enter what acting guru Stanislavski called, "the vortex of life." We have truths fossilized in the body and if we spoke honestly, our words could shatter our solitude and we would be exposed to each other again. None of this is just political but also spiritual. Language seeks the knowledge of its untranslatable origin and the suffering of our bodies is the map of its hunger.

What I've done falls short of Method Writing but it is a beginning. Two tracks run parallel – memoir and journalism are positioned like mirrors that reflect the truth that life is elsewhere. Using levers, I tried to open myself, to be a different man at the end than who I was at the beginning. It almost worked.

"The subtlest change in New York is something people don't speak much but that is in everyone's mind. The city, for the first time in its long history, is destructible. A single flight of planes no bigger than a wedge of geese can quickly end this island fantasy, burn the towers, crumble the bridges, turn the underground passages into lethal chambers, cremate the millions. The intimation of mortality is part of New York now: in the sound of the jets overhead, in the black headlines of the latest edition."

E. B. White – *Here Is New York* – 1948

9/11

"NICKY, COME HERE," Uncle Junior yells. I jog to his bedroom where he points at the TV, "A plane hit the World Trade Center!" I see one of the towers on screen billowing smoke then blink and blink again. Instinctively, I pull inside myself until the screaming TV is a small light at the end of a tunnel. I turn to him, "Was it an accident?"

"I don't know."

"Well, did someone fly into it on purpose?"

"I don't know."

"It was an accident then?"

"Jesus, Nick, *I don't know!*"

My body feels like cracking ice. The air is charged with immense terror, so I talk trying to use words as a sponge. "It's going to be alright Junior," I said and put my hand on his trembling shoulder. "They're built strong. I mean it fucking sucks to be inside them but they won't fall or anything. The fire fighters just have to put the flames out and then they'll get the people, some are already dead but most of them will be rescued…"

Another jet   flies   across the screen   *AND HITS THE TOWER*
A GIANT ROSE OF FIRE   *blossoms*

OH NO OHHHHH NOOOOOOOOOOOOOOOOOOOOO

I stomp   in   circles   GODDAMN IT! GODDAMN IT!

OH FUCK!

OH FUCK THEY DID IT ON PURPOSE!

Uncle Junior turns to me, red-faced. Swallowing hard, I cross my arms and stare at the Towers. My vision is a beam of panic. "Okay, it was an attack," I pant more than speak, "but those towers are built strong, they won't fall. They won't fall, they won't…" I chant this over and over until one tower dips and…

f

a

l

l

s

Icarus

"Nuke the rag-heads," he spat out the words.

"No man, stop that," I said.

"Drop some nuclear bombs on the Middle East and fucking wipe them out," he closed his grizzled mouth and tugged at his baseball cap. I studied his gaunt face, hoarse voice, eyes like burning coals. He was filled with the Fury. When the Twin Towers collapsed into a mountain of rubble, icy terror rose from everyone's groins, shot past the belly and into the heart where it transformed into rage. Now it spewed from the mouth. People on street corners were openly talking of killing Muslims.

Here on the N-train, swaying in our seats, I tried to reason with him but he shook his head, "They gotta get payback!"

I leaned in, "You know the pain your feeling right here," I grabbed my chest, "you want to bring that to innocents? A few guys did this. We bomb the Middle East and we'll kill a bunch of people who had nothing to do with this."

His mouth puckered as if he was going to spit out what I just said but he stopped. I felt his struggle and aimed my voice at the space inside him, "You know they're watching us."

He looked up. Our eyes locked and our faces seemed enlarged by magnifying glasses. "Everyone who died in those towers – they're here," I lifted my eyes up and around and then back to his, "do you think they want us to become like their murderers?"

His shoulders slumped, "I know. I know what you're saying. It's just I lost my…" he covered his mouth. I held out my hand and he took it, squeezing nameless agony into me like a Morse code that I deciphered into —*I'm hurting. I'm hurting.*

Seconds After

Seconds after 9/11, the telephones of New York lit up with panicked voices asking for a return call or if so and so went to work at the Towers. Most of the time, someone picked up and the caller exhaled in relief as they heard, "No, I haven't worked there for months," or "I'm fine."

What about those who did work in the Towers but missed that day? They repeated in the months to come, stories of near misses, alarm clocks that didn't go off or a flu that kept them from going in. And they would laugh, wildly, nervously feeling how close death was. How hands ran through the hair and large breathing steamed the phone.

And then there are the thousands of people who called and called but no one picked up or heard it ring, endlessly ring. They poured into the streets, holding candles next to photos, asking have you seen my father or have you seen my sister, have you seen…

Altars

Fire trucks blared and honked and we waved to the ragged men on top. Coated with dust, they wore white air filters like hospital patients who gasped for oxygen.

They were coming from Ground Zero, where they tunneled under twisted steel to find survivors. The city, nation and world beyond knew that only hours were left for anyone trapped in the rubble to be found alive. The men here were the only ones who could reach them in time.

After the wailing faded, we gathered around the altars. I stared at the faces in the photos, knowing each of them was an emptiness a family had to cover with prayer. A dreadlocked woman circled, taking photos. People delicately wiped tears. Some broke down into chest heaving sobs. And then another fire truck wailed up the street and we looked at the weary men on top. A panic filled my throat. I wanted to scream for us to march to Ground Zero, all eight million New Yorkers and scoop it, hand by hand until the rubble was cleared and the survivors emerged with white dusty faces, coughing blood like ghosts from the afterlife ready to live again.

I wanted to yell but every thought was echoed as if my head was filled with an ocean. Tides of despair flowed through the city and cascaded into the black holes under the wreckage. It was like our voices were a waterfall into the void.

In the park, I saw a circle of faces around a bushy haired man yelling and pointing. Walking closer, his voice became clear, "You can't bomb other people like America has and not think it'll come back to you." Standing on the outer rim, I watched him pave the road from the past to the present with scenes of U.S. military jets slicing the skies above foreign capitals or arming young men to topple the government or propping up a dictator. Everyone stared in rapture as if the chaotic, torn apart world was now fitting back into place. A cop waved his arms above us, "Ok people, you can't crowd the street. Take your little seminar somewhere else."

The speaker ambled away but kept talking as his audience trailed behind him. A man standing next to me said, "The city is out of control right now."

"Yeah, it really is."

"Like I'm totally free to do whatever I want," he said but his voice had a razor's glint. "I could rape someone," he whispered, "and no one would know."

"What the fuck is wrong with you!" I shouted as he walked into the crowd and disappeared.

Vertigo

I was in bed, staring at the ceiling, tracing my path from Boston to New York. Born in Gotham, I left with mom as she searched city after city for work. One day she came home and saw me playing with a switchblade on the corner as older boys laughed and egged me on. She sent me to a boarding school where I graduated from high school, went to Boston for college, graduated again, fell in love, got engaged and worked at a newspaper.

It was a good life but in a fever of ambition, I applied to graduate schools and got into CUNY. My fiancé was so proud. She began looking for a job in the city and would join me in two months. We kissed goodbye. Once on the road, I drove the U-Haul van over bumps, hoping to knock its doors open and send my stuff bouncing across the highway. I wanted to be a blank slate, written on by New York. Turning onto the ramp, I saw a cemetery, behind it was the Manhattan skyline and for an instant the tombstones lined up in front of the skyscrapers.

I moved in with my uncle in Astoria, got an adjunct job and each morning took the train to Borough Manhattan Community College. It was the college my mom went to and it seemed my life was a spiral of hers. The pay was shit. I took out loans just to eat but I felt "real" living in a city of dangerous hungers that constantly changed shape. And I was seeing it through Theory. In graduate classes, we read volumes of criticism by Derrida, Foucault and Lacan. My mind became filled with strange electricity like the voltage lamps in novelty stores where lightning followed your hand when you touched it.

One day I was going to teach class and, for the first time, stopped in the B.M.C.C. plaza and studied the metal statue of Icarus, son of Daedalus who fashioned wings for them to escape their island prison. In the Greek myth, he warned his son not to fly near the sun or the wax in the wings would melt. But Icarus, overcome by the joy of flight, soared too high and frantically flapping his crumbling wings, fell into the ocean.

Staring at the statue, I always thought it an odd choice to put in front of a college for working class students. Shouldn't they try for greatness? I looked at the statue of Icarus with the Twin Towers in the background. Are the well paid workers in those offices flying too close to the sun?

Blinking away that memory, I dug up an earlier one. It was years ago, I watched the Trade Center being used as a stage for the dancers in *The Wiz*. Cast as Emerald City, it was a site of power and decadence. Moving in sinuous synchronicity, they hustled, waltzed, shimmied and jumped in unison to the changing colors that bathed them.

But then another memory surfaced, one too old to date and nearly soundless because the years had washed away the voices. I was a child, visiting the World Trade Center with family. My uncle had me lean against the wall of one of the giant skyscrapers. Looking up, I saw the North Tower arcing over me as if it was going to fall.

Am I upside down? Dizziness tickled my balls, flew up my spine and neck and head. I stumbled away, clumsily crisscrossing my feet as the sidewalk spun around me. "Look," someone said, "he's going to fall."

Dancing in the End Times

"I'm going out to dance," I said to my uncle and jogged down the stairs to the night. It was too late to sleep, too late to think, too late to be terrified. In the sky, Air Force jets circled the city. I hurried to the subway, where soldiers with heavy black machine guns chatted about sports.

How bad would it get? Would they start sifting our bags or patting us down in the streets? No, I thought, I look black or Puerto Rican not Arab or Muslim. Standing on the subway platform, I studied the people waiting. They were an old couple sharing a bag of nuts, a black woman fixing her shoe, a group of young friends and an Arab-looking man. I could see an empty circle around him as if he was being quietly quarantined.

He was jittery as if our paranoia zapped his face muscles. Like a blank screen, he was lit by our projections. We saw a wild terrorist and under that image, a scimitar slashing Bedouin and under that a scowling pharaoh, arms crossed as slaves heaved giant rocks into a pyramid. In war, no one is an individual but part of a group whose history submerges your face under layers of imagery.

Staring at the empty circle around the Arab, I knew the "Eye," that roving suspicion of crime that had targeted my body since youth, had now moved on to anyone who looked Arab or Muslim. After the attacks, white people greeted me in stores and elevators with the gossip of shared exhaustion or rage at terrorists.

The train came and I walked in, sat and closed my eyes, imagining the Middle Eastern families getting visits from the F.B.I. or being pulled into police stations. I thought of the "Osama Wanted Dead Not Alive" poster at the corner store as young men stood around it thrusting their voices like swords. "You see this," one man pointed to the poster as I left with my groceries, "we're going to get *this* nigger."

Arab was the new black. But how long would I not be a spic or nigger? How long before the "Eye" swung its spotlight back on to me? Under the question lingered guilt that the hate that drained away from me now filled Arab bodies. And we who were black not brown, Christian not Muslim, Western not Eastern could wear the American flag like a new skin.

A few nights ago, I walked with my uncle in Astoria as he pointed at the houses with the American flag. It hung on doors, out of windows, on poles, on cars and mailboxes. He joked, "It's like Passover. You have to mark your door with the flag or the Spirit of America will jail your first born." He pointed to one house with a huge flag that made the porch look like a carousel, "You will be spared." He pointed to the only house on the block that stood bare, "But your first born will be jailed."

My subway stop came and I bounded up the stairs to Chinatown. Fingering the invite, I peered at the far ends of the avenue when I saw a line of people in flashy clothes snaking into a thick door. Hard thumping beats rattled my bones as I walked into the building, spread my arms for the bouncer and entered a steamy sauna of human heat. Inside, people moved their limbs like pistons driven by an invisible engine. I let the groove fill me. It was good. It was a normal night until the DJ began mixing into the music the terrible truth of our city. The large speakers thundered out the roar of a passing jet and a crash and then he cut the beat.

We stood panting, faces turned up, questions curling our foreheads as we heard a news recording of the attacks, "Oh my God. The North Tower is, oh my God it's falling." Deep rumbling shook us as the speakers blasted the sound of the collapsing Twin Towers. My face flashed hot and cold, eyes needled with tears as a heart-like beat thumped our feet and legs, carrying the pain up, up, up and we raised our hands as the beat quickened, rising inside us until it slammed down a hard rhythm. We howled in pain and release. Fog spewed from the ceiling and red lights flooded the room and we looked like people writhing in a fire. Many of us had secretly imagined the last moments inside the World Trade Center. Now we reached out and stroked each other's faces. We embraced as if we were in the fiery towers, as if we were dancing as we died.

After the Fall

It was the first day of class since the terrorist attacks. I walked to B.M.C.C. where gusts of air condition made the sweat under my armpits feel like ice. Pausing at the door, I heard my students murmur and rustle papers. When I stepped inside, everyone stared at me. Studying them, I saw chewed lips, jittery eyes and panicked stares.

Holding my arms out, I began, "We're scared. We have no idea about tomorrow but let's take control of today." I asked them to hold hands and pray. They did and then as they looked up, I asked them to take out paper. "Words have to be connected to what we feel," I circled my hands in front of my chest. "Connect what you feel with language – let it be your testimony."

And they did. Heads bent like monks, they filled pages with their screams and prayers. I felt the pressure drop like a bathtub being emptied. Afterwards they put the papers into their folders and filed out of the room. Some shook my hand, "Thanks Prof." and "That felt good." One student held the folder to her chest, whispering that she couldn't write. I told her it was going to be all right, she would find a way to say it. When the room cleared, I went outside and rubbed my temples. In the plaza, I saw again the statue of Icarus, against a sky filled with memory, trying, always trying to fly away.

The Subway Prophet

"The people are suffering and the government is lying. We know war is upon us and we need faith in God," he chants. I look at our subway prophet, his eyes burning like hot coals in an ashen face. His beard is yellow and the shirt flaps open at the belly. He's a mess but sincere and I watch him waving the Bible in his dirt caked hands. Every day he rides the train at same time, same incantation.

"Would you like to hear God's Word?" He hands me a pamphlet which I take to use as a bookmark. What a lonely man, I think, but aren't most prophets? In every age, in every city, they shout in the midst of rushing crowds, demanding we stop and save our souls. They offer us redemption but their sizzling eyes and bad smell are a warning of its price. And New York has many prophets, except ours rant under the neon signs. Thankfully, few of us listen. I know I don't. But sometimes I'm scared of the infinite directions my life can take and I want to know which way is forward? And when I'm weak, I'll mistake their madness for courage and feel small and greedy in their presence.

"Would you like to read the word of God?" He gently asks the next passenger and surprisingly she takes it. I look around and see that everyone is cradling the prophet's pamphlets in their hands like paper doves. The train shoots out of the tunnel and over the bridge. Above their bowed heads I see the gray sky and the smoke rising from Ground Zero.

Letter from Burning Man – 2002

Dear Bridgit,

God, I miss you. In the letter, you asked about life in New York. It's terrifying. Walking through the city is like entering a low-level electrical field. Sparks of fear zap you at random moments. But after this summer, I don't feel it as sharply. A layer of wonder insulates me. I rediscovered faith in the desert.

In August, friends took me to Burning Man, a giant art festival in Nevada. As we drove from the last small town, I saw a flashing river of cars, RV's and U-Haul trucks pouring into an ancient dried out lakebed. The cracked earth was like a vast white jigsaw puzzle and on this flatland we built a city. People unloaded power tools, lugged water and unrolled tents. They erected steel scaffolding that was draped with miles of bright cloth. They built through hot days that baked the ground and cold nights where stars swayed above us like chandeliers. Each hour more people arrived by the thousands, some stared in awe, some laughed and some wept at the beauty of it.

But it was hard for me to open up. The first few days I was there, anger bubbled in me like hot tar. 9/11 was in my hair, my skin, my sleep. My body was an iron coil from living in the shadow of the absent towers. The heaviness of fear had become my armor. I was angry and muttered, "Who are they to dance naked in the desert while my city smelled like the burning dead?" Rummaging in my bag, I pulled out black clothes and a white rope and knotted it. My campmates flinched when they saw me dressed like a shadow with a noose around its neck. Fuck them, I thought. This is what terror feels like.

Later that night, I was rooting around for a hammer to nail my tent down and this guy asked me where I was from. "New York," I huffed. He looked at me and said, "Me too." Quiet moments fell between us like ash. His name was Tony. "How are you holding up," he asked. My shoulders slumped and I rubbed my chest, "Feel tight. Can't do this Burning Man thing, you know, be open, love everyone." He walked over to me and reached into his pocket and pulled out a tab of LSD and Ecstasy.

"Shamans used drugs to heal," he said and dropped one then the other in my palm. "Take them," he said, "it's not a cure but a door. Go through it." I took them and we hugged. A few hours later I gulped them down and walked out to the desert. Within minutes I felt my spirit floating around my body as if being blown back and forth by night wind.

I walked past strangers kissing in the shadows and poi dancers spinning fire like comets around them. I walked past techno tents where DJs experimented with faster and faster beats. I left them behind and aimed my face toward the dark horizon. The city shrank to a thin glitter of light in the desert. At the far edge, I hopped over the pink plastic fence separating us from the vast wasteland.

I wanted to be lost in wind, dust and darkness. Stumbling in the night, I looked up at the stars that seemed like pollen floating down to my face. Suddenly my whispering turned into one long ragged scream. Falling on my knees, I punched the earth as the memory of the Twin Towers hung over me. I grabbed fistfuls of dust and wept until the terror of it – the grief at the death, the smell of ash and the flinching at loud sounds finally poured out on the land. Coughing, I slowly stood up and felt the thump of my pulse, turned and saw the twinkling city.

With each step I heard the distant roar become music and joyful yelling. Ahead of me was a fire and around it a circle of bright-faced drummers pounding a heartbeat for the city. They guided me back in from the desert. Later, when I found my camp, everyone was tripping on LSD. No one wanted to talk through the clogged straw of words so we danced, moving arms around each other like tree branches entwining in fast motion. We became knots of warmth in the cold of night, then loosened and ran off, each a wild human flame.

I felt at Burning Man the rhythms of synchronicity, experienced the cycle of small and great things, from the tiny pulse of my blood to the roar of planets above. We are a part of everything that lives.

And that is odd to say because religion was always a point between us. I was the Lacanian Atheist, too clever to believe in God. You were the devout Christian, making your life into a sacred scripture no one but you could read. We were more loyal to words than to the experience they failed to describe.

Maybe now we can trust a hug to say what is impossible. Or, being that we live miles apart, let's try to listen to each other without judgment. I trust our love more than any descriptions we have of ourselves.

Flags

In the Graduate Center, we sat at a table writing answers to the First Year Exam when I smelled the rustic odor of smoke. I turned my head, searching for it and then followed the scent to my sleeve. Pressing my nose to it, I inhaled the whiff and a memory sparked in my brain of a rowdy crowd swirling around an 80-foot statue called The Man.

The day before, I took a red-eye flight from Nevada where I was at Burning Man, a carnival tent city of 30,000 people which had at its center a giant wood effigy called The Man. I smiled when they told me its name – it was 1970s slang for any oppressive power structure. Growing up, I often heard mom cursing The Man for the Vietnam War or the poor or for her own problems. He sent soldiers into foreign streets. He was the cop in our heads, the priest in our sex and the silence in our throats. Now almost forty years later, He again ordered our soldiers overseas to kill faceless people in Iraq and Afghanistan. But here in the desert, Burners made The Man into a tall wood figure and cheered the last night of the festival as He collapsed in a spray of sparks.

Dancing near the fire, I saw people unrolling a large billowing American flag over the orange coals where it flashed into a blaze. A grey haired woman shook her head, "I'm not cool with that. I'm not down with that." I stared at the Stars and Stripes curling into black ash and finally, after a long struggle against fear, began to applaud.

Opening my eyes, I saw no one at the table. I finished my essay, closed the exam booklet and turned it in. Scanning the English Department, I saw students on couches absentmindedly reaching for coffee cups. A year ago, I moved here from Boston and came to the new student orientation where I drank wine from a plastic cup, walked from face to face, my dreadlocks like a curtain. Older faculty created a gentle roar of good humored banter. We, new students, shot ideas back and forth like electric ping pong, driven to show our intellect. How did one relate to power? Were we beneficiaries or victims? In the era of Black Studies, Queer and Feminist Theory and Cultural Studies, teaching literature meant being a witness to the pain left in the wake of power's passage through history.

But we lived in a time of war and the shadow of the Twin Towers hung over us. A jittery fear twitched in our faces as patriotic rage filled the airwaves and streets. I climbed the stairs to my World War One in Literature class and sat next to my friend Anna. She glanced at the other students, "Remember, homeboy, we're the only two brown people in here," she said like a knife, "so you better get my back if the semiotic cross-burning starts."

The professor came, we opened our books but a question pulsed above our heads. Who'd say that these books by World War One soldiers, whose faith was blown apart by bombs, whose minds were lost to suicide, predicted what awaited our soldiers as they marched into and eventually out of Iraq?

Anna turned to me, eyebrows raised but when I said nothing, shot her hand up, "Professor, it's important to see how the analysis in *The Rites of Spring* of mass propaganda to advance imperialism fits in with our post 9/11 moment as we're about to wage war for oil in the name of a war on terrorism." The professor lowered her glasses on the table and said, "I was wondering who would have the balls to say the truth."

Nearly everyone threw their hands up, hitting the president's war speeches like a piñata. After class, Anna walked outside, patted her bag, "Homeboy, you want to hit this joint or not?" I told her next time and jogged down the street into a tourist store and bought a U.S. flag, a McDonald's flag, a Gay Pride flag, a Pan African flag, a Soviet flag and a Chinese flag, and bundled them into my book bag.

On the train to Astoria, I pulled each one out, admiring the color and history. When the train got to Ditmars, I ran through the streets with flags waving out of my arms, opened my uncle's apartment, dashed past the living room and climbed out of the window on to the roof. He stumbled out of his bedroom, "Nicky, what are you doing?"

I asked him to hold them and took out a lighter. He winced as I grabbed the flags and waved the flame under them. Fire ate black holes into the Stars and Stripes, Hammer and Sickle, Golden Arches and I swung them above my head in a fiery arc. The light reflected on each window as if the whole neighborhood burned flags in their homes as if everyone wanted to burn the Man.

Samson

"A nuclear bomb explodes in Manhattan," I told Michael, "like a sun igniting over a city." My hands opened as if shaping a bubble. "A soundless blaze," I held the moment and clapped, "followed by a shockwave that incinerates buildings to ash. Across the river, in Brooklyn, a man sees the flash, runs down to a street of screaming people, many bloody from flying debris, staring at the mushroom cloud rising over New York."

"Jesus, that's intense," he said, eyes wide, seeing each detail. "What's the name of the guy on the roof?"

"I don't know yet," I stroked my chin, "he's the nameless hero of the novel."

"Almost done?" he asked, holding his elbows as people walked by. The story pulsed in the air. "Working on it," I licked my thumb and acted like I was counting money, "it's my big 9/11 novel."

Story Telling

Rows of glazed eyes stared at me. My students were waiting for something to make sense. "Please look at the next highlighted section of Freud's *Creative Writers and Daydreaming,*" I pressed my voice on its words. "The psychological novel in general, no doubt, owes its special nature to the inclination of the modern writer to split up his ego, by self-observation, into many part-egos and in consequence, to personify the conflicting currents of his own mental life in several heroes."

A sullen quiet washed the room. Pencils seesawed in fingers, cell phones were glanced at and doodling grew on the corner of my handout like vines. Freud's ideas seemed an endless maze. The more my students read, the more they failed to understand until finally they shut their minds off.

"You all are modern writers," I said, "every day you split your selves into many characters. When your boyfriend or girlfriend asks if you love them, you say yes whether or not you do."

They chuckled and a woman in the front row slapped her thigh. "You have experienced being trapped not just in a relationship but in whom it is that relationship needs you to be. One of the reasons we crave new people is we are a new person with them." I mimed taking off a mask, "None of us is just one person but a whole cast of actors on different stages – work, home, school, bedroom."

They stared at me, sucking in the words. A few leaned forward in their chairs. "Our assignment is to follow Freud and split ourselves into characters. I want you to write down two versions of yourself. First, create a version of you that is everything you want to be but aren't. What does he or she look, act and live like? Next, create a version of you that is everything you are but wish you weren't. At the end, write one scene where they meet."

Au Natural

"I want to be white," her paper read, "and have long flowing hair." It was the fifth student paper that described their ideal self as one whose skin was bleached, hair straightened and who hit the lottery. My students wanted to become corporate advertisements they see around them. In the next essay, I read, "My best self has Italian hair."

The words struck a memory in me that rang like a bell. "She hated my hair," I heard a blurred face say; it was obscured by other faces. Slowly I remembered mom doing an angry reenactment of her mother. We sat in the Toyota hatchback she drove many years ago. I was studying the sunlight sliding across my hands. "She'd pull my nappy knots out in tufts," mom grimaced, "always saying I was too dark to be her daughter."

Face gnarled, my mother seemed possessed by her mother. Icy terror sloshed in my belly as she acted out the scene. I worried that she'd never return to normal.

Like sliding down a tunnel, I fell from that memory into another one where I was digging through mom's closet. It was cool, dark and smelled like stale perfume. Rummaging through high heel shoes, I found a brown doll with black hair. "Mom," I yelled, "whose is this?"

"God, I thought I lost that." She hugged it, "I wanted to have a daughter and I got this for her." Stroking its black nappy pigtails, she gazed into a distant fantasy life, blinked and handed the doll back to me. When she left for the kitchen, I kicked the fucking thing and tried to tear out its hair. "Hey, what's going on in there?" she asked.

"Nothing," I hollered and twisted the doll's neck.

The Nazirite

As I left the train, a Rastafarian saw my dreadlocks. "One love, Rasta," he intoned, eyes lowered like a secret, his fist held up. "One love, bredrin'," I said, hand over my heart. We nodded, briefly warmed by the heat in our stares and then let each other vanish into the crowd.

In glittering New York, a dark tribe of men gave each other furtive signs of brotherhood. We knew each other by our hair, knotted like tree roots that drank the history flowing under the modern world. We looked with pity upon the red eyed poor who drank on their blistered stoops to numb hopelessness. We were Rasta living in Babylon, waiting for the End Times.

Like a Greek theater mask, it was the face on top of my face. I had molded it years ago, in college, to be seen as the son of men like Malcolm X, Bob Marley and Gandhi. I hung posters of them in my room, read their books and replayed their music. Tonguing LSD one night, I listened to the crackly tapes wheeling in my radio and Malcolm X's voice. His words entered me like a sculptor's hands. I converted to Islam, carried a prayer mat as my friends warily watched from a growing distance. The black mask struck fear into people.

After college, a friend got me a job as a reporter. My first day, I saw on my editor's desk a large photo of a Rasta from Kenmore Square. We knew him as The Preacher. He was a tall ragged man, shaking a Bible in our faces, screaming about sins only he could see. One day I was walking with my nose in Nietzsche's *The Will to Power* when I heard him shouting. I pulled my dreads back, they hung like chimes but it was too late. "Yes Rasta," he slurred and clasped me in his dirt-caked hands. I smelled liquor, saw fireworks in his eyes. "Yesss Rasta, Babylon is," he pointed in all directions then pounded his head with the palms of his hands. He wobbled off as his dreads spun around like spider legs. I asked myself if he was the man I was destined to become, if I too would someday be driven insane by morality?

While smoking in basements with Caribbean men, I sensed a great pain fueled their fierce pride. When not playing drums or debating theology, they told me of childhood shame for being dark skinned or poor. But in searching for beauty outside the West, they became trapped in a fantasy of the past. The Bible or Koran were our holy books and in them was the plan for the ideal society we tried to recreate in the present. But it was a "paradise" that banned gays, silenced women, and scorned science.

After I left those cloudy basements, I wondered how my life would change if I lived Rasta. Friends I loved would be banished and books that I cherished would be trashed. Shaking my head, I chose to instead use my "mask." When applying for jobs, I waited until the boss or secretary realized I wasn't "scary" because they would wave me in faster as if to apologize for their prejudice. Each step from cubicle to classroom led me into the vast interlocking institutions that connect across society like a maze of paper-filled rooms.

By the time I moved to New York for graduate school, the street had receded into the background and the Rastas who worked hard jobs and believed in God or sacrificed their sanity for righteousness were shadows waving at me in the distance. "One love," they said in a religious baritone, "one love."

Samson's Journey

"So, the character's name is Samson, he has long dreads," I said as we sat on a bench in Tompkins Park. Whenever Michael was in the city, we met and continued the story which seemed like a giant moving film being created in front of us.

"Samson runs on Fulton Street and sees National Guards in white hazard suits leaping from a truck. He waits in a side street. People are running like balls on a pool table, bouncing madly everywhere. He takes a brick and knocks out a National Guard, strips him of the hazmat suit and puts it on. Knowing it will protect him from the radiation, he runs, runs, runs to the piers where waves of people are swimming, scalded red, skin peeling as they scramble up the wood poles, trying to get on land."

"Jesus."

"He sees a man on a boat and yells," I say in a panting voice. "No words are needed. They both know what they're going to do and why. He guns the engine and they swerve into the East River to Manhattan. Skyscrapers are like black volcanoes, spouting red fire and oozing streams of bloody people into the river who thrash near the boat, begging for rescue. Samson beats their hands off the sides with an oar. He can't help them. He's trying to reach his wife who is lost in that chaos."

"Jesus."

"Word," I say smugly, "it's going to be a best-seller."

The Rock of Etam

"It's been a few weeks," I said, "let's talk." She let the quiet stretch until my nerves almost snapped. "Six months," she said, "I need six months before talking about us again."

"Are you going to the anti-war protest?" I asked and the phone felt like a large anchor. "Yes, I'll be at Penn Station," she said and we hung up. Uncle Junior came in the room and shot me a glance, "I don't know if she's going to take you back."

I studied him, stomping through the apartment in his underwear, grizzled, pot-bellied and balding. Junior said I was the son he never had and as a boy, he taught me chess, gave me beer, porn and Twilight Zone episodes. He was a father figure divining the world outside school, church and mother. Years later, when I moved to New York for graduate school, he let me stay with him until my fiancé could find a job in the city.

One morning in September, he yelled for me to come to his bedroom and when I did, we both stared, open mouthed at the Twin Towers burning on TV. The phone rang and I heard my mom screaming, "I'm fine. No, I don't have an escape plan." The doorbell rang. Junior buzzed it open. Footsteps stomped up stairs and then Elisa, a married woman he smoked and had sex with, dashed into the apartment, pulling tangled hair from her sweaty forehead. Eyes gushing fear, she hugged him then me but I was a rock, holding in a flood.

She threw her bags and coat on the couch and began talking. Her words bounced off the walls. "Are you okay? Do you know anybody in the towers?" She kept reaching but I turned to the TV. The Towers were falling over and over. We sat on the bed, "Emilio, let's play chess."

He unfolded the board. I looked at him, "I'll be the terrorists." He nodded. "You," I said, "can be the U.S. government." We placed the pieces on the squares. Elisa was in tears on the bed. I didn't look at her but at the chess board, angling lines of attack. "Maybe they'll hit Indian Point nuclear reactor," I murmured. Elisa hissed, "You really do know how to play this game." Quietly, I pushed my pieces forward, driving through his lines and cornering Emilio as the Towers fell in the background.

The day after 9/11, I eyed him suspiciously. In the weeks after, I choked back odd spasms of rage that convulsed my fists. Strange fantasies of hurting him shook me and I was thankful when my fiancé moved to New York. We found an apartment and made it a nest, the TV like a glowing egg. We lay in bed, laughed and made love like in Boston. But every night, I untangled myself from her arms and left for poetry slams and drinking with homeless men until sunrise and when I came home she was awake staring at the TV like a frozen stranger. And then I met Nadja at a bar, came home the next morning, packed my books as my fiancé wept and an hour later, knocked on Uncle Junior's door.

Now I studied him as we sat on the couch, handing me a joint as we blew smoke out of the window. "I don't think she'll take you back," he used a fatherly tone, "you spend nearly every night at your new girl's place, what's she again?"

"An actress," I ran my hand through my hair.

"Don't you think you should make a decision," he pushed but I shook my head.

"I think they're being made for me," I said and rubbed my temple, "feels like I'm repeating the family's history. I think of grandpa and how he raised the family in Brooklyn and now I'm back there again, on the same streets, making the same mistakes that he did."

"He haunts the streets," he said, "Pop was one of the first Puerto Ricans to come to New York."

"You said he was in the merchant marines," I said, glad we moved on from my problems. I continued, "Mom told me he was a mean old man."

"Yeah and they left me with him," Junior said bitterly. "Everyone left. Eddie, my oldest brother, left. Margie got married. And your mom left. I was stuck with dad." Half his face was lit by the moon and the other half in shadow.

"When he was old, Pop would walk around the apartment naked, talking aloud and masturbating, I couldn't bring girls home. I couldn't tell anyone about it," he spoke as breath spilled out of his deflating words. Silenced hummed between us. I watched his face, saw the struggle between the anger and grief. Grandpa was a myth to me, the Old Man, a bald grim giant whose shadow fell on the family but now I saw a shriveled invalid yanking on his cock, spilling his useless seed on the floor as his son, my uncle, watched in helpless terror.

Somehow I knew this was why I came back, that these stories were what I was searching for in the streets and bars and poetry slams. I felt in the electrified air of 9/11 that our memory had magnetized and things forgotten began to surface. But staring at Uncle Junior, I felt a roaring in my head and got up.

"I'm heading out, Emilio," I put on my jacket as he waved a numb goodbye. On the sidewalk, I panted and felt the endless movie reel of my family memory burst into flame. On the train, I scribbled a poem and when it pulled into the 2nd Ave stop, I bounded up the steps to the Lower East Side. Dizzy, I walked into the Bowery Poetry Club, drank and took my poem on stage, nearly screamed it and then lit it on fire, waving the burning pages back and forth like a man lost in a dark cave.

The Morning After

In the morning, I stumbled back to Emilio's apartment, woozy and coated with city dirt. Hosing down in the shower, I heard him enter the bathroom, piss and leave which shot my anger up like a hot thermometer. I stepped out, wrapped a towel around my hips and was going to my room when I saw him in the living room, staring at me without blinking.

"I did something to you," he said blankly and it felt like a bright flash exposed our spirits wrestling over a secret. It faded as he went to his room and closed the door.

The Philistine's Shadow

"He steps into a burning city," I act as if my hands are feet, "fires spew from the buckled streets, people scream and run past him as he searches for his wife."

"Your novel makes me see it," Michael said and smoothed the hairs on his arm.

"He gets to an odd quiet place, walking under a building that fell on another building when a wave of nausea hits him and he vomits in his suit," I mocked throwing up. "He falls and looks and sees his shadow in front of him. It begins to move without him and rises, taking form and substance until it stands. They stare at each other and then his shadow laughs and runs off. Samson is wracked by terror, knowing it is searching for his wife and will hurt her if he doesn't catch it first. Stumbling, he gets up, vomits again and begins to jog through the jagged concrete rubble under an orange nuclear sky."

"Is it real?" he asked, a line of disbelief on his forehead.

"I don't know," I say, "it could be a radiation induced hallucination but the point is that it's his shadow, the evil part of him has escaped control and can hurt those he loves."

The Jawbone

"Jesus, even the pizza box has an American flag," I said to Nadja, my new lover, "and my tissue paper, my trash bag, my coffee cup and my napkin." I threw it into a small pile. "Oh wait," she held up her forefinger, rummaged in her purse and pulled out a wet-nap we saved from an Indian restaurant. She pointed at the American flag on one side, flipped it and read in serious newscaster monotone, "We humbly offer donation for attack on America."

Slapping knees, we cackled.

"What will kill us first, the terrorists or bad grammar?" She asked and we hiccupped laughter. "Bad grammar," I said. "You know, they're Indian, they can't make mistakes like that. Someone will think they're Arabs and call the F.B.I."

"Knowing the yahoos here, they already have," she muttered and went into the kitchen and then came back, imitating every white New Yorker we ever met. Her face was a cascade of voices, thick with beer and patriotism. "Hey rag-head," she slurred, "polish my flag."

"Okay, I better get to the anti-war protest," I pulled my bag on my shoulders. Nadja had an audition to go to and so we left together, pinching each other and laughing but in the street, a woman passed us, smiled and said, "Beautiful locks, brother."

My girlfriend's hand became like a rock. I tried to squeeze it soft again, "She didn't mean anything." But her ears pulled back and her face was hard. "You always say that," she hissed, "but you don't mind getting a lot of attention for your dreads. They don't know who you really are."

Silence pushed us apart and we rode the train, staring at nothing. Her stop came and she left. I took out my journal and wrote, "Notes for the Novel – Samson chases after shadow self through the fiery rubble when he sees it standing in a shattered window store, it yanks out one of its dreads and Samson feels one of his own fall off. The shadow has the power to kill him. Samson takes his helmet off and shouts at it, What did you mean that you 'did something to me?' But his shadow does not answer, it just dashes off and Samson follows."

I ran up the steps and felt a kind of static electricity crackling in the air as people gathered in a swelling crowd. A river of protesters splashed against the buildings, banners billowed above us as cops on horses nervously trotted on the sides. As it surged forward, I was caught in the vortex of chanting, drumming and dancing. We the People thundered the air and shook the ground. We rocked police barriers until they fell and, streaming into the open avenues, we raised our hands and hollered. In my bag, I had a U.S. flag and tied it around my hands, shaking them as if I was chained. People roared as I ripped it apart and threw the red, white and blue rags into the air.

The Return

After the march, I slept on my girlfriend's hot sticky couch when her yelling woke me up. "Mom, why didn't you tell me this?" She gripped the phone, "It would have explained a lot." She hung up and her hand drifted down. Sitting on the couch, she turned to me and said, "My father's uncle forced him and his brother to give blowjobs."

It happened to him – I think against my will and rubbed her shoulders as she wept.

Samson's Blindness

"What the hell is this?" She pointed at the computer screen. On it was an e-mail to my ex-fiancé asking for forgiveness, love, home. "Are you some kind of schizophrenic?" she yelled, chest heaving like a furnace billow.

I began to laugh as she shrieked at me. I closed my eyes and saw Samson being held by his shadow self. It gouged out his eyes and ran off as he fumbled blindly in the rubble, bald patches on his scalp from where his dreads had fallen off.

"I want my mind back. I want my mind back. I want my mind back," the words spooled out of me. Rocking back and forth, I cradled my head as tears streamed down my face. She sat next to me, scared, wondering. "What's going on?" She touched my back but I was lost inside myself – *Why this pain, am I lying? Am I? Why am I drowning? Why am I drowning?*

Huge dark waves lifted out of me and thoughts flashed randomly like a buoy bobbing in a storm. Somewhere in the distance, I heard myself say, "What happened to your father happened to me." She leaned me back on the couch, rubbed my chest, pulled a blanket over me. "Shhhhhhh, it's okay, it's okay," she cooed and held me until the night became morning. "Sleep, sleep," she said and drew the blanket to my chin and I slept a long dreamless sleep.

Smiting

We got on the N-train, our hands a knot so I would not fall or run. It pulled into Astoria station. "I'll be at the diner," she whispered into my ear, "give me a call when you're coming back." I nodded. She hugged me as if to squeeze me into a solid man. I kissed her thankfully and walked to Emilio's apartment. Questions tumbled out of my mouth. People looked at me and under the pressure of their gaze I turned down a side street and kept practicing my questions until the building was in front of me. I rang the bell, went upstairs and saw him by the door. Inside, two chairs faced each other by the window as if he knew somehow that tonight we'd break through the secret we shared.

"Nicky," he hugged me but I was a statue. Syrupy anxiety oozed as I walked to the chair. "Emilio," I lit a joint and inhaled "Emilio, remember when you said, 'I did something to you?' Remember that?"

"No, Nicky, I don't."

I pointed at the living room where the memory shined like a movie being projected in the air. I saw us standing at the edge of words that opened to a secret that if ignited would illuminate every dark corner of our lives.

"Look, Nicky, if I did something to you, I'm sorry but I don't know what you're talking about."

"I know you do," I gave him the joint. "You remember when I was young, almost too young to remember but I did," I tapped my head, my finger like a small hammer, "I did remember that you came into the shower while I was in it."

He looked scared.

"My memory goes black after that," I said, "which is funny since I clearly remember events before that and after. Why does my memory go black after you stepped into the shower?"

A terrified dog-like smile spread across his face. My hands began to itch and I knew I could kill him. His pulsing neck artery could be ripped out like a hose and his life spilled on the floor.

"Emilio, I can't stay here. If I do, I'll hurt you," I got up, left, nearly ran down the stairs, panting, wiping tears from my face, screaming into my sleeve.

I saw my girlfriend at the diner. She held me like an open wound as trains came and went, came and went.

Pulling the Temple Down

"Your mom's here at Burning Man," they guffawed, shook their heads. Unbelievable, my friends said and cheered her coolness. We sat under the dappled shade of a billowing parachute on a dusty carpet, handing a glass pipe around as marijuana smoke spilled from our mouths like fog.

Around us was the carnival city of Burning Man, tents swayed in the white chalk wind, partiers in goggles danced to bumping music booming from art cars. Our talk floated up and away, everyone adding who they wished came to the desert – aliens who'd fuck us with tentacles, cops who could be spanked with their batons. Wild laughter shook us but I kept looking afar, imagining my mother, her face heavy with worry as she pitched her tent and waited for me to arrive.

At night, Nadja walked me to my mom's camp, our arms swaying together like cables transmitting high voltage emotions. The desert was as dark as the sea bottom. Bright camps thumped dance music as people walked around us, pulsing with LED lights like multicolored lantern fish.

"Scared," she said to me but not as a question and lit her flashlight. Its beam waved in the night like a sword. I lit mine and we leaned on each other, clashing our beams and then overlapped them and stared at the tall light as if it was a ladder we could climb into the sky.

She stopped at the edge of mom's camp and said to meet her later, kissed me and left. I walked into the dark and saw mom emerging from the night like a spirit becoming a solid body again.

"Mom," I embraced her. We stared silently like a subliminal tug of war over who would say what and where it would lead. "I know Uncle Junior said I was acting crazy but look at me," I raised my hands and turned side to side. I said, "Do you think I'm crazy?"

"Emilio said you were on drugs," she searched my face, "but you seemed fine when I talked to you."

"Mom," I held my breath, "for years I've known that he abused me in some way. I remember him coming into the shower and then it goes black. Even if I can't see the details," I gestured to my mouth and my chest, "it's been here for a long time."

She seemed to stare into my eyes and see the whole of me. And I felt free, felt the great weight that sat in me rise and evaporate on my face. Shame, fear, disgust became transformed between us into a charged presence. But I trembled, waiting.

"I know. I know," she said. "The same thing happened to me."

The words struck me and shattered my image of her, one common I think to children, that our parents are huge indestructible beings. *Why did no one protect you?* The thought hit me over and over. *Why didn't I discover this sooner?*

"Mom, I'm so sorry."

"My father came into our bedroom at night. He would touch my breasts, then go to Margie and do more. Grandma knew. One time, she was at the table and said 'He's no good. He even touches the kids.' But she never stopped him."

So much time flooded her face, eyes like portholes through which I saw an ocean churn and spray. I saw the wounded scared child and the adult struggling. And when she finished, I felt wonder at how much can be let go, released, and that a truer self can survive and remain standing, breathing, living.

"I am so proud of you," she held my arms, "I always knew you were the smart one." She moved in and hugged me tight, "I knew you'd figure it out." Around us a giant dust storm blew through and when it cleared, the tents were gone, the desert was gone and we stood at the center of a vast atomic blast hole. Right beside us were pillars holding up a temple, I looked up and saw a giant statue with many faces on it.

In the distance, New York City collapsed into fiery ruin and I saw Uncle Junior walk up to us, and Grandpa jerking off, and Grandma trailing behind him holding tufts of dark nappy hair, and Samson in his white hazard suit now blind and bald, and holding the hand of his shadow self that tenderly guided him. They stood there and I saw mom was now a small trembling girl trying to cover her breasts which had bruises on them. I placed my hands on the pillars and saw that everyone in my family had gathered and were waiting, and then finally, yelling that I loved them, I pushed the pillars apart.

Epilogue

Taking a shower, I bantered with my girlfriend about going to Downtown Brooklyn to pick up supplies for a trip. Casually, she tiptoes into the tub with me.

"Oh, you're like a shower bunny," I squeeze her slippery body next to me.

"Oh no, that sounds like something that visits children," she says but her eyes change from the jolt of surprise to worry that I'll see my uncle again, which I do but with a hard baying laughter that shakes my ribs.

"Is that what visited me as a child," I asked, "a shower bunny!"

"Hey kid," she deepens her voice, "nibble on my carrot!"

"It'll make your eyesight better," I zing back.

"So you can spot me in a line up," she cracks. "Hey, rub my rabbit's foot for good luck!"

"Sure that's your foot?" I ask and we collapse in the tub, rolling and slapping the walls, laughing silently then exploding in hoarse barking, gasping laughter.

"Oh my god," we say, "oh my god."

President Bush and Bob Marley

My girlfriend Nadja and I were at the 2004 Republican National Convention yelling and pumping our fists. She tied a flag around my mouth and collared my neck. My four foot long dreadlocks flapped in a wild frenzy like a lion caught by poachers. She was dressed in a President Bush mask and a red-white-blue suit. People laughed from behind the police barricades. Bush was dragging Bob Marley on a leash down the street.

In the fever of protest, she grabbed my dreads and jerked my head back. Very S/M. Very fun. But it was hard to breathe so I asked to be untied. We stood on the hot pavement, being passed by bright-faced protestors and argued about my freedom. "No, c'mon, we having fun," she said. I was heaving air and pointed to my chest. She shot me a look, "Okay, okay. Get some water."

I jogged to the corner store. The brothers by the door nodded, I nodded. It is the Universal Sign of Respect among men of color. They stood, arms crossing their chests, staring at the carnival on the street and here I came, one of its clowns leaving the stage. "Yo, you let her drag you around like that?" one asked. He was young, hands in pockets, excited but cautious. I knew the unspoken question. Was it cool to protest?

"I either have fun being yanked by my girl," I pointed to her as she grabbed her crotch at the spectators who booed, "or get dragged into war and get my dick blown off." He smiled. I used the global metaphor of men, castration, after that he eased up. His two friends looked over. Since I had their ears, I kept going.

"Besides, I'm used to getting beaten by a woman," I said. "My mom beat me all the time. Didn't she beat you?" They looked at each other with the where-is-this-nigga-taking-it look. "Yo, let's start a new protest," I exhorted, arms raised like a preacher, "let's protest getting beaten by our moms." They shook their heads but laughed. The silent glue that held bodies back dissolved. Arms fell. Hands slapped thighs.

"Maybe then we can lay off the girls," I offered. Now it was is-this-guy-a-homo look. I lifted my chin and said, "Isn't that what we're known for, black and Latino men, gettin' them pregnant and beatin' them? Knocking them up and knocking them down." Gusts of air fell from them. The young blood who first talked to me had his head in his hands. "Yo, this nigga is crazy."

"No man, this situation is crazy." I waved my arms around us, "How did we get to be so angry we attack each other? We're not just protesting the war in Iraq. We're protesting the war in our homes, in our heads. That war is killing us every day." I was in full Rasta-self-righteous speech mode. They were feeling it, staring and nodding. Then I got brave.

"Walk a few blocks with us," I suggested. For a long, slow moment they looked to each other.

"No, we cool."

"Sure?"

"We cool."

One of his friends turned and spat on the street. Arms crossed chests again. I began tying the flag around my face, "Don't let me see you in an army uniform," I said. My girlfriend yelled for me to hurry. I jogged back. "Where's your water?" she asked. I looked in my hands, "Fuck, I forgot to buy it." She rolled her eyes and began tying me up.

We began our act again but I glanced back at them. The one who asked me how-I-could-let-her-yank-me held up his fist in a Black Power salute but his friend pulled it down. I lost sight of them but not of the barricade; it was there the whole route. People leaned on it and watched us. I rushed up to them and pointed to the American flag tied around my mouth and begged for them to take it off but no one did.

The Indypendent

"Progressive New York newspaper looking for writers," the ad read but I tossed it on the English Department table. Nearby were flyers for academic conferences, old theory books interpreting this or that novel, dirty napkins, empty sugar wrappers and someone's half finished essay.

"Words, words, words," I muttered and skimmed a forgotten dissertation from the shelf. In the academy, words piled on top of words like snow until a blinding white horizon surrounded the mind. As if to free myself, I took out my lighter, flicked the flame up and circled the tip in front of my eyes. It being an inch away, the fire seemed to spiral over every paper, book and flyer. "Burn every illusion," I laughed, "even the illusion of not having illusions."

An hour later, I walked into the Indypendent office for their new writers' meeting. People smiled politely, chairs scraped as we got close to let newcomers in. One of the heads of the meeting was John, a long faced man with Texas in his voice. *He looks like Abraham Lincoln*, I thought. Next to him sat Arun, a barrel-chested Indian man with flashing eyes who held court. And then there was a beautiful woman whose number I wanted but she was leaving for Africa in a few weeks.

We talked of the war, people disappearing into detention centers, corporate news, but above it all was the State, its large white pillars made of bones, out of which flew jets, marching soldiers, rolling tanks, lawyers with papers, newscasters reading lies and politicians with business money in their wallets. The State, it was a Parthenon sitting on the shoulders of the people who lugged it through history.

When they asked me what I wanted to write, I told them an event was coming up, a Burning Man spinoff, where artists create an ephemeral utopia.

"It may be good," I said, "to let people read about a world made of dreams, where progressive values are lived out."

An odd silence thickened the air. "But isn't that just escapism?" Arun asked.

"I don't know," I responded and took out my lighter, flicking the flame on and off, on and off, "I don't know."

Report from Playa del Fuego — The Indypendent, June 2005

"Why am I here?" I asked as partygoers clinked bottles of rum near a Vietnam-era army helicopter. It sat atop beams at the center of a veterans' park where Playa del Fuego, a spin-off Burning Man event is held. I stood in the shadow of the helicopter, knowing that my nation is again at war and our soldiers are killing, being killed and coming home crippled.

Across the field, a DJ played a clip from the 700 Club show in which Pat Robertson interviewed a Christian Conservative who went to Burning Man. "Pat, I saw a man point his ass to the sky and tell God to kiss it," he said. Robertson replied, "Dear Jesus." The man, in a bewildered, exasperated tone, listed orgies, drug-fueled dancing and obscene art.

They agreed that Burning Man threatened America. But walking around Playa del Fuego, it seemed the secret of this underground art scene was that it exposed the idolatry of religion. Fetishizing rules doesn't guarantee goodness. Burners break rules to release desire from shame, even as they tell God to kiss it they also search for God in each other.

At Playa del Fuego, our alienated desires transformed us into who we wanted to be. Strangers fed each other. A sauna was built and kept going all night so people sore from dancing could relax. Drum circles pounded rhythms that lifted Vietnam vets, scarred and limping from a forgotten war, to wave their hands. People leaned over a fire, smoke whispering around their hands as if feelings burned words away. Standing alone at the bright blaze, I mulled my place at the gathering when a man gave me magic mushrooms. He didn't want money and scooped some into my palm. I had been "gifted."

Gifting is the core of Burning Man. Its founder Larry Harvey repeatedly says that what's important in any economy is the social bond it creates. Looking at the mushrooms in my hand, I felt gratitude soak through me and how it contrasts the tense haggling of New York. In graduate school, I began reading Marxist theory and saw how when we sell labor for money, take our wages and buy, buy, buy that we grow a crust of false consciousness. In the day to day life of capitalism, we rarely reach through to the person on the other side.

Gifting destroys false consciousness; it does not define the other by what they have to sell or buy from us. Instead, we value exchanging experience. I could see it at Playa del Fuego, in the naked slip and slide where people zoom down a foamy plastic runway to the wild applause of vets, or the sun drenched yoga, or the open love-making.

But beyond our art festival cocoon is the world. If Burning Man and its regional spinoffs like Playa del Fuego are going to be more than a Saturnalia festival, a brief eruption of creativity, it must be surrounded by a sustainable economy in which common needs are met. We need our everyday lives to be a journey that transforms consciousness rather than sporadic escapes into an ephemeral hedonism.

Weeks ago, I researched Burning Man founder Larry Harvey and read his 1998 speech. In it he used the cliché of black ghetto kids creating Hip-Hop as an example of real American culture. Yet no one in the ghetto can afford this make believe, made real world of utopia. A tense contradiction exists between the grandiose, world-changing, New Age rhetoric of Burning Man and how few people can actually go to it.

When it was a free event at San Francisco beach, open to the public and within reach, it was a radical "happening" that could transform society. But when Harvey dodged the police by going to the Nevada desert, he abandoned any hope of lasting social change. And it is the same for Playa del Fuego where we drive hours from New York to the Delaware countryside to escape the law.

Until we connect with those in permanent poverty it will be an escapist utopia for the white liberal elite. And we know this, for all the radical self-expression, hardly any art offers political critiques. Racial and class privilege subsidize Burning Man.

I do ask if my questioning hides another silenced question within it. *Do I deserve this?* As a politicized man of color, it's hard to trust free beauty because all the freedom one achieves in America comes with such a price. Gifting is an emotionally vulnerable act. It creates a feeling that, along with the mushrooms, spread buoyant joy through my body.

Some unknown man gave me freedom from myself for a night. I stumbled about laughing and crying. *Yes I do deserve this*, I thought and so does everyone else in the world, including ghetto kids. As I danced around the fire, I hoped for a night when we would dance in the streets of New York, around a fire that burned real authority not just its effigy.

Say Anything

"Can I hit it raw?" I asked Rocky. Nestling her face in my hands, she teased, "And if I get pregnant?" I sensed the desire in her dare. "If it's a boy," I said, "let's name him William Bennett." Her face pulled into a question, "William Bennett? That is the whitest sounding name."

I turned on my back, "He's a conservative pundit and said stupid shit on his radio show about aborting black babies to bring down the crime rate." Her fingers unknotted from mine as heat filled my throat, "Babies aren't born criminals. Our society criminalizes them. What a fucking genocidal thing to say let's get rid of a people to get rid of crime."

I saw the perfect symmetry of my own voice in the air like a crystal and stared at it, as I often do, forgetting the person next to me. And it was too easy to forget Rocky because we both met after rebounding from other relationships. Nadja and I broke up just as Rocky and her boyfriend split. "You know, I just started this internship at *The Village Voice*," I told her. "Maybe I'll pitch them an article and interview you about it."

It was a big name newspaper in the city and since the internship began, I had this habit of name dropping it every thirty seconds. But she wasn't listening.

"What's up?"

Her sigh washed over my chest, "I had three abortions, RU-486 each one." Her voice was formal as if talking about someone else. Having a baby, she said seemed the only way to be loved. It was a reason to live, to work and triumph. But the dream hit against the reality of no money, against the nagging suspicion that she did not know, much less love, the father and that she wanted more of the world than a child.

Lying stiff in my arms, she braced for judgment. I circled her navel with my hand and remembered, years ago in Boston, sharing a bed with my then fiancé after an abortion. She curled in bed sheets for the whole weekend, lights off, afraid of judgment staring back at her from the mirror. Always, always it seemed that someone was staring at her, me, at us from inside our heads.

"Who's in your mirror," I turned to Rocky, "when you close your eyes, who looks at you, judges you, who tells you that what is here is not enough?"

She turned to me and said, "You."

Muddy Waters – The Village Voice, October 2005

I went to New Orleans to be saved. During the summer, the days were getting bright and every flaw in my life became incredibly vivid. Nothing in me felt real except a loud emptiness. When I saw New Orleans fall apart it was my chance to join a cause that was undeniably good. The poor were fighting against nature and losing. They were innocent and could cure my guilt but such a shallow reason for going left me helpless against their desperation. I was an emotional carpetbagger, a northerner going south to re-create himself.

I packed food, medicine and flew to Baton Rouge. At baggage claim, people glanced around anxiously and tightened their grip on their bags. A black family camped near the wall, using their coats as blankets. A Southern white woman turned to me and said, "It's awful what happened in New Orleans." Leaning in, she whispered, "Many of them were already homeless." She searched my face for agreement which troubled me and I pulled my dreadlocks back into a knot. It's a nervous tic. They are four feet long and heavy—their weight anchors me to blackness. I'm light-skinned, nearly her complexion but black enough, I hoped to be safe among people driven mad with hunger.

In New Orleans I met Reverend Willie Walker. A friend had given me his name and number and we'd talked on the phone before I left New York. He was raised in New Orleans and had been rescuing people since the flood. We met in a parking lot. He hopped out of a Mustang and said, "Get ready, dude. It's crazy in there. You won't believe what you'll see." Immediately I thought: *Player*. He had the easy confidence and busy eyes of the best hustlers. Later I would find out how wrong I was.

We put on rubber boots, he strapped a gun to his waist and we wandered into the flooded streets. I stood knee-deep in dark water as a boat sped by. Inside it a rescue worker named Tim hovered over a skeletal black man curled in a fetal position. A bloody defibrillator wire coiled out of his chest. Tim fanned the man's face with his hat. "Hang on, ya hear? We're gonna get you out," he said and looked around. "Can we get him to shade? He's cooking." We pulled the boat under a tree and yelled for help.

A van drove up and we hoisted the man in. After it left, I saw him in my mind: old, voiceless, begging with his eyes for help. Around me, men packed equipment and pushed boats into the water. Many of them had swallowed what they saw, but the shock of it never left their faces. I looked up. Ahead of me lay a city silenced by water.

I joined a rescue mission. We splashed in the murky water and then jumped in the boat. Many of us were reporters. We focused our cameras and held our notebooks like poker cards. Downtown New Orleans was a wide shimmering lake reflecting sky and buildings. A web of power lines drifted in the tide. Car roofs were hazy squares under the water. The captain cut the engine and drifted up to a home where a family stood. "The federal cowboys are coming," he shouted, "we wanna get you out before they take you by force."

She agreed and tugged at her son to come inside. When the reporters hollered at her to wait, she held up her hands, "Please don't take pictures. I don't look decent." They aimed their lenses at her. She crossed her arms over herself, "Please."

The cameras clicked and clicked. She stopped asking and pressed her mouth into a grim line. They would not give her the dignity she asked for because degradation sells papers. The most valuable thing she had was her tragedy.

Would those photos haunt her? Would she be reminded of her helplessness? Before coming to New Orleans I was surrounded by images of myself that scared me. I saw a man whose ex-fiancé would not take his calls, whose family was broken by pride and silence, whose mother was dying from overwork while he wrote poetry. I thought the time, money and sweat I gave to the poor would return an image of me as a decent man. It would be my reward. Instead I learned how small a part of their burden I could carry.

Later we passed some families on the road. I pulled over and handed them diapers, water, toothbrushes and drove them to the military post to search for their relatives. I saw mothers quickly wiping their tears away so the children would not be scared but the children knew. Their faces were made gaunt by knowledge that only the old should have, that nothing we own can be kept. They saw me looking at them in the rearview mirror and turned away.

We shuttled families until dusk. I went to a crowd to offer rides. A woman asked me how long I'd grown my dreads. "Ten years," I said. She said they were beautiful and held them like ropes that could pull her out of the chaos.

"We're a beautiful people," I said.

"We are," she agreed weakly.

"This sure is some beauty," a man in the back said sarcastically.

"We are," I repeated, "but we can't see it unless we have money. Money is soap in America. It don't matter where you come from, you can be Brown, Yellow, Black. Money will wash you white." A ring of people gathered around me.

"Why do you think no one came for you? Your life is not valued."

Their faces glowed. "Go on man," someone yelled, "spit it."

Words erupted out of me, "If they don't value your lives then don't value theirs. This is the latest battle in a war that began on the slave ships. They threw people overboard—they drowned them back then and they're drowning you now. Don't let them kill you." I was panting. My hands pounded the air as if it were a wall. Reverend Willie called from the van. I pulled away from the circle and climbed into a seat, quiet, sullen.

It was a long ride back. The rage that escaped in my rant still burned in my throat. I saw them in my mind, asking me for food and water. Reverend Willie drove us to his church. We got out and sloshed through brown water and entered the building. The floors were rotten. Slabs of the ceiling had fallen on the pews. When we sat, we began to argue about God, or at least I argued. "Just put your faith in God," he kept saying, "don't doubt Him." I did more than doubt. I sat on the steps and twisted my dreadlocks around my wrists like chains and yanked and yanked. I wanted to be free of caring for people I could not help.

The next day we went on our last rescue mission. Five men abandoned their flooded homes and came with us. One of them sat with me in the boat. "Thank you for talkin' sense into me," he said. "When you hear about all that craziness at the Superdome it seemed safer to stay." He kept looking around at the city, as if seeing it for the first time. The more he saw, the quieter he got. I asked him what's lost of New Orleans that may never come back. He turned, wiped his face, and closed his eyes.

"I'm sorry," he said. He walked to the end of the boat and wept as we drove through the ruined city. I sensed what he lost but it was too immense to fully feel. Numbness had settled into me. It kept feeling from getting in the way of action.

After four days, I returned to Baton Rouge airport to catch a flight to New York. When I first arrived, I'd seen a small chapel room in the terminal. Now I saw it again and like the first time avoided it and went to the bar, the restaurant, and the arcade. I walked around in blind exhaustion and saw the chapel again and this time opened the door.

In the back was a dimly lit area with pews. I sat down and held my face in my hands. I saw them again, women who carried children too weak to walk. Men who asked for help I could not give. I saw pain flooding their eyes and leaned over and pressed my palms to my face. My chest heaved and all the water I saw and waded in came streaming down my fingers.

Drown

Deep winds are blowing from the South and against my will I see New Orleans. Laying in bed with my lover, I see on the apartment walls a corpse floating in the street and families or people walking in the hot sun, saying the same thing, "Jesus, please help us, Jesus!"

After coming home, I tirelessly walked New York but at each corner was exposed to the great overwhelming need driving the city. The new vision came from the people I left in New Orleans who lingered in my eyes. Their haggard faces were superimposed on the crowds in New York and, like magnifying glasses, made visible our subtle misery. In Brooklyn, I saw faces heavy with quiet agony, faces haunted with exile or tight with terror, faces of panicked hunger. Each expression of pain was magnified by the memories of the drowned city until dizzy I leaned on a building and looked up at the slow clouds.

Last night, I walked to the subway and a couple passed by. The man had the same hard eyed panic I saw in New Orleans. I asked if they were living on the streets. "We's homeless," he said, "how'd you know?"

They wanted to tell me their story, to share the loneliness they survived but I could not hold any more. I gave the homeless couple five dollars and left, disgusted by New York because its lights hid more than they showed. I wanted to scream in the streets a wild, loud testimony of the suffering we walked over and around. But instead, I returned home and stared at the walls that flickered with memory.

Now lying in bed, I wonder if I could just let go of this life. Why live amidst pain? So I imagine cascades of water gushing through the window, splashing against walls. Closing my eyes, I see the dark tides lift the bed and me out of the bed. I float in cold water, blowing out bubbles of air. Descending, I see silhouettes of people float by – some I remember from New Orleans, further down some wear shackles, even deeper I see rotting wood ships and skeletons entangled in a giant coral reef, bound together by chains.

The imagined scene relaxes me and the world is dim and far away until I wake up and feel Rocky caressing my forehead. "While you slept," she said, "you kept gasping for air and saying, 'Jesus, Jesus.'"

The Coral Reef

I lit candles until the apartment looked like a cathedral, waved burning sage in a double helix of smoke that encircled me and faded.

After five years of graduate school, I was going to write the last page of my dissertation. Over the past year, I read the fiction and slave testimony from the Middle Passage, finding rapture in their voices when they broke through the master's voice and reclaimed themselves. Lifting this whispery idea into words, I shaped it into theory. Now it was done, save for an image to bring it together, I felt it glowing like a star in my head.

I touched two photos near the candles. One was of a dead, mentally challenged homeless man named Eddie who floated by me in New Orleans, body bloated like a balloon. The other photo was of a 19th Century slave caught in a net, eyes wet and hopeless, bright like moonlight in wells. I began to type:

I would like to end this work where it began. My first images were of two photos. One was a slave shackled and the second was Eddie, the homeless man floating through the streets of New Orleans. They have been on my desk for over two years. When the words led nowhere, I looked at the photos and pushed through my fear or boredom to a thought with consequence. At each try, I lift some of the weight from me into words. I don't have to carry the sight of men screaming in the street. Mothers weeping as children slept in their arms. A city drowned and people walking the highways.

Dark energy zapped my fingers as if typing lightning.

In August I go to the Middle Passage Ceremony at Coney Island. Santeria and Vodun acolytes come dressed in white. Drums are set in a circle on the beach and it begins. Hands hit skin layering rhythm on rhythm, building a cascade of music that gets in the muscle. We dance, leap, shimmy. It goes on for hours, the rhythms interweaving. One fades, another rises. We ride it with our hips.

Later the sun sets and sky cools. We go to the water's edge, pray then lay flowers and fruit in the tides. Each wave rolls higher up and pulls farther back, soaking our feet and taking our gifts. I stood on the shore and peered into the past. My imagination would shape the images of slave ships. I saw people jumping into the ocean and felt their cold shock at breaking water. I imagined the weight of chains pulling me down and thrashing as the last bubbles of air left my mouth. The descent quickened. The ocean squeezed my body until the light in my mind was snuffed out. It was only an act of imagination but it was enough to feel too much. The drums would begin again. I'd return to the circle and stomp my anger and sorrow into the sand. On the way home, I realized that what remained of the Middle Passage were the numbers on the ship log, the margins of money made or lost and the rare narrative of a survivor. So many bodies sank into an ocean dark as the ink of their bill-of-sale.

Words are fossils left behind. Language is the coral reef of humanity. After our bodies decay into wind, earth and water, our words remain. Into them new generations are born and grow and live.

Panting, I felt the whole manuscript in that image – The Coral Reef – and saw a moving ocean filled with people. Its currents were their voices pushing out, pushing those around them who were caught in the voices of those who lived before. Everyone was carried against their will into the spiky hard reefs that were history and institutions and buildings, all the unyielding fossilized residue of humanity that greeted the newly born who had to make a home in what the past has left for them. And as they lived, their words hardened into new deposits, new colors, new spikes in the giant coral reef. And when they died their voices carried on, flowing with the force of all they said and did not say, all the secrets they spoke of only in touch, all the hope that flowed into their descendants, everything. Everything. And I let my head fall back, then forward and held the two photos of Eddie and the slave and said, "Is this what you wanted? Can I stop seeing you floating downtown? Can you forgive me for wanting that?"

I climbed the stairs to the roof and saw sunrise. A great red rose of dawn blossomed in the sky that made the morning into a rainbow. I fell on my knees and cradled my head, saying, "I want my mind back. I want my mind back."

Notes from the Underground
For Jorge Luis Borges

"What's your name?" I asked.

"Hypatia," she said strumming her guitar, jasmine and sunflowers fell from the strings to the moneyless case. An empty glass jar with the words *My Father's Voice* scrawled on it, rolled back and forth under her left foot.

We smiled at each other as the F-train whooshed by, rolling newspapers along the platform with the wind of its passing. I leaned in and she cradled my hair.

"Growing these dreads for so long must have taught you a thing worth knowing," she said and stroked the dreadlocks and muttered, "I need toilet paper."

I put fifteen dollars in her case and asked to listen to her sing. She hefted her guitar, chipped fingernails chopped a rhythm from the strings and then she lifted her voice, a clear soulful wail carrying me with her. She pushed it higher, wider, louder and sang of hard love that was a rest from no love and I knew everything she said was true and clapped.

"That was amazing," I said seeing her hips and wanting to feel her beneath me. "Where can I hear you perform?"

"You already have," she smiled, her arrowhead face pulled back as she hung a question around my neck. "Remember, you're writing this scene after six years of us being together. I love you so much but it won't be enough to hold you, to stop you from judging me too poor, too messy, and too religious, too much like the mom you spent your life escaping. I will give you my virginity but it won't stop you from cheating on me."

We stared at each other and I saw my reflection in her eyes sitting at this desk writing these words and blinked. "Is there any way to stop it from happening?" I reached out and brought her to me. She held me and we swayed, "No, it's already done."

"Is it too late to be forgiven?" I asked.

"After we've died, after everyone who knows us has died," she said into my ear, "after this book you are so feverishly writing tonight is forgotten, after you and I are just symbols swirling in history, it will be up to someone to rediscover us, to make us into who we should have been and then it can be said you asked for my forgiveness and that I gave it."

The Ground Below Zero — The Indypendent, August 2006

People are still drowning in New Orleans. It's a year later and the waters have receded but those of us who waded through the city's death, we carry the flood. Driving in downtown, I saw dry streets, people walking to work and blink back the memory of dark waters lapping over the roofs.

I came to review Spike Lee's documentary *When the Levees Broke*. And it's a morbid return. After the flood, I came back to New York, wrote a dissertation and got a job but the crisis of New Orleans bookended my conversations. On Friday nights, I stared at people laughing over drinks in the Lower East Side, knowing that the money spent here in just one weekend could rebuild the homes of hundreds of families. When I called friends in NOLA, I heard survivors were popping pills and a few, drowning in nightmares, simply shot a hole in their heads.

Shaking the thoughts out, I parked the car and joined the thousands of people on a red carpet that led to the Superdome. Survivors and celebrities shook hands and hugged. Each camera flash made visible the victims, who in the borrowed light of fame became part of history.

In between the hellos and trading of business cards, I felt a nervous tension in the air. What would we see? Will it be our story? Lee walked to the podium and introduced the film. The screen lit up and it was like a door opened in the dark and Hurricane Katrina swept us with hard, wet winds into the past. We saw ourselves sloshing through chest-high water, screaming for help on roofs, dying in the Superdome. We laughed and cried and prayed until the theater was loud with the "amen" of baptism.

After the film, Reverend Willie who guided me through the flood was guiding me again. He introduced me to actors, politicians and survivors then brought me to Mayor Nagin whose head seemed like an egg in a nest of microphones. In the crush of questions, I asked if we could have an interview about the 9th Ward and the thousands of homeless left in the trailers. His eyes glazed over and I knew we would never talk.

FEMA

The next day Willie, my friend and photojournalist, drove me to the FEMA

Diamond site to find answers. Rows of white trailers shined in the sun. Weeks ago we couldn't have come. FEMA blocked reporters from talking to evacuees. If a family had a complaint it was kept inside the fence. After public pressure, they reversed policy and allowed reporters into the camps but by then the media had moved onto Iraq and Lebanon. The world was blowing itself apart and the homeless of New Orleans could not be heard in the deafening explosions of war.

I parked and saw there were no public phones. Evacuees walked around aimlessly in the heat. Few had cars and those that did drove in slow circles. There was nowhere to go except the bottom of a can of beer. A portly man came out of an office and shook my hand. He was the park manager and gestured for us to follow him. "A lot of them hang out and get drunk," he said, "that's how they lived before the hurricane."

Walking the camp, I saw men on cars drinking as if to numb the passing of time. Mark St. Anne, a coppery man with fuzzy corn-rows, told me of his tour in Iraq. "I got shot at, lost friends and my heart tells me it was just for oil," he said. I asked him how his spirit was holding up. "Not a 100% there but I'm able to…you know," he shrugged.

Everyone said they wanted to leave but without a car or phone it was impossible to search for jobs. When work is found it is taken on any terms. "I got a job on an oil platform. Had to stay on it for twenty-one days," said one man, dapping sweat from his brow with a washrag. "It was luck. I'm trying to find more." In the middle of his story, his girlfriend leaned on the rail and yelled, "Don't come over with that shit. I'll knock your fucking teeth out." I had no idea who she threatened until I saw a small girl hurrying away, head down.

Willie had left and came back, told me of a kid with swollen lips and bruised eye. The pressure in the camp was being let loose on the ones who could not speak. How many children were dodging words and fists? I wondered if the parents would try to stop me from talking to these abused kids the way FEMA once stopped reporters from talking to them? It's an impossible question but I could see the silence dividing them from the world was now dividing them against each other.

Almost everyone had cell phones turned off because they couldn't pay the bill. Night came and kids played basketball on the unlit court until a man parked his motorcycle and left the headlight on. There was nothing to do but play games in the dark.

While they live in FEMA camps, Mayor Nagin allowed their neighborhoods to be demolished. With his approval, New Orleans City Council passed ordinance 22203 that declared homes not gutted could be bulldozed. A race between land developers and home owners began. If the real estate moguls won, one of the oldest black neighborhoods will disappear. Here was where jazz was born. Here was where former slaves gave birth to their first free babies and passed from their generation to the next, music to remind the world how sweet freedom is. And in weeks it would be bulldozed away.

The Ninth Ward

I went to the 9th Ward where volunteers slung tools over shoulders and entered houses, scraping them clean so people could claim them before the city did. The largest group was Common Ground whose members live in St. Mary's Church of Angels. They hauled rotten furniture and moldy drywall out of the homes. Each day they came back sore and exhausted from trying to resurrect life from the ruins.

While driving, I saw a plastic skeleton on the fence. It was the kind doctors have in their offices. I pulled it down, danced with it for a minute. It dangled in my arms. "How does it feel to be dead," I whispered to the skull, "can you forgive the people who killed you?" I leaned it over as if we were in a tango, kissed its grin and put it in the car. The whole trip we collected memories of dead lives, dead places, dead hope.

I parked close to where the levee broke. We got out and felt the wall between the city and the water. Willie looked at me with the same question – *It seemed too thin* – Did they learn nothing from the flood? A construction team was clearing debris. A tall black woman in a green vest and construction hat directed the men. She was stern, proud and strong. "Not a lot of women could handle this," she said. We walked for a while. She told me about her home being flooded away. "It took a toll on me," she pointed at the raw wreckage around us. "When I rebuild the city, I feel like I'm rebuilding myself."

Later that night, I visited Curtis Muhammad, an old-school activist from the Civil Rights Movement. He looked like an angry black Santa Claus, portly, a big bushy beard and he hobbled on a cane while prodding and pushing the people around him. He founded the People's Organizing Committee and with a staff of twenty volunteers was gutting homes for free. They had a second mission, to amplify the voice of the masses. "Instead of forcing some ideology on them," Muhammad said, "we let them tell us what they want."

We sat down on the porch and he created in the air a living portrait of Black America. He told me of the first generation after slavery, of freed people working under the eye of the KKK, working to raise homes and families in New Orleans, a bowl shaped city built near steaming swamps and at the rim of an ocean, a city filled by the passing storms that left its people wading in the debris of broken dreams. "It's the Black belt," he said, "here are the darkest, poorest black people who were stranded as the economy became global and industrialized and didn't need them." In his vision, I saw Hurricane Katrina as just the latest disaster to hit. I shook my head, angry and then angry again at being so far removed from knowing what to do.

We got up, I shook his hand but as I walked away, huffed steam from my lips. Reverend Willie said, "Why you let him get to you like that?" I shook my head, "It's not him," I said, "it's that when I look at this shit from his view, everything looks like a fucking crime."

The Reverend laughed, "Everything is."

The French Quarter

On Saturday, the People's Organizing Committee held a Survival Council meeting. A circle of chairs was set up and thirty residents fanned hot air to their faces. Muhammad sensed their exhaustion and doubt and got up. "We take our orders from you," he said, "if you want us to clean your home, get you a trailer, tell us and it's done." The people listened cautiously. "I know they mean well but it's hard to believe any promises," an older woman said. "It's been a year and I still ain't got electricity."

Later that night, Willie and I drove to the brightly lit French Quarter. We strolled along Bourbon Street, drank cheap drinks and pointed at the strip joints that lined both sides blasting tourists with music and sex.

In the street, I met activists of People's Organizing Committee who looked bored and anxious. "It's awkward," a member said, "we're here to help the people and I know this is what they want but the misogyny of this place is…" She shook her shoulders, "Yeah, it's time to go." They left in a huddle, protecting their purity from the loud violent pleasures of Bourbon Street. We stayed, bought more beers and watched college kids stumble around and circle a passed out drunk, holding his swollen limbs and smiling for a picture.

In the window of the strip joint *Bewitched*, a young woman spun and slid on a pole. It seemed like a good photo op and I asked her if we could take her picture. "You a reporter?" she asked. In a few minutes she told me her life, the fight with her mom, dropping out of high school, running away to the city and her dream of being the next Keyshia Cole.

"I'm a singer," she said, "I strip to make money but I sing to survive." The manager came, asked who I was and pinched her nipple as if twisting a cow's teat. While saying I was a reporter, I shot him a look and he left. She put her bra back in place and sang Sam Cooke's anthem *A Change is Gonna Come*. Her voice carried me the long distance she traveled since leaving home. It stunned me and I stood there surrounded by drunken leering men and wondered if they could hear this, if it snapped the spell they were in. It didn't, they just clapped and yelled for her to slide on the pole. But she kept singing and through her came the music of the slaves who knew how sweet freedom is.

Maybe it was anger. Maybe I wanted to remind the tourists of the culture New Orleans was losing one family, one demolished house at a time. I asked Willie to get the skeleton we found earlier. He came back with it and I grabbed it by the ankles and dragged it up and down Bourbon Street. People assumed it was a joke and asked, "Hey, is that your wife?"

"No" I said, "it's the 9th Ward."

Some scowled and walked off but I kept dragging it through the streets, laughing at myself. For the first time since my arrival, the memory of the flood didn't overwhelm my sight. I don't know how but while dragging the skeleton through Bourbon Street, laughing from my belly, I finally, after a year of drowning, felt the waters recede.

The Ecstasy of Exile — The Indypendent, September 2006

"Welcome home!" He shouted and hugged me. I kneeled, scooped dust on my head and shook it out like a baptism. For a moment, I studied the ephemeral city of Burning Man shimmering in the vast Nevada desert. After missing it last year, I returned to pour out the last water from New Orleans. Rage and sadness sloshed inside me and I hoped the desert would soak the last of it away. But I didn't know if it was possible for me to "come home."

After wading in flooded New Orleans and seeing its people made homeless, I wanted to let go of the memory. But how could I let go of pain here, a utopia where no one wanted to be reminded of it? After parking the car, I went to Center Camp, a gigantic billowing tent where the sun beamed on New Agers entwining limbs in a slow dance. A woman leaned to me. "Why can't this be the real world?" She paused, "Is the real world even real?"

Attendees describe the event as truth and the outside world as illusion. It is easy to feel this in an empty desert used as a stage to act out fantasy. On the white, canvas-like playa, our hidden desires are lived out in hopes of revealing the true self. It is the core value. "Don't be a spectator," Burners shout when they catch you looking rather than doing.

And they speak of the event with religious intensity. But it's a euphoria created by escaping differences not overcoming them. Real world poverty is not alleviated, hunger abated, war ended or disease cured. We just fled to the desert and, isolated from the pain of the world, simply pretend we created a new one.

Near my camp was a Hare Krishna site where whites with Hindu facepaint swayed and chanted, "We're all one interconnected cosmic consciousness." They smiled sweetly and fed me. Their sincere kindness eroded my guard and briefly I felt a genuine openness.

I told them about New Orleans and 9/11, I tried to say how both tragedies exposed the chasm of race and class into which millions of people fell but they kept repeating, "We are all the same cosmic consciousness." It sounded less a profound truth than an escape of reality through denial. Like the many attendees with dreadlocks and saris, they wore a mask of ethnicity. They enjoyed the freedom of Third World otherness without the exposure to power that real people of color endure.

The next day at camp, a friend saw me walking surlily to my tent. He gave me two pills of ecstasy. "If you don't find what you're looking for," he said, "these will help you forget you tried." We laughed and I pocketed them, walked out to the playa, the vast expanse of hard desert floor on which the city was built and at the far edge found an art installation with rows of crosses for soldiers killed in Iraq. A veteran knelt and wept.

When I was a boy, the Christian cross was a symbol of sacrifice to me. Years of questioning it made it an empty icon. But seeing him crying over the crosses moved me. I walked back to my campsite and saw a Common Ground activist. We had met in New Orleans. "I was here when we heard about Katrina," she said, "people said in that hippie way, it was meant to be." Her eyes flashed, "I was like what the fuck is wrong with you." We shook our heads. I gave her a pill. If we could not believe in joy, we could induce it.

On the climatic sixth night of the festival, when Burners set fire to the giant wooden effigy called The Man, I took half a pill. After He blazed and crashed, I circled the inferno. My friend from New Orleans sat and stared into the fire. I hoped it burned away her memory of the flood.

After walking in the desert night, I found Nexus, one of the large clubs. It looked like a giant half egg flashing with lights and a dark river of people flowing in and out. The mild glow of ecstasy began to make me float in my body. It left me knowing I have this small gasp of time on earth and the only meaning it can have comes from how I share it with others.

Nearby a young woman stood stiffly. I remembered the crosses and said, "Here," and put the last pill in her palm. She smiled, "You totally read me." I leaned in, "Remember the story of Jesus feeding the masses?" She nodded. "Maybe it wasn't a physical miracle," I said, "maybe he had them split bread until each had a useless bit and realized they sacrificed hunger for togetherness. No one was left out. Maybe that was the real miracle."

She hugged her thanks. The ecstasy I took had worn off but a stronger joy reached through me. I gave away the pills that could numb my exile. It left in my mind a self-image I could believe in and, while dancing, I held myself like home.

My Brother's Keeper — The Indypendent, December 2006

"C'mon, jump," the man yelled to the cop on the roof. We were rallying in front of the 103rd precinct in East New York. The officer laughed as people pointed at him.

"C'mon pig, jump," the man next to me taunted. Suddenly, cheers erupted from the crowd as two boys, both gang members, one a Blood, the other a Crip, were hoisted on the shoulders of the New Black Panthers. Held up by the men beneath them they waved their gang colors. The Crip yelled, "Yo, we endin' this beef, we all black. Bloods and Crips unite and we ready to pop!"

Behind the barricades, police eyed us. Seeing our strength in their fear, we yelled louder. We wanted to strip them of the power to kill that they held over us. It was a power that New York cops used on black and Latino men in a careless indiscriminate manner. It was as if blinded by the glare of the badge every brown face seemed like a deadly monster to be killed.

Killing Sean Bell

On November 25th, undercover cops followed Trent Benefield, Joseph Guzman and Sean Bell out of the Kalua nightclub in Queens. The threesome celebrated Bell's upcoming marriage until two rude-boys pushed their way into the bachelor party. Each side traded threats, saying they had guns and the icy cool to use them. Bell, who just wanted to leave, broke the rising gamble of rage and pride by saying it was time to go.

As they got into their car, one of the officers who heard the threats walked up to them, hand on gun. He did not show his badge. He did not say he was N.Y.P.D. "He got a gat! Be out!" shouted Guzman. Panicked, Bell rammed their car forward into the van, reversed and rammed it again. The cop fired repeatedly, and the other police fired, a cross fire of high velocity metal broke bone, splattered flesh, severed arteries.

In the car, glass shattered as their bodies were punched around by bullets. Benefield fell out pleading, "Stop shooting at me!" Inside the car, Bell's neck was shredded. He gasped until he had no more air. His life blood soaked his chest red. The cops shot fifty bullets at the four men and no gun was found in the car.

The next day, New York read about the killings. After hearing that fifty shots were fired many of us had the same question. Did they enjoy killing him? Officer Mike Oliver fired thirty-one bullets. He shot, reloaded and shot again. When did fear and panic become rage?

The New Emmett Till

I went to Bell's funeral at Community Church of Christ where he and his fiancée Nicole Paultre planned to marry. Men in dark suits guided us in. "No cameras please," they said and we turned off our cell-phones. A local news crew was in line and he shooed them away. "They never came around before," the older black woman in front of me said. "They don't care about Sean, they just here to make money." I hummed agreement even though I was there as a reporter.

The line going into the church was black. Across the street, the line of reporters was white. They wanted to wrap him in headlines and tell us the meaning of his death. Even I, who covered the funeral for my newspaper, felt a different need: it was not just to see the body but to make him into a symbol of my own.

We entered the rose-scented church and I watched people lay prayer over his face, blessing him. I didn't want to feel sadness or anger, I just wanted to look and go but when I glimpsed his grey face in the coffin, my eyes flinched. His death was my death too. They shot fifty bullets into the blackness we both share and now the value of my life depends on the price they pay for his murder. Walking away, I knew whatever is said must bear the weight of his lost life.

Next to the church, media trucks glowed as TV anchors waved their microphones like metal detectors searching for treasure. Activists worked the crowd, handing out flyers. I took one and read it but could feel ambition in the air.

Faces circled the camera-light as if to audition for the Revolution. Only a few spots were open and activists who never came to the neighborhood before were now speaking for it. A white woman held a sign that read People's Organization for Progress over a man being interviewed. "You don't know Sean Bell," a black woman screamed. "I live in an African-American community," she pleaded and touched her chest. "What! Get out my face," the black woman hollered, "you don't even talk black!" The white woman hurried away, pelted by curses. Reporters aimed their lenses at the heckler and she took out her camera and took pictures of them.

It began to rain and everyone opened umbrellas. In that silence, the family came out of the church singing *Amazing Grace*. The pain they sang stunned me. Behind the fence we chanted, "No justice, no peace!" Our rage and their sadness rolled back and forth over his coffin as it was placed in the hearse.

When they drove away, activists and reporters surged into the street. Men and women screamed and moved around blindly as if inside a boiling pot. The Bloods showed up and as I passed them some of us looked at each other with the same question. Finally I asked out loud, "Don't they kill black men?" A black couple raised their eyebrows and blew frustration out soundlessly. But then an older man said, "They're just kids. They're lost and they need some direction."

A black woman with a camera walked up to the Bloods, "Brothers, what do you have to say about police brutality?" It was her test, if they were going to be tough then what do they say about a death that could so easily have been theirs? The Bloods eyed each other over the red bandannas and stepped back. They had the same awkwardness I had as a boy. In that gesture, I saw how close and far we are from each other.

They were children and we feared them. Are we this broken, I asked myself. Has it gotten so bad we need Black Nationalist rhetoric to do something as simple as love each other? Next to me, a Rasta-man intoned, "Burn the city down." A black girl looked around in wonder, then at him. "We can't burn the city down," she said, "we got to live here."

River of Rage

Next day, Saturday, I followed the flyer an activist gave me to the Kalua nightclub. The New Black Panther Party called for a rally and we gathered at the altar for Sean Bell. Candlelight protected him against forgetfulness. Many Panthers are ex-Nation of Islam and their national chairman, Malik Shabazz, has used his life to complete Malcolm X's half lived one. Malcolm X wanted to be a lawyer. Shabazz became one. Malcolm X died for the Cause. Shabazz would live for it.

The Panthers used the "Black Power!" war-cry to keep the air warm until Shabazz came. He held a white bullhorn that boomed out his voice. It was raspy,

I wondered if he gave it a little gruff to sell the speeches. Performers can't sustain the flow of feeling without being worn down, so they give signs of passion without being lost in it. Except now, it was us at risk. It was our delicate bodies caught in this struggle for power. "We don't need a permit," Shabazz challenged, "how are you going to ask for permission from the very people who are killing you?"

We marched down Jamaica Avenue like a river of rage. Cars and buses turned to the side. Shabazz stopped us in the middle of the street. "We have to hit them were it hurts," he pointed at the stores. "Fifty shots, fifty day boycott! Don't buy from these stores!" I saw people staring from sidewalks, it was obvious they wanted to join but were too weighed down by shopping bags.

We were freely moving down the street and the power got to some. A Blood turned to a white female cop, "You a bitch yo, yeah you, cop, SUCK MY DICK!" Her eyes locked and her arms stopped swinging and tightened. An older brother, eyes flashing like knives cursed a black female cop. "You should be ashamed of yourself for wearing the uniform," he yelled, "a woman should not wear the authority of a man. Read Deuteronomy!"

We gathered in front of the 103rd precinct. Men took turns hollering through the bullhorn. "Revolutionary greetings," a brother in a leather jacket got up, "we got black men in the army who know how to shoot," he said as his face flushed red, "we can get a tank and roll it through here and blow up this police station!" The guys around me covered their laughter. He overstepped the line between fact and fantasy and snapped our suspension of disbelief.

Shabazz raised his hand and we listened. "If there are more murders," he aimed his bullhorn at the cops, "we will kill you!" It was dangerous theater. Fear and excitement pulsed through us like a heartbeat. No one wanted to get beaten or arrested and no one wanted to seem weak. Shabazz pulled us back from the momentary dizziness. "But we are disciplined," he assured and, in the back, I sighed.

In the headiness, two boys, a Blood and a Crip, were hoisted on the shoulders of the older men and embraced. They reached beyond their pride, their arms like stitches over the wound made by 50 bullets. I put down my pen. The whole day I kept my hands busy taking notes when they shouted "Black Power!" I knew enough history to be suspicious. Usually, "Black Power" became the personal power of whichever leader called for it. Except now, for this, I held up my fist too. The Panthers called for a march to the hospital. I wondered what permanent good would our marching achieve and not just this one but all the marches that began at Bell's death. Who would we be at the end of it? What would be the price?

Later that night, I received a call from the New Black Panther Party secretary. His voice had the eager sincerity of someone trying to catch up to his ideals. We rapped for an hour. I told him my muscles were in knots. Some of the rage was ugly. "I feel you," he conceded, "some of it was…"

He said our people were mentally poisoned but we could recover. "Your melanin makes you morally superior to the white man," he cooed, "it's just not in their nature, brother." I silently studied my own yellow hand and laughed at the idea that my color made me more or less prone to sin. If anything, sin was too fun to give up for righteousness.

"Holiness isn't for everyone," I said. We hung up but my muscles were in knots even as the euphoria of togetherness filled me like helium. I shook my head and my dreadlocks fell down. Am I my brother's keeper? I tugged on it like a chain. Am I?

The Fire This Time

On Wednesday, I went to the rally at Police Plaza One. The cops had set up a maze of barricades that squeezed people into a pen at Foley Square. Inside it, hundreds of protesters shook the air with "Kelly must go!" If Sean Bell became the symbol of black innocence, Police Commissioner Ray Kelly became a symbol of white racism. Neither was the truth of the man but a crime had been committed and we needed a target. Ideas are not as satisfying to destroy as a man.

In the crowd, smaller stages were carved out by the camera light. Black Israelites in full ancient head dress talked of the Original Black Man. Nearby a tall gaunt black man in army camouflage yelled repeatedly, "Daniel in da' Lion's Den!" Communists wove through the crowd, holding their newspapers. Most of the audience was young with no ideological loyalty or party membership. Our skin color was our nation.

A man was selling pan-African flags. I bought one and waved it around to save my voice from yelling. "We're marching," they shouted as the crowd walked to the street. A wall of police stood grim faced, arms crossed. "Go back to Long Island, pigs," young men cackled. They held a banner with the spray-painted slogan "Police Number #1 Enemy" that tilted back and forth as the police and protesters argued. The police crumbled and the march moved ahead. A helicopter chopped the sky above us as we banged drums and chanted, "Fuck the Police!" In the star-like spotlight of helicopters we became black silhouettes indistinguishable from one another.

We escaped the maze of police barricades and marched into the larger maze of the city. I looked at the skyscrapers where money traveled through electronic signals far above our heads. So much wealth and yet half of New York's black and Latino children will not graduate high school and half will be unemployed as adults. Generations of New Yorkers have been abandoned by the city and herded by police into prisons. I stared at the lights and remembered Shabazz calling for revenge, Sharpton for a federal investigation, and Barron for community control over police. Would any of it change the historical forces that kept these office buildings lit, school doors shut, and prisons full?

After the march, Barron spoke. "Remember," he said tapping the end of each sentence with his finger, "on December 21st, we shut down Wall Street!" Camera flashes lit Barron as if he was a statue. He passed the microphone to activist Viola Plummer. "The next cop who kills one of us," she promised, "will go the very same way the bullet goes." Plummer warned of police surveillance and advised us to look out for each other.

As I left, young brothers were hollering into microphones, each heating up rhetoric to keep the night from going cold. Two men walked by me, one had communist leaflets crumpled in his hand. "How they trying to tell me about the truth," he said, "nigga, I've been living this for twenty years!"

In his complaint, I saw two cultures, the white Left and black radicals, struggling to lift Sean Bell's name high enough for everyone to see. A new movement was in the streets but the direction it would take is unknown and the divisions within it are already clear. What will happen as the winter comes, will Bell's murder become layered over by snow and gift wrap? Or will, in his name, black people go on a consumer fast and not buy from white-owned stores? I held the Pan-African flag in my hands and swore to follow the boycott yet a part of me wondered what am I really buying into?

Cursed Bits

"You call your vagina 'cursed bits?'" I asked while laughing and slapping the table. Hypatia half grimaced, half smiled. "It's just that how we talk about things, you know," I tried to reel my shock back in, "it's just the language we use shapes how we relate to life. And 'cursed bits' is so Christian."

"I did go to church," she stabbed the table with her finger, "for a long time. I even thought being gay was a sin. So Adam and Eve covering up their 'cursed bits,'" she made air quotes, "was what I learned."

"But there are thousands of religions made up by people," I used the tone of shared complicity, "why follow one that sabotages you by making your body your enemy?" I flung my hands up in mock incomprehension. Her lips pursed as she followed the logic to the warmth between her thighs. "I'm a twenty-six year old virgin," she held her voice up like a stop sign, "and I stayed one this long by making my own decisions."

"Yes," I said, "consent is sexy, especially between one's mind and a two thousand year old religion. Anyone ask your consent while teaching you this nonsense?"

The Broken Pot

"I don't know, man," I hurried across 2nd Avenue, "she's a twenty-six year old virgin. If I take her virginity, that's a huge deal." The phone was quiet for a second. My friend cleared his throat. "Hey, do you remember what Colin Powell said to Bush about invading Iraq?" He asked.

"No," I said.

"If you break it, you own it."

Playa del Fuego

"You're doing what," they said.

"I'm driving overnight to New York to pick her up at the airport and bring her here to Playa del Fuego," I said and crossed my arms as if knotting the idea to my chest.

"Dude, that's like an eight hour drive at least," one of the guys said. We were lined up at the bathroom at the festival, towels slung over necks, our feet in sandals as across the field partygoers emerged swollen eyed from tents. The line was just guys, so instantly we gossiped about our hook-ups, during which I told them about my trip back to pick up a 'maybe' girlfriend.

"Yeah man, she's a *maybe girlfriend*," another joshed, "I think you can find a lot of *maybe* girlfriends right here." We laughed and as the chuckling faded, I remembered her, a petite woman with a face like an elf carrying this huge guitar on her back. "You know, she's been traveling for a long time," I said to them, "for once I want her not to feel tired when she gets home." An odd silence hung in the air and then one of the guys said, "Go get her."

Later that night, I sped through the midnight highways, opening the window so cold air blasted me awake. I parked at J.F.K. airport in the morning and walked to the arrival hall where she saw me and we kissed blindly.

We kissed while I drove, we kissed while I parked, limbs clamped on each other like wrestlers. We kissed between eating and kissed between words. Our lips were bruised by the time I rolled into Playa del Fuego and our groins ached from wanting. Humping in the tent, we licked and stroked and sucked our way into each other until our bodies were left behind and we wordlessly flowed through each other, bruising old fears with hard thrusting and the pain was welcome as proof that we arrived.

Outside the tent, someone heard our slippery noises and cackled, "Does it taste good?"

Laughing, we fell off each other, blinking in amazement. We kissed as we danced around the fire, her body lit orange by nearby flames and she said to me, "This is like the backstage of the circus."

"How would you know," I shouted.

"Didn't I tell you," she laughed, "I ran away from home at sixteen and joined the circus."

Daddy's Girl

"I was my father's daughter," she said while on my chest, her voice like a geyser, "we did everything together. He made me into a little warrior Amazon. Then I went through puberty," she wiped her face. We laid in the backseat of the rental car, her body a breathing accordion on mine.

"He dropped the hammer," she said. "Don't do this. Don't do that. Dress like a girl. It was like I was in jail and I didn't get it. How did we go from being best friends to me being a porcelain doll? But he was and is an old school black man from the South. Girls had to be girls." A long breath snaked out of her, "One night he was in the kitchen and I had just come out of the shower, topless, and went and hugged him. He was visibly shaken. Weeks later, we were on a family trip and he yelled at me and when I yelled back, he climbed out, opened the back door and tried to beat me but I kicked and punched him silly."

She covered one of the air condition vents with her feet, "He was so embarrassed that his girl defied him. He told my mom I had to leave. And she didn't defend me at all. She just kept saying, 'It's what your father says.' My sisters cried. He didn't care, he just kicked me out. I stayed with my aunt and then others until I left on my own and joined the circus."

I massaged her neck as she wiped her eyes, "No one said, 'Maybe you shouldn't kick your sixteen year old daughter out of the house.' *Think that would have been good to hear? Someone saying I was worth keeping even if I was trouble.*"

We lay there and I rubbed circles into her chest as if to break the rusted pain and keep her words flowing. But I saw the battery light was blinking and tried to start the engine but no power stirred the pistons.

"Fuck," I looked around the car, "battery's dead. I left the AC on too long." Getting out, I looked around for help and saw a guy with a dog squirming in his arms and asked him for a jump. While he got out his jumper cables, I saw police and New Orleans insignia stitched on his shirt.

"You a NOLA cop," I questioned.

"Oh no," his eyes seemed to focus on some faraway scene before tightening up. "No, I work for the New York Police but, you know, I went to New Orleans to help. After 9/11, honestly, all I want to do is help people."

We leaned on the car and I told him about my trip to New Orleans and a dark river of memory carried us back there. It carved a trench in us where what flowed was not just the death of New Orleans but every destroyed life we saw afterwards.

"You know," he said, "a lot of people ain't got homes, I mean not just physical ones but the one here," he touched his heart. Clearing his throat he said, "This fucking world is real good at throwing people away."

In my mind, I heard my 'maybe' girlfriend say – Think that would have been good to hear? Someone saying I was worth keeping even if I was trouble.

Ceremony

"We just had graduation yesterday," I told Hypatia while dropping my backpack on the floor. "Funny, I imagined you coming down the aisle as your whole family cheered."

"Even my father?"

"Even your father."

"I'm not the graduating type."

"Of course you are. Didn't you know you graduated? You survived the streets and now you're on the other side. You didn't get turned out or hooked on anything. You didn't hurt yourself or others or let others hurt you. I can tell you, I've seen thousands of people lose their city, their homes, their lives and some of them are killing themselves. No, you graduated."

She was staring at me, wide eyed. "Hey, let's make it official," I said and got up, grabbing the blue college graduation robe and cap we professors wore at the ceremony, flung it over her, put the cap on her head, lit a candle and gave it to her. She stood there as a shy smile opened her face.

"Please come forward," I used a heavy voice. She stepped slowly, blue robe shimmering in candlelight, her eyes spilling wonder, hope, thanks. "For surviving the loss of home and family and for keeping yourself intact through celibacy, for creating art inside the nightmare of capitalism, and for being a black woman who beat the odds, we the School of Hard Knocks award you a diploma in Spiritual Freedom."

She took the rolled up paper I had in my hand and we kissed, softly, deeply, joyfully and she laid on the bed, in the blue robe, legs opening and when I entered her, our rhythm carried us to an oceanic darkness that was neither blessed nor cursed, just patient and waiting for her to give it a name.

Getting Frisky – The Village Voice, March 2007

I hurried into the Franklin subway stop and saw five cops circling an older black man. His mouth tightened as he held out his wallet. He seemed helpless and bewildered. The cops arrogantly pawed through his pockets. I glared at them and the sergeant saw me and scowled. Our stares locked into instant hate. The C-train whooshed into the station and I was thankful for the rush of wind that pulled me away.

Leaning on the doors, I felt guilt for not staying and telling them in a loud voice – no one is above the law, not even its enforcers. But my choice to leave wasn't made out of fear but selfishness. I'm a virgin. For black men, being stopped and frisked by the police is a rite of passage. But I've never been touched by a cop and am proud of it. Over the years the anticipation has built and now I'm trying to save my first stop-n-frisk, my first arrest for a big, momentous event like a riot or protest march. Losing it on a subway platform isn't special enough.

A stop and frisk is state sanctioned groping, it's a strange cop's hands feeling up and down your body, fingering pockets and cupping armpits. In New York, nearly a million people, mostly black and Latino men, have been stopped and frisked. The police sift the city like a miner panning for gold but their endless shakedowns only get a few guns and drugs to fall out.

I never asked my friends if they've been stopped and frisked. Are they virgins like me or are they experienced? When my roommate Esse and his friend Justine came home, I asked them. Esse looked up. "My first time, hmmm, I was buying a loosie from the bodega. When I left and walked home two cops rushed me," he said. "The female cop warned me her partner had a gun and I was like what are you going to do, shoot me?" I asked Esse why I haven't been stopped. He smiled, "Take off your glasses and wear a hoodie. You'll get all the love you want."

When I left the apartment my suitors were on the corner, badges flashing as they watched the street. Years ago, cops were rare and Myrtle Avenue was known as Murder Avenue. Then the 1990s came and gentrification began, which means white people and cops suddenly roved up and down the block. Esse and I laughed saying cops are the shadows of white people. When they arrive, the police follow.

Walking through Bed-Stuy, I see brownstones for sale and think that buyers must see stop-n-frisks and zero-tolerance policing as insurance. But when long-time residents complain at having cops' handprints all over them, the problem is directed back at them. It's not the policing, it's the policed.

Conservative pundits always blame the poor. They repeat the same argument – we're animals that need to be kept in open air pens lest we go wild in the streets. But I asked myself – *Isn't poverty a crime?* Unless you believe that we are biologically lower beings, ruled by primal passions, you have to shift the cause from people to the society around them.

I thought of the tall, dapper president of the National Urban League, Marc Morial. We met in New Orleans at the showing of *When the Levees Broke*, afterwards we shared flood stories in the damp summer night. I dialed his number and asked him about the stop and frisk policy. He said, "Policing is a relationship with the community. If people don't trust you, if they don't show up to juries, if no one offers information then police can't solve crimes." His analysis of the climate of fear and resentment rang true. I saw it last summer in the Stop Snitchin' t-shirts that young black and Latino men wore like shields.

Morial says conservatives conveniently forget half of crime reduction is economic justice. "In suburbia, mommy or daddy can pay for their child's sport league membership, gear and drive them to practice. In the urban context, parents who are working poor can't afford it. The most important part of policing is prevention. Stop and frisks are not as effective as investment in after-school programs."

As he talked, the question bubbled up. Was he a virgin? I asked him if he was ever frisked. "I haven't thought about it for thirty years," he said. His voice was like a Southern breeze opening the pages of a diary. After a high school football game, he and a friend were driving home when a police car flashed lights at them. They pulled over. The cop ordered them out, on the car and frisked them up and down. "I felt violated," Morial said, "as we drove home the questions rang in my head. What was that for? We weren't doing anything." But he never told his parents. "I didn't want them to think I had done something wrong," he said.

Growing up, Morial said school was a safe haven and I felt how true that was for me too. My own choices took me from high-school to college to graduate school and I learned new dialects of English along the way. Men of color learn to be multilingual by speaking street-slang, intimate home talk and corporate English. It sends the signal that you are not dangerous. It's a choice we make so early in our lives that it becomes unconscious when we get to be adults. Sometimes we don't ask what the consequences are of how we see ourselves or others.

I asked my friend Leron if he'd been stopped and frisked. We've known each other for years at the graduate school. "I never had the pleasure," he laughed. "It's how you carry yourself. I don't wear my pants around my knees. When I see brothers doing that, it reminds me of *March of the Penguins*."

The question burned in me like a light bulb. Who else do I know has been groped by the police? Scrolling through numbers on my cell phone, I called ex-Black Panther and current city councilman Charles Barron and asked if he's ever been frisked. "I won't allow it," he asserts. "If a cop tries to frisk me and I haven't committed a crime, we're going to rumble." Barron admitted he's not a good example being a city councilman and political celebrity. Still, it seemed ironic. One of the most militant voices in New York is a virgin.

Yet Barron spent forty-five days in jail so he can't wear pure white. Rather he's a V.I.N.O. or Virgin in Name Only. He rides around East New York providing a knightly service by policing the police. "If I see someone is pulled over, I get out of my car and tell the cop they are violating constitutional rights," Barron said. "We have a right to move freely. Being a black man in the hood is not probable cause." Of course he brings up the latest police killing of an unarmed man, "They are stopping innocent men and look what happens. Sean Bell is dead."

Barron sees crime as an effect of economic inequality and he doesn't mince words on which side he's on. "If I see brothers on the corner in Hip-Hop clothing and on the other corner rookie white cops with guns," Barron said, "I'm walking by the brothers."

After we hang up, I think about that statement. It's the choice many of us have to make – what side of the street do we walk on because there is always this one street, dividing the working poor from the moneyed, the bad schools from the good, and the candlelit restaurants from the bodegas.

The Street – it is an invisible class line that divides the clean white neighborhoods from the dark troubled streets a few city blocks over. The police are working-class recruits, hired by the wealthy to guard the gates against the barbarians. The Street – on one side are armed cops with badges and a code of silence who track us. On the other side are black and Latino men, angry and betrayed with "Stop Snitching" T-shirts. Depending on who wins the standoff, the name of the street will go from Myrtle Avenue to Murder Avenue and back again.

Yet for those of us who live behind that line of scarred black men, who love them but are afraid for them and even worse, of them, the choices are few. I called my friend, True, who told me, "One time a car pulled up on the sidewalk. Cops got out and frisked me." He was left with the same ringing question – *But I didn't do anything wrong*. Yet he said, "I own a home in Bed-Stuy and even called the police asking for more patrols, so I'm happy they aren't apathetic."

True jokes that as a 6'3" tall black man with long dreads, not many people test him. While he doesn't feel danger, his friends, especially those who are gay, are often viciously profiled not by cops but by black and Latino men.

His gay friends had been cursed and beaten near the Utica Avenue stop, so True organized BE SAFE, which stands for Bedford-Stuyvesant Accepts Everyone. "We met at the park where gay bashing took place," he said, "I wasn't there but Lloyd and this kid got into it. They did the I'm-going-to-fight-you dance but no blows." We talked about a mutual friend, a bi-sexual black woman who avoids those streets because men curse her. Later I called her and she said, "Just holding hands with another woman can cost me my life."

Quiet as It's Kept

"There is a conspiracy of silence in black communities," said Bill Fletcher, former president of TransAfrica forum. "People want to say 'I want the cops to be here' because we are more victimized by crime. But we don't because when it's said aloud it gets folded in with a racist attack on black and Latino men."

Of course, I ask him if he's a virgin. He mulled the memory over, "My first time, I was a senior in college. A man in a leather jacket came up and yelled, 'up against the wall, you fit the description!' I freaked out." He sighed heavily, "I was already a political activist and rationally prepared for being stopped but not on an emotional level." Another time, he was driving and a jeep cut in front of him. Fletcher thought he was going to be assassinated. White men jumped from the jeep and flashed a light in his car. "This isn't the one," the cop said and drove away as Fletcher's panic slowly eased.

He said that the violence within the neighborhood can be even more corrosive to much needed solidarity. Bitter men, who don't have the money to settle the question of their manhood, target the weakest among us. Gays and women are preyed on by men who need to remind themselves of the power in their cocks and their fists. "We have to challenge the criminal as role model," Fletcher said. "A community is created by individuals interacting and if they can't interact, the community is destroyed. We have to see crime as a counter-revolutionary act."

His words made me look in the mirror. Not only has no police officer ever touched me, neither has any criminal. I've never been mugged – hassled for money, yes, but never mugged. I walk the streets at night and brothers see my nearly four foot long dreads and tell me stories of prison, of women they lost, of knife fights that carved scars into them that never feel closed. It's as if they want to entwine their short brutal lives in the centuries of struggle my hair symbolizes. Sometimes they just ask me to use my metro-pass and get them closer to home.

But home is hard to go to when too many people live in it, when you're being chased out by high rents and unpaid bills and escape means wandering the maze of city streets. And being in the streets means exposure to the rough hands of the police. And the violence the police use to clear the working poor from streets the middle class want is translated by black and Latino men into street-level machismo. If our rite of passage is being groped by the police then for black women, it is being groped by us.

And I know this because my ex-girlfriend Nadja often called me on her way to the Franklin subway station, so street corner men wouldn't hassle her. We weren't married but she waved a ring I bought her in order to ward them off. When she came home she acted out scenes from the corner. "Shorty, let me talk to you, c'mon Shorty," she imitated them, trying to make laughter out of fear and anger. But the staged humor became open hurt as she repeated them cursing her, "Fuck you then, bitch!"

Every woman of color I know has been through the gauntlet of sullen men who yell at them less to be answered than to prove their power. Every sister I know has a tactic to deal with male desperation, a quick nod and "no thank you" to give them the small victory of being heard without the sacrifice of being had. Some wear a mask of stony silence and force their way through the web of taunts, pleas and crotch-grabbing. Some trade barbed jokes to let the men know pain isn't private property. And some are caught behind closed doors and forced to be the evidence of his manhood.

It's the secret violence that leaves the longest scars. At an Afro-Latino conference at CUNY Graduate Center, I met Maria who paints bright images of black women with butterfly and angel wings. Over coffee, she told me that years ago she was raped. The attacker tore her sense of safety away, leaving her exposed. Slowly, after years, she began to bandage her body with art, painting black women as angels.

The art healed her but it was still just a thin layer of paint covering terror. Once, we walked home from a restaurant with bags of food and brothers on the corner eyed her, one whistled. Her eyes locked and neck stiffened. Later she said, "They're always out there and they never let me feel safe."

When I left her house, the men were gone but others took their place. Kneeling on the sidewalk, I reached into my bag for chalk and wrote, *"When you harass women, they take it out on their children who grow up to be you. The cycle of violence continues for generations."* An older black woman said, "Thank you." Two younger sisters stood for a while, "That's so true." I gave them chalk and kept writing. Folks gathered and the men on the stoop got curious. They came and read the words but it was the open despair of the elders that shocked them. I offered them chalk but they laughed nervously and left.

It felt good to write but I knew words on the sidewalk could not help her. By the time I got home it was raining and they had washed away. Leaning out the window to wet my face, I felt my political virginity, how clean my body was with no handprints from either cop or criminal to remind me of my weakness. How did this privilege become mine?

I looked at my college diploma on the shelf and my dreadlocks. Angry black and Latino men don't hurt me because I'm a symbol of our shared history. If anything, they confess to me their hidden shame. Here I am, in the vortex of conflicting privileges of race, class and sex, which crushes so many of us, yet somehow creates this upward wind that allows me flight. Maria and her paintings shined in my mind. How lucky I am to have her wings.

The Dissertation Defense

Mother, I remember you sitting at a desk hour after hour trying to pass the Bar Exam, to be a lawyer, how the sun made your hair into a frizzy halo and your palms left sweat prints on the book covers. I cleaned your room but you yelled, saying you didn't know where anything was anymore. Grandma didn't call to say good luck.

"The slave sublime is the return to the self," I said as if laying my voice down like stone. I was at the Graduate Center defending my dissertation and eyeing my professors for doubt. "It contrasts the European sublime of the 18th Century, where wealthy men stood on mountaintops staring at a storm or a heaving sea and being overwhelmed by the spectacle, as if the concepts that their minds used to place reality in categories broke causing a rapture to lift them out of themselves. Against this sublime or maybe running underneath it is another one, a sublime experienced by the millions of slaves who were shipped across the Atlantic."

You came home, defeated. You didn't pass the Bar Exam. You sat on the bed and wept. I was defeated with you.

"Slaves were ripped out of their bodies by whips, rape, linguistic isolation and homesickness. It was a forced transcendence that did not lead to a romantic ego but a traumatized alienation," I stacked sentence upon sentence, hoping my high tower of theory would not fall.

You tried again at everything, the Bar Exam, Grandma's love, a man's love, losing weight, starting a business. You slept with the TV on because it kept you company. I was gone already and not calling either, angry, embarrassed. One day you told me you were not taking the Bar Exam again and that's when I knew how tired you were. I wanted to win something for you.

"When slaves were freed, again and again they used the language of the sublime to articulate the freedom not to transcend but to return to their stolen bodies," I circled my hands as if scooping water on my chest, "and this return to the self is the engine of history, it is what forces the world to see its own suppressed truth and beauty. It is the slave sublime."

Do you hear my professors clapping? Do you feel them shaking my hand? Can you feel their hugs on your shoulders? Can you see how clean this room is?

300 Quincy Street

Gunshots cracked outside the window and screams rose from the street. Heads low, we ran to the curtain. Fey peeked, her face creased with lines as she studied the panic. I saw women curled under tables. Mothers wedged into doorways, arms crisscrossed over children. People ran like pool balls knocked apart. In the chaos stood a young man in a red shirt watching the street empty. He belt-tucked his gun, walked backward, arms out to welcome challengers, turned and ran.

The 300 Quincy Street block-party was officially over. Tony, my downstairs neighbor, sprinted across the sidewalk. He was the DJ who stacked speakers to boom bone rattling beats, one hand on the headphones that cupped his head like ear-muffs, the other flipping records. When the gunman fired, Tony cut the music and ran to his daughter, a girl who just spoke her first words and who was calling for him now. Fey turned and said, "You can tell we're used to this. We didn't hide. We ran to the window to see what happened."

She's right, we are used to this, we don't hide; we decipher the shooting. Which is it this time, random drunkenness, drug business gone bad, or the easily bruised pride of a boy? My guess, it was the pride.

I opened my mouth to say something about the woman clutching her friend and crying, or the family huddled behind a tree or even the loud humming in my head but instead I gripped the window. The silence swelled like a heavy rock. "I know we shouldn't be used to this," she said, "no one should. The whole point of our lives is to make this unacceptable."

I met Fey at the Graduate Center Library where books rose around us like a maze. We talked of school. I just got my doctorate, she just began hers but neither of us knew a way out of this labyrinth of words to our former world. The abstract dialect of the academy had made our lives the strange symptoms of hidden forces. Wading in theory, we frantically analyzed everything we knew to make it ours again. But however we deciphered the world, it spoke its own rhetoric of raw power. We said theory, it said fist. We said social construction, it said crotch-grabbing. Tonight we said alienation, it said gunshots. My head was roaring.

"Thanks," I squeezed her hand and pointed below at my neighbors carrying children. "No one knows if someone's going to shoot back," I said. "A kid got shot right on those steps a few months before I got here. Every summer boys kill each other while the rest of us just try to get out of the way."

She rubbed my shoulder and we scooted to the next window. I leaned out and saw Diane, an older lady who lived downstairs, who welcomed me to the building, smiling as I came and left until one day we sat on the stoop trading stories. Her voice was a Southern breeze blowing through Brooklyn brownstones, warm, open and full of pollen. But now I saw her running down the street, pointing at someone and yelling for them to come back inside. I hated seeing her terrified.

"Let's go to the roof," I said.

"Yeah, good idea," as she poked her arms through coat-sleeves, I clenched my keys, we ran up the stairs, flung open the roof-door and stepped out into a night mist that speckled my glasses. In the street, police sirens whooped. Red and blue lights splashed the buildings that looked like cathedrals where people watched from windows, misty halos around their heads as if they were spirits studying the human agony below.

Cop cars circled the street, lights a bright whirlpool. Old men yelled to women who crouched under tables holding their children. Nearby stood baby-faced boys, excited by the violence, studying the young men in the center grinding fists and vowing revenge. It was a boiling pit of rage and fear. I could witness it because in Bed-Stuy the rent was cheap and I spent the extra money on white poetry groups or white Leftist parties. Those were safer worlds where no one ducked gunshots but where it was a ritual to eulogize those who did. At the parties, we spoke about the violent streets with pity or righteousness but here those words were sucked out of me and into this vortex of terror that could not be stopped simply by describing it.

"Look, people are coming out," she pointed and it was true. Women, looking first, rose slowly from under tables. I saw George, an older man, turning and turning as if lost and I worried for him. His son was the boy shot on the front steps of my building, Tony told me how blood spilled from him as he wobbled to the sidewalk where the last of it spread in a red pool. Ever since, George will sit for hours on the stoop like a living tombstone. I watched him spin around as if looking for the world to fall back in place.

A white couple, skin glowing in the dark, clambered beside us. "Did you see the shooting?" the man asked. My friend eye-rolled and ignored them. I glanced over and saw their faces overflowing with unasked questions. *Are we safe yet? Can we leave now? Do you know who did it?*

"No," I turned and mumbled, "we heard it then came up here to get a better look." She jabbed my arm to show me motorcycles light up, rev thunderously and angle through the police cars. They were Tony's friends and I hoped they hunted the shooter down. I glanced at the whites who lay next to us and envied that they could feel terror but only terror; I also felt pride, shame and vengeance.

"Cold?" my friend asked.

"Cold," I nodded.

We went down, back inside my apartment. "Let me walk you back to your place." We headed downstairs but the entry was jammed with people. Tony and his friends angled huge speakers through the slim doorway as we flattened on the wall to let them pass. His face met mine. "Your daughter safe?" I asked.

"Yeah, thanks," he veered the load into his apartment then walked back out breathing hard and fast, "She was inside."

"Anyone shot?"

"No, he just wanted to scare us," he said. "Why niggers got to be so ignorant. We're trying to do right, you know, have a peaceful fucking party," he slaps his hand on his palm on each syllable. "And-this-shit…"

Tony's wife stood cross-armed at the door and shot a look at me, "Now you really live here." My sleeve was tugged and I saw my friend, jutting her jaw to the street, asking silently to go. "I'm taking her back home," I said, "I'll see you later." We slapped hands as if sliding an invisible envelope between us, one that read I-got-your-back-you-got-mine. As we walked away, the loud shouts faded to a murmur until our footsteps echoed around us. I studied every man at the corner-store, every silhouette under the streetlight.

Love Thy Neighbor — The Indypendent, July 2007

On Sunday, I went to the *International African Arts Festival* in the Brooklyn Navy Yard. Thousands of Afrocentric black folk, men with long dreadlocks, women with afro-puffs, walked the maze of tents. They were my neighbors. Even if most of us never set foot on Africa, we shared it as an ideal.

It was a classic scene of commodity fetishism. Our relationship to each other was materialized in cowry-shell bracelets, Afrocentric books, bright African dresses and sculptures. We came to buy our "blackness." Each purchase committed us to our color, our hair and African past because its ancient glory, we hoped, would someday shine in our lives.

As I asked a seller about a dress, my cell phone sang. It was Delia, a friend at the international aid agency CONCERN. When I told her of the festival, she said, "You know most African clothes are made in Indonesia or the Netherlands." I stood hand on hip, "Delia, no." She laughed, "No, I'm serious. Even in the Democratic Republic of the Congo, where I'm going, Mobutu banned Western clothes so more people dress traditionally but none of the clothes are actually made there. It's fucked."

We cackled bitterly. "So what's real here?" I asked. "Maybe the people," she said. We hung up and I looked around. Hard-faced Nation of Islam men stood silent as a video of Minister Farrakhan spoke for them. Black Israelites in Lord of the Rings costumes sold books "proving" we are the original Jews. A Nuwaubian in a turban held a book to a woman, "It tells the truth about our Egyptian origins." In stall after stall the fantasy of Africa was sold and black Americans could buy into it but the fact was Africa, according to Delia, couldn't afford to buy itself.

In the crowd, a black woman with "Save Darfur" scribbled on her shirt, clip-board in hand, studied people. If someone lingered at a stall, she asked, "Hi, my name is Herlena Lewis, will you help stop the genocide in Darfur?" Sometimes guilt made them sign. If not, they brusquely waved her away.

I approached her and we talked under a painting of Samson asleep as Delia cut his locks. "When I heard about the genocide in Darfur I couldn't ignore the emergency," she said and pointed at the ideal imagery around us, saying it was irritating. I told her that I was going to Chad to interview refugees from Darfur. We shared stories of women gang-raped, of boys with guns and men thinned by AIDS. It was an Africa concealed by the romantic images that flooded the Afrocentric mind.

We traded numbers and barbed jokes but as I left the festival, my ex-girlfriend Rocky called, "Can I ask you something?" She told me her friend was losing it. "He's really Afrocentric. We were hanging out and a few Hasidic Jews walked by. He yelled, 'You're not real Jews. We are!' and stomped off." She quietly pulled her breath into words, "He has so much hate."

Glancing back at the tents filled with glorious Africa, I could see the source of his anger. Closing my eyes, I remembered my own dabbling with the Nation of Islam in college. Basically, I was a fellow traveler, who hoped a militant, proud Islam could transform my confusion into power. The Nation of Islam's weird mythology promised us that we were the chosen people and that our suffering was part of God's plan to return us to glory. But I let go of them after realizing the price of God's glory was hatred of whoever else claimed it, specifically Jews.

Afrocentrism led to a strange apathy. How can suffering in Africa be meaningful to us when we need it to be a pure homeland, where we can escape the suffering in our lives?

Expensive Sympathy

Black Brooklyn was not alone in pretending to be a neighbor to Africa. On Monday, I went to "In Darfur," a play written by Winter Miller, a research assistant for *New York Times* writer Nicholas Kristof. It was at the Public Theater at Central Park West where workers wore Save Darfur shirts and guided us to our seats. It was a stark contrast to Lewis and her homemade shirt because these shirts were professionally designed. Here, sympathy had a budget. The audience was mostly white and earnest. The play began with three characters: the reporter Maryka, an aid doctor named Carlos, and the English-speaking refugee Hamida. They are in a car racing away from the Janjaweed toward a checkpoint.

Maryka came to Darfur and heard of Hamida, a refugee who witnessed the Janjaweed pound her husband's skull into pulp with their gun butts. They raped her over and over. After they left, she stumbled through the desert to a camp. Maryka knows this story could break the front page but if she uses names, Hamida will be killed. The editor refuses to print the piece without a name.

Maryka gives up Hamida for "the greater good." Afterwards, as she files her story, Hamida is alone again in the desert. The stage goes dark and machine-gun fire echoes.

After the play, Nicolas Kristof, Samantha Power and others gathered on a panel. They recited the grim facts and hopeless history of American indifference. Against the despair, an earnest young man told the audience, "You can be Oscar Schindler, you can be a moral giant." But what was his strategy? We enlist on a website and call our politicians a lot. Everyone applauded but it seemed too loud for such a small act. No direct action was called for.

It struck me that he gave the audience what they wanted: they could enjoy the self righteousness of bearing witness within the comfort of everyday life. Like the African Arts Festival, we were encouraged to consume empty signs of our moral identity. At the end of the panel, actress Mia Farrow held up a melted child's shoe she found in the ash of a burned village. "This shows how real it is," she said, "if you want to touch it, come see me afterwards."

As I left, I met Reverend Spencer of Concord Baptist Church of Christ. He, Representative Charles Rangel, and Reverend Herbert Daughtry were arrested for chaining themselves to the Sudanese Embassy in Washington D.C. On the way home to Brooklyn, I asked him why are there so few black people at the official Save Darfur rallies?

"If you cut our community," he says, "half are Christian and half are Muslims. A lot of Muslims don't want to get involved, saying it's a Jewish conspiracy." His hands wheel in the air as he draws into focus the reasons. "I hear brothers say, 'Why should we do anything for them? They don't help us.' It's the wrong way to look at it." His voice shoots out, "I say, it's not about if they love you but can you love them." I ask why altruistic love is so hard for us. "We bought into capitalism. It's the I-got-mine mentality," he said then sighed. "We got too much hate in us."

I got out of the subway and walked down Nostrand Avenue where long-robed Muslim Africans passed bearded Rastafari, and round the way girls in tights swaggered past women in long black hijabs. We shared the street but we are not neighbors because we did not share a vision. It was obvious after seeing Afrocentric blacks at the festival and liberal whites at the stage reading of "In Darfur," both posing as good neighbors to the estranged African. Is it that we can only love a neighbor who is a distant reflection of our own goodwill?

Six Months

It's been over six months since I returned from Africa. I went to Chad, to the edge of the Sudan, where the earth desert had soaked up blood, and memory lay ripped across land. I went to bear witness to genocide and came back safe. I feel a heavy guilt for being safe, for having only listened to stories. Again, nothing I did was real. Again, the measure of my voice was taken and found infinitesimal. Whatever is worth saying will be buried in media noise. Whatever is done will never be enough.

It's been over six months since I came back. My friends ask me, "Where is the story?" I think the story is not there or here but in between us, in why we don't challenge the comfort we cling to, in the reflections we build into a fortress around ourselves. And I am beginning to hate myself. I hate my cowardice at knowing horror but letting that knowledge drip into me, one word at a time so that daylight comes before I finish writing the truth. I just want to live my sweet life again.

It's been over six months since I had a dream about Africa. Friends ask if I ever went and I say no, I never did. It was only a strange night and a strange dream filled with screams and shadows asking for escape. What a ringing it left in my head. What a hopeless way to sleep.

The Genocide Tourist — The Indypendent, January 2008

I learned about Darfur from TV news stories where sorrow-creased faces begged for help. Each one reminded me of the faces I saw in flooded New Orleans where families on rooftops lifted arms to the helicopters, hoping for rescue. I got a plane ticket, flew there and waded through the 9th Ward, giving food and recording stories. It took almost two years to stomp the water and screams out of my mind. The body is a sponge soaking emotions from others and my only relief was to squeeze them into words. It was too early for me to return to a crisis but the genocide in Darfur narrowed my vision until everyday life became a blur.

At Outpost Café, between gulps of beer, I told friends, "I'm going to Darfur." They shook heads and one let her fingers linger on my arm. I enjoyed the heroic halo that lit my face but it came at a cost. I saw a globe at the bar and touched New York, spun it until Africa was under my palm and touched Chad. The distance was dizzying. I'd never been there and I don't speak French or Arabic. I speak dollar. And there is the terrorist imagery that casts a shadow over Muslim nations. In a truly dumb move, I went to see the film *A Mighty Heart* where American journalist Daniel Pearl is beheaded by Islamic hijackers. After it ended, I stood on a subway platform lightheaded with fear.

I taped a map of North Africa over my bed and studied Darfur. The war appeared in the media in 2004 but the seeds of it were planted in the 1890s when English colonialists drew borders that boxed the Arab north and African south inside a nation called Sudan. The English paved and lit the north but left the south a vast, poverty-stricken desert. After Sudan gained its independence in 1956, the Arabs saw themselves a degree better than the Africans and since then they have fought over the nation's identity.

In between the rounds of war, old rituals continued. Each season, Arab herders drove cattle to the southern region of Darfur where Fur, Masaaleit and Zaghawa African tribes welcomed them. The cattle fertilized soil and helped carry supplies. In 2003, a drought in the North dried wells, turning earth to sand and forcing Arab herders south. They wanted more than grazing time for cattle, they wanted new land.

Rifles were handed out to African tribesmen. Anger crystallized into rebel groups, among them the Sudanese Liberation Army and the Justice and Equal-

ity Movement. After rebels raided a military outpost, the Arab-dominated gov-
ernment, flush with oil money, bought weapons for the Arab herders creating
the militia we now call the Janjaweed. They galloped into villages and shot the
men, ripped women apart and stuffed bodies into wells. Refugees fled to the
neighboring nations of Chad and the Central African Republic. In the years
that followed, 2.5 million people were driven from their homes and up to
255,000 were killed.

Journalists took photos of the refugees and sent their faces to float up
through the pages of Western magazines. Wedged between the ads, their pain-
bright eyes sparkled like diamonds and it seemed to me those eyes were the most
valuable prisms in the world. In them was condensed the pain of humanity and
if I could see through them would life finally become intelligible?

Days before I left, my poetry group met. They asked why I was going. They
weren't satiated with easy answers and kept weighing my words against the risk
to my life. They wanted to know why I was so willing to go. Was it bravery? Was
it a death wish? Was it guilt? I sat at the table surrounded by their worried faces
as my fingers fiddled as if untying a knot. Finally I admitted, "I want to feel what
I did in the flood at New Orleans. Everything was clear. Everything was real."
One of them leaned in, "You're trying to distill life into a pure moment," she ex-
plained. Another turned and said, "It's dangerous to chase that and you may not
need to. If you look around, you'll find that purity is here. It's smaller, sometimes
harder to see, but it's here too."

Days later, I was on my first flight of three. My hands shook in my lap. I was
going to Chad, one of the poorest nations, to travel to its farthest border and in-
terview refugees. I didn't speak the colonial or local languages. I didn't have a lot
of money. I would need more than luck and began to exhume old fantasies from
my mind. In a strange desperate turn, Jesus glowed in the dark of my closed
eyes. I haven't been a Christian in years; in college, I left religion. But my athe-
ism was more a fashionable gesture than a real questioning of the Bible. It was
a cheap pose that sometimes cracked under pressure.

In Amsterdam, during a layover, I took a train from the airport to Central
Station and scissor-walked to the red-light district. Men hosed the booths down
from the night before. As foam swirled into the cracks of the cobblestones, I turned
a corner and saw three African whores who hurried me in. "Let's go upstairs,
fuck!" she shouted. "No, no fuck," I pointed at her feet, "let me massage them."

She studied me, took my Euros and lay back in the chair. This thin scarred woman put her feet in my hands, closed her eyes and hummed as I pressed. "Where are you from?" I asked. She replied, "Ghana – oh good – came for work but stuck here – softer – I want to go home but no one will marry me – harder – yes – good." She eyed me. "Will you marry me?" I smiled and shook my head and pressed thumbs harder into her sole.

Her friends, one short, the other tall, glared, "Why don't you fuck?" I was glad she asked because I had a line ready, "I came for your blessing." My cheeks flushed. I told them about going to Chad to interview refugees and that I was scared shitless. But instead of laughing she patted my hand to cool my embarrassment.

In the Bible, a fallen woman washed the feet of Jesus with her tears and dried it with her hair. And here I stood over a prostitute's feet, drying it with my dreads. Looking at her oiled up legs, I realized how stupid, romantic and silly I was. "Thank you," she drawled, "your God is strong." I looked up surprised.

Her friends vigorously cleaned my hands. "Bless you. God bless you," they said and pressed their palms on my chest and prayed. As I ran back to the train, a wild grin jangled on my face. I have a whore's blessing, I thought, nothing can touch me.

Careworn

On Sunday, I stepped down the jet into the African night. The earthy musk told me how far I was from home. Even the sky smelled different. I hired a cab to the hotel, eyeing dark empty streets, watching soldiers with machine guns chat. The driver turned, stopped at the hotel gate. It was laced with ribbons of barbwire. A guard opened and I went to the desk, paid and fell on the bed but couldn't sleep. Minutes later I was in the courtyard staring at an orange lizard crawling by. Its scales shined bright against the memory of the grey concrete of New York. "Africa," I wondered aloud. "I'm in Africa."

The next day, I sat in a taxi speeding through dusty streets of N'Djamena. In New York, I read articles on Chad in which each author contrasted its poverty with our wealth. It's easy to do. One can imagine above each dirt road our superhighways, in place of their broken streetlights, our gleaming ones blinking automatically, against their crumbled buildings, our glinting skyscrapers. When I arrived at CARE, the international aid agency that agreed to be my host, a compact studious man named Joseph met me.

We went to his office. "First thing to know is people are afraid to say what they think here. It's dangerous," he said while his eyes searched the air for the right words. "The rebels reached the city April last year. French troops helped President Idriss Deby keep power."

"Even after liberation," I asked, "France has troops here?" Joseph nodded, "They never left. Deby needs them. The country is poor, prices are rising. Oil money is flowing but not to the people. The other tribes want power." My pen stopped. I tried to ask a question but didn't know how to phrase it. I tried to speak in bright clear words while siphoning English through his accent. We talked at the edge of our cultures, our words spilled in the air as if we were swimming around each other.

Slowly, we got into a rhythm, I asked what tribe president Deby is from. Joseph said, "He is Zaghawa and here tribal identity comes before national identity. Tribes wear the mask of a political party to benefit themselves. But no one feels they belong to the nation." I pushed him, "Is the Zaghawa a minority?" He looked up, "Yes." The picture he described of Chadian politics seemed a slippery slope to violence. I asked if the imbalance of power could someday lead to the kind of ethnic bloodletting that occurred in Rwanda in 1994. Joseph, who is Rwandan, sighed, "I know what happened in my country but…" He blinked and then glared, "I hate tribes. I hate African politics. It uses you in a way you don't want to be used."

I asked him if he lost anyone in the genocide. "Yes… I lost many friends, many relatives," he stared into his hands. "But," he lifted his eyes, "we must keep things straight."

As we left the CARE compound, Joseph said, "Be careful." My eyebrows scrunched. "You won't get shot," he said ruefully, "but men will stick you up. It's a poor country. People are desperate."

The NGO Economy

Each day in N'Djamena someone told me of a murder or mugging. Every warning was a brick in a wall surrounding me. If I traveled, it was by car. If I bought water or exchanged money, a local was hired to do it. I rode around staring out of the windows of CARE jeeps.

I met BBC reporter Stephanie Hancock at the Café Glacier. We sat, ordered coffee and she began the rundown. "Chad is corrupt. President Deby signed a deal with the World Bank to develop the oil supplies. The World Bank insisted that eighty percent of the revenue go to development. After the rebel attack last April, Deby had Parliament dissolve the laws. The World Bank tried to get Exxon Mobile to freeze the account but they didn't. They are completely spineless. Now the oil money is wired to him and every penny goes where he decides. It goes into his bank account and on weapons for the army."

"Deby is shrewd," she continued, "he used the crisis in Darfur to position himself a victim of the Sudan, saying Sudanese President Omar Al-Bashir is helping the Janjaweed and the Chadian rebels. And Deby is right but in turn he supports the Darfur rebellion by allowing rebel groups to go into the refugee camps and recruit. One hundred and seventy thousand Chadians are displaced. Deby hasn't given them food or stopped the fighting. Instead, he armed Chadians, handing out three to four hundred Kalashnikov machine guns to the men of the Dajo tribe in the Gouroukoum camp. He is just as guilty as Al-Bashir in the Sudan. So when I hear the Save Darfur Coalition blame the Sudan, I think it's because it fits the American War on Terrorism narrative. Arabs, Al-Bashir and Muslim Terrorists are folded into one face."

I rubbed my temples, "Stephanie…" I hesitated, not liking what I was going to say, "It seems NGOs are the only business in town that brings money to people." Her eyebrows rose as she nodded, "I know what you're getting at. War is an industry. Every Chadian with an NGO job supports twenty people, unlike the government. Even now, the schools are shut down and teachers are on strike because they haven't been paid in six months. Just five years ago, the main road was quiet, no cars, only goats. Now it's busy with NGO Toyotas and motorcycles."

We shook hands and I saw her walk into the street. Instead of calling a CARE driver, I followed her lead and tried to find my way back alone. As I smiled and waved at everyone, people began staring at me in a weird way. A sick woman, wrapped in a shawl, rocked on thin legs and begged me for money. Quietly, people began to circle me and a hard-eyed hunger shot from their faces like a net. It set off an inner alarm and I got into a cab but the fucking driver didn't understand English nor could he read the address I wrote down. Rubbing my temples at the dizzy feeling of being lost in a ruined city, I called Joseph who talked to the driver and within minutes we were parked in front of the gate.

Feeling safe behind the walls, I wanted to stay inside them forever. "Tomorrow you will go to Abeche," Joseph said as he greeted me, "we have a plane for you and from there you go to the camps." My hand went to my chest. I looked at him for a moment. "Joseph, the way you say tribes. I've been speaking English for thirty-two years and I've never heard anyone say the word like you. It's like you grind it." An angry smile cut his face. "Tribes," he grimaced, "I hate tribes."

An Endless Border

On the following day, I flew to Abeche, Chad's main eastern city and headed to the local CARE office. As I left the airport, young men circled me, offering to take luggage and guide me through town. One had eyes like radars as if scanning for the smallest want to fill. He followed me to the corner. "I want to go to America," he said, "fuck Chad, Africa is nothing." We didn't share enough common words to talk, so we simply stood, quietly watching the road disappear under the desert dust.

A CARE driver came and waved me in. On the way, we saw two boys fighting in the street. One had curly Arab hair, the other was African. I watched them in the side-view mirror, struggling in the dirt and wondered how many years before someone gave them guns to finish what fists could not.

We pulled into the compound where CARE officer Françoise ran around showing workers floors that needed brick, electric wires to be routed, and computers to be installed. "We just moved in so you came at a bad time," she said. I sensed her fatigue and figured that many reporters before me had come through and like me they wanted shelter, food and, most importantly, a sense of safety in a strange land. How like eager children we must seem to her, coming here with stories already written but needing the experience to fill in the details.

I waited until we sat down and asked for her story. And she traced her life across Africa. "I was in Mali, in Kenya and now here," she leaned in, "I'm not an expert in All Things African but what is very obvious is tribal identity starts young. Adults will interpret what a child does as Zaghawa or Yoruba. It creates division in the child's mind that grows as he grows and finally it becomes civil war."

During a hot afternoon, a staff member excitedly motioned to me. I followed him to his office where he showed me photos of U.S. senators, grimly smiling as they shook hands. One, a tall black man named Obama, seemed relaxed, more at ease. "Probably thinks he's in the 'motherland,'" I muttered, tired of empty goodwill. But the staff member shoved his I.D. at me, "See the date of my birthday!" My face is a tight knot, I read it – January 15th – thinking *what's the big fucking deal.* "It's Marteen Luther Keeng's birthday," he smiled, "it means I will go to America, yes?" Smiling, I nod and say, "*Of course* it does."

At night, the European staff tumbled on the sofas and watched African sitcoms, French news and dubbed *Law and Order* episodes. Mosquitoes buzzed our faces. Weather worn ex-pats came in with liquor and we drank, entangling German, English and French as the hired Chadian help sat outside silently watching TV from the porch.

I wondered what they did with the images of wealth pouring from the TV. Did the flashing sitcoms of the First World make their night darker by exposing the failures of their nation? TV was a telescope into a faraway world, a world whose wealth magnified every flaw of Chad. And we stepped out of the TV to help. We had money, bought cars, hired drivers and were protected. We had plane tickets that returned us to the land of commercials as they sat, left behind, watching us from the dark.

Into the Image

"So you are going tomorrow to Iriba," Francoise says, "I made the trip myself, it's beautiful. You'll be going with good drivers." We left the next morning. I watched the dry yellow land rise and fall. I waved to a peasant who stood up from tilling red, hard soil to wave.

My camera lay in my lap but it was useless. A photo is important to a public for its composition or context but she was not a fucking image. I watched her scrape the earth open as her child, dressed in rags, sat on a mud wall. This is real, I thought.

It was naïve wonder and I knew that but it was also a much needed epiphany. I couldn't turn the page, turn the channels or click the computer mouse. She was not an image frozen in the safe distance of consumer spectacle. I was physically here and however briefly shared time with her, her child, the driver and the soldiers guarding the roads, the boys hustling for money, the child beggars holding bowls up on the road and the Western aid workers smiling under the weight of hopelessness. Soon I would be in a refugee camp where survivors huddled under the UN logo for safety, giving pieces of broken lives to journalists who sifted through them as if looking for jeweled sorrow.

We wrestled the land with the jeep, swaying as the driver lurched up hills. We stopped at a rain-swollen river. On our side, a large semi truck puttered. The driver tied a rope around an older boy who waded into the foamy currents, hands out like a tightrope walker. He was sucked in. The men reeled him from the river and the boy stumbled onto land, wiping his face. He went out again and was sucked under again and reeled back again. On the fifth try he wobbled out on the other side of the river. They took the rope, tied it to the truck and signaled the other driver. He started his engine and drove pulling the truck in and through the waves. My driver turned to me, "Chadians don't build bridges but we know how to cross rivers."

After the trucks passed, we grabbed stones and filled the rushing waters. The current wrinkled, creased and spilled around the rocks. We got in and drove over and onward, again heaving over ridges and dry river beds. Day faded from the sky. Our driver turned on the headlights and we passed like a submarine, illuminating other trucks buried in mud, hoods open, engines gutted as men slept on tires, their heads resting on the barrels of their machine guns. We passed, taking the light away but the afterimage floated in the night.

We stopped at an outpost and our guide got me beers. Inside a hut, we gulped them down and I heard crying, turned and saw babies crawling on the dirt in the next room. Women squatted over them, fanning flies off their faces. No one said a word. What would it take, I wondered, for me to get used to seeing my children crawling on dirt, flies circling their faces?

On our way back to our trucks, our guide greeted a lieutenant. "An American," he says pointing to me. He looked around, "American, where?" Our eyes met, I shook his hand and said, "Brooklyn." He shouted, "BROOKLYN!" I smiled and later asked is he with the rebels or government. "He was once with the rebels but now he's with us," our guide said. At first I thought how slippery loyalties are but then remembered the hut where we drank beers, how they spoke in warm tones. I sensed that Western agencies wrote laws, built large warehouses filled with equipment and paying work. It was a vast but fragile infrastructure teetering in the older currents of African culture. My grand anthropological musings were broken when bored soldiers shot their guns. I entwined fingers around my hair and whispered, "Whore's blessing. Whore's blessing."

Iriba

In Iriba, I met Paul, a tall, gentle-eyed CARE officer. He showed me my room and instantly I saw that it was a small square with a bed. Later, I looked for the bathroom and the cook pointed over to a side door. Seeing a shower head and a latrine cover, I kicked it open and watched roaches scurry around the rim. "Oh come on," I muttered.

After staring down the hole, I unbuckled, pulled my pants down and tried to aim but my trousers were in the way. I waddled around asking, "How am I going to do this?" A pole was bolted near the latrine and I remembered the first scene of *Roots*. In it, Alex Hailey traced his lineage to Africa and the series began with his ancestral mother holding a wood pole, squatting and giving birth to her son Kunta Kinte. So I grabbed it like she did, edged myself past my pants and over the hole, chanting, "C'mon Kunta. C'mon Kunta Kinte." It worked and I walked back to my room thinking finally I found a good use for Afrocentrism.

At night, we watched TV. Paul and his friend lounged on couches, bantering. He turned it to an English language CNN channel. "Thanks," I said as we clinked beers. In one story, a panicked newscaster was shouting that a major American bridge had collapsed. On screen, I saw cars piled in a river as people were pulled out of twisted metal. His friend laughed and I heard an ugly tone of revenge against the West. Paul scolded him, saying everyone deserves prayer. His friend shrugged and changed the channel to one in a language I couldn't understand.

The Refugees

In the morning, I met my translator Zoubeida and as we rode the jeep to the camp she said, "Each NGO has their own camp. The ones you will see are CARE's. The two main tribes are Zaghawa and Fur. In 2003 they came over the border into Chad. They were hungry, afraid. Women were pregnant, delivered babies that died. Their feet were blistered from walking." Our truck heaved over a hill and I saw a burnt tank buried in the sand. Ahead of us, a pick-up truck of soldiers turned into the camp entrance. "In the beginning, they sit all day and cry," she said. "When you ask them questions, they cry deep."

We stopped at the entrance so the guards could stamp my papers. The lieutenant asked me something. Zoubeida translated, "He wants to know why your hair." I lift a dreadlock, "It means respect for the Africans brought to America for slavery." She translated, he said something and they nodded and pointed at my hair. I asked her with my eyes. "He said if a woman had your hair," she rolled her eyes, "she'd be very beautiful."

We rode into camp, got out and she walked me through a maze of huts. "CARE gives material and opened a library and school," we approached a small mud hut with a tattered U.N. fabric roof. "It's not enough," she declared flatly. We enter and Zoubeida tells a young woman who I am and why I am there. She nodded and we sat. "Her name is Saida. She is twenty-two years old," Zoubeida told me, "when she was sixteen her father engaged her to his sister's son who was in Libya. He never came back to marry her so he told her to marry the man's brother instead. Her father told her if she did not agree to marry she must leave the house. She had baby from husband's brother. It's with the grandmother now. After she had the baby, she didn't talk for a year."

I asked how wide the age difference was. "He was thirty, she was just sixteen," Zoubeida said. I angrily tapped the notepad. "Where is her family?" I asked. They talked more and Zoubeida said, "She is alone now."

Later, while we walked between the tents, I asked Zoubeida how the women were treated. She lowered her voice, "Women have many problems. Woman to woman, it's easy to talk. Woman to man is hard. A lot of beatings happen. Men are angry. We see women with…" she circled a finger around her eye. We entered a building where men sat on the rug, the women in the back. The chiefs held court from chairs. One wore a white turban and he directed the meeting. His face was a rock until I asked the universal question, "Do you get paid enough?" They laughed long and hard. "We need four times as much," he said.

"What would you like to say to Americans," I threw the question into the room like an inflated beach ball. The chief spoke with confident joy for an endless time. When he finished, Zoubeida translated, "We know about Malcolm X and Martin Luther King Jr. We know when the African American people hear our story, they will help us." I winced, knowing his solemn words would be drowned out in the music, movies and celebrity gossip that sloshed in our ears.

I wondered what Zoubeida would like to ask and said, "With all the anger and pain from the war, does it cause violence in the home? Is there abuse of women?" They squinted, shook their heads, "No, we don't have that problem here." His smile was innocent and forced. "Whore's blessing indeed," I muttered. "What?" Zoubeida asked.

"Nothing, nothing," I said but quietly thought of his smile and the casual violence it concealed. How like water violence followed the gravity of powerlessness. It hit those too silent to speak or too invisible to be seen. It carried the victims away, out of sight into the grave, into madness or into the brothels of the First World where they are used as the raw material for men's fantasies of sex or salvation.

The next morning, I asked Zoubeida about the Janjaweed using rape as a weapon. She took me to a hut where a young woman sat on a mat. Her body was still and she seemed focused on a scene that flickered in front of her like a film. She was told who I was and spoke through Zoubeida. "My name is Fatime, three years ago the Janjaweed came on horse and helicopter. We ran. Some of us were separated from family. I saw them kill my uncle. They shot him. We were running from the village, crying and shouting. Five men on horses pulled me away. They raped me. I remember the whole thing. I couldn't walk. I lay there for two days. I thought I was going to die. I wanted to die. Someone saw me and gave me water. At first I didn't say anything because I was ashamed. I told my husband. He knew the situation with us. I'm always thinking about what happened. I want to go home. There is nothing new here."

Her eyes were wet and bright. Pain emanated from her like a ringing bell. I stumbled out and we drove back to the CARE compound.

Night came and I left my room, climbed on a parked truck and rubbed my chest. It was tight as if my heart was pumping Fatime's voice. A lightning storm struck the land and I sat there seeing her face every time my eyes closed.

Leaving

In the morning, we met again at the CARE office. Paul announced, "Today you go back to Abeche." It seemed sudden and I wondered if they were getting nervous at my questions. Zoubeida and I stared at each other, not knowing what to say. The past three days we shared the same stories. Our English created a common light that showed unseen parts of each other's worlds. I took out my copy of *Beloved*, "You said you wanted to learn to read and write English." She nodded. "Take this, it's the best English to know," I said and she smiled. In a jerky, clumsy dance we almost shook hands or hugged but the veil got in the way.

On the UN flight back to Abeche, I studied the land below, I saw grass trail the underground veins of water. My trip has been similar. I flowed into Chad on the veins of Western aid, riding its jeeps, sleeping on its beds, flying its planes and writing its story. The small trickle of Western money and equipment sustained life here.

At the CARE office, Francoise shook her head. "I can't believe they drove at night," she barked. "They are like little boys. They think nothing will happen to them until it does." She leveled her eyes to mine, "They are planning to send twenty thousand soldiers here. Where are they going to stay? The only way peace will come is if there is a framework for their return and I don't see that happening for years."

Hours later, I stood at a landing strip as a U.N. plane zoomed in and rolled to a stop. The man who drove me here asked excitedly, "Can I have your email? When I get to America, you will help me, yes." I grinned and wrote with long precise letters a fake address. "Please, look me up and I will help you." He smiled wide, "Thank you, my friend."

In N'Djamena I said good bye to Joseph. During one of our talks, he told me of wanting to bring his children to America to go to college. I gave him my real email and number. It would be years before they were old enough for me to help but it was my debt to him and one I could pay.

At the airport, Texan oil men peered over each other's shoulders to the plane. One had a Confederate flag on his cap. We filed into the jet and flew into the night. North Africa was a black desert with small patches of light like spilled glitter. Above us was endless space where I saw a red meteor arc across the sky. The stars were bright chandeliers. In its darkness, I saw my face in the window and wondered what home meant to me now.

After two flights, I sat in a cab zooming to Brooklyn, gazing out of the passenger window. In Chad I measured their poverty against our wealth. Now I measured our wealth against their poverty. My mind imposed a dirt road on every highway, a mud hut next to every skyscraper. In my apartment, I stood over the toilet and flushed, amazed at the endless swirl of water.

In the street, I walked without fear. Buildings lined the sidewalk. Businesses were open to whoever walked in but I superimposed the tall steel gates with coils of barbwire in Chad. In the distance between these worlds, I could react in one of two ways. Either lay my life down as a bridge between them or let daily life chip at memory until I forget what I learned. And I chose to forget.

Days went by, then weeks and months, falling like snow until the pulse of the memory was too faint to feel. I went to work or out to play in the city. But after being in a place, the mind may forget but the body remembers. On the internet, I read a report by Stephanie, who I met in Café Glacier. Gunman barged into aid offices in Eastern Chad and beat the staff. A shiver went through me. It was late, the sun spread blue into the purple night and in that new light I began typing, "It's been over six months since I returned."

Space Station New York

Caught in the currents of memory, I see how small our fears are and float above them. A homeless man spits on his chest and the crowd arcs around him. I place a napkin in his palm. His dirt caked hands grip mine. In the subway, a man glares at a woman with hard beams of hate and lust. I tell him to leave her alone and he shyly mumbles, walks away and then from a distance saws his finger over his neck and points to me. I shrug and smile. None of it holds me. None of them are real.

I live among holograms that when reached for leave a puddle of light in the hand. I was once like them, unreal, living in an image of myself but I left New York for the edge of a war and there felt the weight people carry in their silence. When I came home, gravity hardly held me. The fears here seem faint against the more real memory of children crawling through dusty streets on twisted limbs, of women moving like sharks to offer themselves to tourists, of boys with machine-guns guarding roadblocks. That is the world. New York in contrast is an insulated space station. Here we live amongst our trivial freedoms and endless reflections. Here we lie to each other and call it gravity.

Letter from Burning Man – 2007

Dear Joseph,

Before leaving Chad, I said when your children come of age that I'd help them get into an American school. I meant it. You gave me transportation from the city to the refugee camps. You drank, laughed and were open with me.

It was a hard trip, Joseph. The faces of the people I talked with are in my head. The young boy whose legs were twisted like pretzels, will he survive? The woman raped by Janjaweed marauders, will she ever feel at home in her body? Such impossible questions, I am not there anymore and if I was the hundreds of thousands of other people with the same wounds, the same fears would overwhelm me.

In your office, you told me that your friends and family had been killed in the Rwandan Genocide. I understood then the heaviness in your core. You keep that memory inside as you work in Chad, a failed state where men settle the question of power with guns. You must guard your family against the desperate hunger that prowls the streets.

I understand the heaviness. I reported from New Orleans when it flooded. It wasn't the dead floating in the streets but the hurt of living people that shook me. When I returned to New York City, I reported on the police killing of a young black man. The faces of his family, twisting in rage, in despair as they sang over his coffin stayed with me long after.

But how do you carry that weight? It pulls me into a black hole. Three weeks after I returned from Chad, I left for another desert, in the United States, in Nevada where I hoped to pour the nihilism out of my body into the sand.

The Nevada desert is very different from the North African desert. It is a white flat earth cracked by sunlight into a puzzle. Every year I go because for one week fifty thousand people arrive in a river of cars and trucks. They get out, erect tents, build stages and bars as people walk from camp to camp, in costume or naked, bottles of liquor swinging from their hands.

Music booms from speakers as dancers grind, swallow pills and smoke weed. It's a huge carnival city called Burning Man, a brief utopia, a wild American Paradise that exists for a week then vanishes. Just Google it and your laptop will be filled with the craziest photos you've ever seen.

I walked around the dusty camps and the memory of the Darfur refugees huddled in U.N. tents moved in front of my eyes like a movie only I could see. Thin black women with buckets searching for water walked past Americans who ate hot meat from plastic plates. Scarred boys in military uniforms held machine guns as naked couples kissed in their tents.

I was the only one who could see both worlds at once, who could superimpose both deserts on top of each other. And I rubbed my eyes to get the vision out. Walking past a large hall, I saw a crowd gathered to hear a lecture. I ducked in. On stage, a man spoke of Burning Man as the future. Sandy haired, lanky with black glasses, he said ancient Mayan calendars predicted our evolution to another level of consciousness and that a new utopia would rise from this old world.

The audience sat blinded by his vision. I imagined next to me a boy from the camps, he was born with stumps for legs and lived tied to a wooden stake. He was so skinny I could count his ribs. I think he is dead by now.

And this is our world, Joseph. Separated by eight thousand miles are two deserts. One is within a failed state where Darfur refugees live on the parched land, the other is where Americans party to fantasies of a utopian future. And they are connected by a history neither can see.

Europe created itself by destroying Africa. It carved nation states into tribal land, it colonized the people, it sold millions of human beings into New World slavery, it stole lives, it stole raw goods. It created America which inherited Europe's global domination. Now Americans flee to a desert to create a world beyond capitalism. But it cannot exist. Not until the thousands of miles between the two deserts and the hundreds of years are bridged and all of humanity can cross over and share life as equals.

And that is how I think of you Joseph, a human bridge between those who are on the edge of death and those with power. You lost so many loved ones. You carry the weight within you. I know. I have it too.

And that's why I remind you to call on me. When your children come of age, I want to help them get here so you can finally rest. You were my bridge, let me be yours.

Obama's Soul

"I'm tired of this Reverend Wright shit," Chris said. Sunlight slid over us as he drove. We were talking about the latest political scandal. The presidential election was nine months off and every TV showed the eager face of a nominee. One Democrat was a black senator from Illinois named Barack Obama and few believed he was anything more than a token. But as he edged close to the nomination, a static charge around his name grew and we began, almost against our will, to hope.

And then ABC and Fox aired clips of Obama's pastor, Jeremiah Wright, condemning America for its foreign policy. After 9/11 he quoted Malcolm X that, "America's chickens were coming home to roost." In his flaming prophecy, the faces of the wretched of the earth were seen and it scared the shit out of white America. Now Senator Obama was being forced to answer why he sat through this angry black pastor's sermons.

"What do you make of it?" I asked my friend.

"The ruling elite are trying to prune Obama of any radical roots he has left," he huffed, "to make him acceptable."

A thought flashes in me but cloudy fear covers it. Why did I close up after glimpsing a truth? I speak rapidly, emptying out words to let the lost idea spurt out. "It's weird how they hammer it in over and over – oh – wait – okay here it is – some of what he said was silly like the government created AIDS to kill black people but they take the one obviously stupid thing he said *to delegitimize* all the accurate things he said like the incarceration of black men, our reaction to 9/11…"

I rant. My friend nods, changes lanes. I mutter, "Something weird happened. I had that thought but repressed it. I felt it close as if it endangered me. Is that how power works inside you, it suppresses thoughts and you have to fight to feel them again."

A sigh spills out of me and I sink into the seat, "That's terrifying." We drive in silence for a few minutes.

He changes lanes again. "What you just experienced," he mulls, "that's Obama's soul."

The Second Death of Sean Bell — The Indypendent, April 2008

Today the value of my life dropped. It was on a scale held by the Queens Supreme Court. On one side were three NYPD policemen. On the other, the death of Sean Bell, a young black man they killed last year. It felt as if all of black and Latino New York stood in the pan with Bell's family.

We stood with them because we'd seen men of color stumble from school to jail, fight in the streets or fight themselves and we knew why they struggled even as it scared us. Police rarely look past the color or swaggering manhood to the confusion beneath. They just shoot and that is our collective experience, the backdrop against which Bell's murder made sense to us. When the trial began, I hoped for justice. And a part of me froze until the day the verdict was due.

I woke, turned on the laptop, typed NY Times, read the headline and sank in my chair. The cops were acquitted. My friend called and told me of a rally at the Queens courthouse. After dressing, I went out but saw no one in the street talking about the verdict. A woman pushed a laundry cart. Workers sipped steaming coffee cups. I was dazed. How could life just go on when its value was being lost?

On the train to Queens my heart felt like an alarm clock. At Union Turnpike I ran to the street and saw cops guarding the courthouse. Next to it was a park where activists chatted. A tingling impatience was in the air as if we waited for the show to start. A sister from the Malcolm X Grassroots Movement yelled in the megaphone. We craned our necks, listening to the incantation of wrongs. After her, a young brother with cornrows, Pan-African flag flapping at his belt, yelled. The rhetoric was interchangeable pieces of the same puzzle, "People's Justice!" or "Revolution!" No one moved beyond Sean Bell the symbol to Sean Bell the man.

The joyful vengeance contrasted the despair I saw in photos from the morning. What I remember from those pictures, from Sean Bell's funeral, from his mom Valerie Bell at the precinct vigil, was deep pain welling up from the absence of a man they loved. For activists, Bell was a symbol to illuminate their politics. There existed two different visions of the same man.

The first vision was nearsighted. The grind of life, the drama of family, of love and loss and money take up the whole horizon. Everyday people can't see the larger system that is their invisible cage. In this myopia, Bell's death is a personal tragedy.

On the other hand, political activists suffer from farsightedness. They see through the prism of history so that *only* that cage is visible. Ideas are more real. Each new victim, like Bell, is reduced to a sign of another domino falling under the momentum of power. Such historical farsightedness can cause blinding arrogance.

"When we chant 'No Justice, No Peace' what does that mean," she demanded. No one answered. Instead, we began to march. A banner with Sean Bell's face and fifty bullet holes was held like a passport; it gave us the right to move across the border between laws. We were a wave. At our crest, photographers walked backward. They bent, angled, clicked. We marched up Queens Boulevard, up Jamaica Avenue. The longer we marched, the louder we yelled. I ran past the stone-faced police, past the blinking cruisers to the front where the march looked more like a festival of rage.

We weren't doing much, I thought. We demand revolution but won't try simple civil disobedience. We can't say the obvious truth that Mayor Bloomberg and Police Commissioner Ray Kelly knew we'd march and let us, figuring correctly that we weren't worth arresting.

We turned into the lot of the Kalua Nightclub where Bell was killed. The march whirlpooled around the speaker. "Leave peacefully," she said, "don't give them a reason to arrest you." She told us what we do afterwards is our responsibility. The structure that bound us evaporated and we bounced around like loose atoms. Revolutionary Communist Party members called for a new march, "Let's keep it going!" We reassembled ourselves, same chants and same movement forward.

I left for home feeling lost. Days went by aimlessly. At school, I watched my students and worried that they'd step in traps they couldn't see. In the background, the tension over the verdict built and then Reverend Sharpton's National Action Network called for six rallies across the city on Wednesday. Each one would march to a bridge or intersection and stop traffic. I hoped it was the beginning of a real resistance and went to Police Plaza One. Protesters counted aloud the number of shots, "One, two, three..." I joined and we held our fists up, yelling, "Forty-eight, forty-nine, fifty." Bored reporters tapped pens on notepads. Women anchors tiptoed on high heels to whoever yelled loudest or looked normal enough to believe. On either side were lines of police eyeing us.

Lawyer Michael Hardy told the National Action Network staff, "Let's keep everyone marching in circles." We spun like a wheel around Sharpton's absence. And then the air electrified as reporters piled on top of each other to see Sharpton, Guzman, Benefield, and Bell's fiancé-to-be, Nicole Paultre Bell, arrive. Cameras wavered above like birds angling over bread. Sharpton walked to the edge of the police barrier and prayed.

After prayer, they turned and walked into the street toward the Brooklyn Bridge. I followed, laughing as bystanders took cell-phone photos like free souvenirs of history. Next to me a tall lanky, young brother was bobbing on his heels as if ready to leap. "You going to get arrested," I asked. He nodded, "Yeah," and dived in but the cameramen around Sharpton were a wall. "Let me in," he yelled, "let me in, I want to get arrested!"

Sharpton, Guzman, Benefield and Nicole Paultre Bell stopped at the bridge entrance, blocking traffic with their bodies. Finally I thought the city will have to wait, even if briefly, for us to be heard. As cops pulled on gloves, we chanted, "No Justice, No Peace," and the words fused into a hard hypnotic rhythm.

We watched them be arrested, plastic handcuffs tied on wrists and walked to the NYPD bus. I saw Guzman looking out the window. He studied the scene as if keeping the image to remember when he was in jail.

As the last protesters were taken, I knew the rally was less about shutting the city down than to show New Yorkers that action was possible. It worked. Often in Bed-Stuy I see black men lined up on the sidewalk being frisked by police. As cops fold the boys into the backseat, we feel deep shame oozing through us. We feel weak and ugly. But at the Sharpton rallies, when black men were arrested, their heads were up, they were not guilty and we were not shamed. A rare light shined from their faces. It was pride.

We need that pride to power this movement and push Sean Bell's unlived life into our collective consciousness. Without it, mass civil disobedience will not happen and Bell will die a second death. His fiancée Nicole said after the verdict, "They killed Sean all over again." She's right. His memory is our responsibility. If he disappears, it's our indifference that caused it. The NYPD killed Sean Bell but only we can let him die.

In the Night of Bodies

Panting in the dark, we untangled our limbs and fell back on the bed. Her breath steamed into my ears. I brought her leg up over my hips. She knotted her hands into my dreads, weaving fingers in and out. Our bodies were a light bulb in the night.

She rubbed my chest but I clenched. Heat needled my eyes and my body was like a hot geyser bubbling desire, grief, rage, hope. *Why am I feeling this? Is this what's been inside me all these years but only now, with her, am I feeling it?*

"You have so much dark energy," she said and palmed circles over my heart, "it's like tar."

"I have a lot of people inside me," I turned to her, "I'm crowded."

She kissed me lovingly, straddled me and rubbed my chest as if scooping out debris. Closing my eyes, I floated in the dark tides that lapped the edge between the self and the unconscious ocean within. She dug into me as if hauling out the raped women and dying families in the refugee camps, hauling out my hopelessness of ever helping them, and even touched the memory of my uncle's too-close face. I grabbed her hands before things spilled out that I could not put back.

In the morning, she left for her place in Queens and I listened to my girlfriend's phone messages asking where I was last night. I picked my lover's hair from the pillow. Each strand was long and straight, I wove them into my dreads and put one in a poetry book I was reading, *The Tree Within* by Octavio Paz.

Months later, I told Hypatia about the affair. She erupted and for months we fought. Every time she cried, guilt scraped my soul like a giant anchor on the ocean floor. I felt responsible for her sex, her life, her future and swallowed the numbness that made me search out another lover in the first place. Day after day, I chewed the hot coals of her rage.

After another fight, we slept with our backs turned to each other. I saw *The Tree Within*, opened it and saw my ex-lover's hair again, next to the lines, "Touch, light in the night of bodies."

Turning off the lamp, I searched Hypatia's body for the tension left by my betrayal, found it below her belly button like a hard rock. I squeezed my apology silently into her muscles. "Can you feel it," she asked but looking away, "can you feel how much you killed me?"

George

An older man sits on my stoop but he doesn't even live in my building. Wearing an Obama cap, its rising sun logo looks like a Third Eye, he watches the boys on the corner, the toddlers, the women drunk and laughing.

Coming home one night, I slapped hands with my neighbor Tony, a light-skinned DJ from the first floor who is the living history of Quincy Street.

"Tony, who is the old guy who is always here," I made a circle with my hand over the chair, "the guy with the Obama cap?" Tony holds a finger up, exhales his cigarette smoke, "That's George."

"He lives in the building?"

"Naw, his son was shot here last year, right in the doorway," he pointed from the steps to the street, "he was bleedin' bad, made it to the street and died. Saw the whole thing."

"Jesus."

"It was rough here for a while," he inhaled again. I held my breath not knowing what words to exhale out. Afterwards, I said hello to George and heard a warm Alabama breeze blowing in his voice. Stillness or sadness, I can't tell which sits in his core. I asked about his son.

"Rashid, he was good. He wasn't into anything. They got him mixed up with some other kids and," he squinted, "it was hard, yeah, real hard especially for his mother. She still broke about it."

"What happened that all the kids turned to guns?" I ask aloud, not to him, just aloud. George shifted in his chair, "You know, before, we just fought. If you got beat, you got beat but now these boys can't take a beating. No one can tell them nothin'," his shoulders slumped. "I don't know. I don't know."

On the anniversary of Rashid's death, a block party boomed through the street. Tony spun records under a tent. I cut through the crowd of teens who were yelling, boasting, teasing and cursing as Rashid's face glowed on their t-shirts. George was on his plastic chair. I waved but his eyes were wet and his arms moved with the slow waviness of someone drunk.

The next day, I saw George on the stoop. Glancing backward, I imagined Rahsid's bloodstain near his feet. He loves his son so much that he has become a human tombstone.

Two Fathers — The Indypendent, June 2008

On Father's Day, two black men passed each other. One stepped into glory, the other emerged from his grief. The first was Senator Barack Obama, a presidential candidate who spoke at Apostolic Church of God to castigate absent black fathers. The other was William Bell, a father who held a rally for his son Sean, killed by the NYPD.

Obama began his Father's Day speech, "If we're honest with ourselves, we'll admit too many fathers are missing." He loosed a cascade of archetypal scenes of black pathology: gunfire at night, boys on corners or in jail, each image ended with a plaintive, "How many?" He demanded black fathers come off the streets, come back home, turn off SportsCenter and raise their kids. Churchgoers stood to applaud.

Obama's biography guaranteed his words. His father abandoned him, leaving a shared "blackness" to cover up the absence. But his speech succeeded because the black middle class needs him to speak their anger. In 1996, they laughed bitterly over Chris Rock's routine *Niggas Versus Black People*, applauded in 2004 at Bill Cosby's *Pound Cake* speech, and made the Don Imus "nappy headed hoes" rant into a debate on Hip-Hop.

Obama is the icon of black middle class and this allows him to work the updraft of two groups united in their resentment of the black working poor — white voters who believe their hard-earned wages are being taxed and given to blacks on welfare, and the black elite itself, weary of carrying the weight of a shared destiny. The shared resentments fused into the image of the absent black father. Yet one father Obama couldn't speak about is William Bell, whose slain son marks the limit of Obama's liberal lyricism.

The Saturday before Father's Day, William Bell organized a rally for his son in Jamaica, Queens. I took the train to Roy Wilkins Park and found the gathering. A scattered hundred people stood politely, listening but bored, hot but willing to stand in the sun for the promise, if not reality, of justice.

Bell sat on stage as speakers took the podium. Some offered simple clichés, others a poignant analysis of a beleaguered people's woes. I looked at him and sensed a father who did right by his son in a hard city. He raised Sean who stumbled from one arrest to another, got his girlfriend Nicole pregnant and had two daughters by her. But slowly Sean was turning himself around. He engaged

Nicole, was training to be an electrician and was going to marry her the day he was shot by the NYPD. At just twenty-three years old, it's that nearly completed redemption that makes us ache.

It's what drew Shane, a city employee to the rally. He told me of his brothers. One killed in a shooting, another in jail for forty-seven years. "These streets play for keeps," he said. "I've got a wife and kids. I don't smoke, don't drink. I keep it real straight but when I was pulled over by a cop who was hostile, I was afraid for my life." He shakes his head as if to pull away from the memory.

As I left the rally, I saw Shane and Bell: two black fathers on the other side of Obama's speech. The former survived to become a father and the latter raised his son who finally became one. Yet the historical violence visited on black people left Shane scared for his life and Bell without his son. It's a cycle of violence that Obama acknowledged in his Father's Day speech as "a tragic history." I remember him leaning into the microphone, "But we can't keep using that as an excuse." He paused, to know if he stepped over the line or nudged it. The churchgoers stood and clapped. His voice deepened to hammer in his gain, "We can't keep using that as an excuse."

But let's do a simple mental experiment. What if every absent black father came home? What if they saw the only way to raise black children is to first change themselves, feel the pain beneath their anger and cure the fear that makes their pride so combustible? What if they saw that that wasn't enough, because city schools graduate only half our children, and too few jobs exist even after they get a diploma? What if they saw their children entering a corrupt society that feeds off their failure?

These fully present black fathers would not use history as an excuse. They'd become history by changing the world into what their children need. And their demands would terrify politicians, including Obama, who would be forced to create a jobs program and free universal health care and free college. But he could never do that because he owes too much to Wall Street and he pays them in the coin of black pathology. As long as crime and failure are seen as rooted in a culture of poverty, we remain blind to the culture of corruption in the ruling class.

During his speech, Obama yelled, "The change is not going to come from the government. The change is going to come from us." I hope so, because when it does, Obama is going to have a lot to answer for.

Masters of the Universe

"Imagine your child self is here," she placed a chair next to me, "and your mom is in this chair. And her child self is in that chair. Now she put you in the orphanage. Milton Hershey, right?"

"It wasn't Charles Dickens," I said. "We had running water, food and clothes. I just felt abandoned."

My therapist patted the seat, "Good, now talk to your child self. What does he need to hear?" I looked at the empty seat, seeing myself as a boy hunched over a book, huge glasses and a questioning look. "Hey little man, you are going to go away and it's going to be scary but keep steady. Mom is struggling and by holding it down, you can keep everyone together."

"Okay, good, now sit in the child's seat and talk to your adult self," she pointed at the next chair. I sat in it, feeling him rise into my voice, "Did I do something wrong? Is she mad at me? Why is she sending me away? Am I bad?"

"Now, mom to child," she urged, her eyes alert to the shifting heat in my face. I got up and sat in Mom's chair. "No baby, you didn't do anything wrong," my voice flew up, "I just need some time to get things together but I'm coming back to get you real soon."

"Now, adult self to mom," she said and I got up, slid into my still warm chair. "Lying bitch," I tasted the sting, "why not tell me I was going to be in that prison of a school for nine years? I could have been prepared. You know, get my shanks ready in case there's a rumble in the yard."

My therapist snorted, laughed, giggled, "Go on. Go on."

"I couldn't believe you anymore," my voice broke, "you were my best friend and you fucking left me there."

"Now, child mom to adult mom," she nodded to the most distant chair which was cold when I sat in it. Closing my eyes, I conjured up the image of her as a girl from photographs, filled it in the tone of her voice, the stories she told me, the restless spark of energy that churned in her.

"I'm scared," the words flashed in my darkness, "I'm running from Grandma's screaming. I'm running from Grandpa's hands at night. I don't know where to go but I just want to feel safe." My throat tightened, feeling the panicked girl at mom's core who ran in an endless dark alley of promises.

"Now, adult mom," she pointed to the next chair, again I got up and sat in a cold chair and felt mom in me, a woman climbing sand hills left by people who chose to silently judge her.

"Never in my whole life was I allowed to be just me," my voice stiffened, "when he went to the orphanage, I was ashamed to say that I wanted to be alone, to be just me. When I saw him, the guilt killed me. It just became easier to keep him there. I lied to him to be able to live with myself."

And turning to the chair where my adult self began, I said from my mother's perspective, "I'm sorry for lying to you."

"Now, sit back in the first chair," she said and I did, rubbing my hands, breathing slowly and then I gripped my knees. "How do you feel?" she asked gently.

"I get it. I get it," inside my closed eyes, I saw everyone, me, my child self, mom, her childhood, merge into a light that filled me with a brief peace.

The Crisis

"Is this what it feels like to be inside out," I said aloud. It amazed me to feel the depths from which feelings well up, knowing each of us has this abyss inside.

Turning the corner, I saw the New School, walked through its bright halls to the class my friend taught on international macroeconomics. He strode in, burly with a big chin and a sly squint in his eye.

He was a mischievous professor, always on the edge of profanity as he charted the flows of money and goods across borders. "Who doesn't want to have a house," he began, "right? We're told from infancy that getting a house is a big fucking deal. It's the last stop on the American Dream, white picket fence, white family and white dog. It's bullshit. The idea that everyone should have a home came after World War Two as a way to sell housing to returning vets. But if you were Black or Latino or Asian or poor, you did not have access to that dream."

"So the masters of the universe on Wall Street devised a plan, sell homes to working poor people, mostly of color, with sub-prime loans. And they lined up to get loans. Who doesn't want a house? The banks bundled the sub-prime loans into larger packages, got credit-rating agencies to slap some fake AAA's on them and sold them to other financial institutions around the world. So here's the picture," he made a tower with his hands.

"The working poor were sold the American Dream and got loans to buy the big house," his hand went up a level, "their monthly payments fed upwards, banks bundled those payments into shiny packages for other institutions who thought they were getting a safe source of constant money." His hands began to rock in the air, "And this teetering tower of lies and money is what we called Western Civilization."

His voice lowered, "But the tiny monthly payments of sub-prime loans were just bait and now came the switch, the payment spiked by hundreds of dollars. The schmucks who took the loans couldn't afford it and defaulted. The money going to banks stopped." His hands snapped together, "BOOM! The tower crashed!"

Stars

After class, I walked on West Broadway past windows glowing with new jewelry. They were like stars. I angled my reflection so I was wearing a gold watch. In how many films has a woman stood in front of a store window, slipping her reflection into jewelry?

I tore my wrist free and thought about those who made the world. I looked at the clothes and imagined swollen-eyed workers stitching miles of cloth. I looked at cars and knew sewage gushed from the factories that made them. I took out my phone and saw the children who dug it from the earth.

Everything we value, everything we eat, wear or drive, is an act of theft. Our civilization is built by the toil of dead souls. I looked up and saw a few stars in the sky and aimed my cell phone at them. Thumbing nine random numbers, I pressed call.

"Hello," an older man answered.

"I'm sorry for lying to you," I said, truly feeling it.

A long silence, then, "You are?"

"Yes, I am," I assured him because he was so cautious but hopeful, "I'm sorry for everything wrong I did to you, am doing and will, I'm sure, do again. I wanted to be a good man and I lied to myself to create an image I could live with but it led to this world that we live in."

"Wait," he flared up, "who is this! Who is this!"

"You know who it is," I said, feeling the moment die, "you know who it is."

Vells

"What's your name?" I asked. "Vells," he said, through red eyes as the superintendent's nephew, Marcel, passed him a joint. I was tired of stepping over the boys' mumbled apologies as they squeezed against the stairwell to let me pass.

Vells always held the joint to me, smoke curling around his wrist like a chain. I always said no and afterwards I'd read *Go Tell It on the Mountain* or *All God's Children* as they cackled on the stairs. They were characters in novels they would never read and I was paid to teach the literature of their destruction. The silence between us wore me down.

One night I came home too tired to care. While stepping over the mumbling boys, Vells held the joint out and I sucked a deep cloud into my lungs. "Cool," he said wide-eyed. I walked up to my door and closed it hard as if to shut out their faces. They were too many to care about and the only way to guide them out was to dismantle my expensive privacy.

On the TV were DVD discs of old grainy Black Panthers newsreels. I put them in, lay on the couch and watched Huey Newton speak from jail. "The police are not in our community to help us. The police are in our community to keep property safe, not to keep us safe." His words were like an open flame. I rubbed my face and went back to the stairwell. Vells was stuffing a Dutch with moist weed. Marcel leaned in. "Got left over?" I asked. They looked up, "We got you, Rasta." Vells scooted over. He twisted the ends of the Dutch and I noted the panic in his eyes. He had the same intense focus I'd seen in other terrified people, focus kept fear in place as if by pressing down hard on each moment one could keep life from shocking you.

"I see police rounding brothers up. Either of you been caught," my hands were held out like empty cups. Vells and Marcel talked at the same time, "Yeah, they catch us and just spread us against the wall. I got busted a couple times but I'm not legal age yet so that shit won't go on my record when I'm adult."

"Yo, yo, yo, in the jails, the toilets be overflowing," Marcel snickered, "it's nasty, niggers are packed in but if you fake a condition they got to take you to the hospital and after the 72 hours are up, they got to let you go."

I prodded, "I work at a newspaper and I want you to tell your stories, your way. Vells, what are you doing after you turn legal age?" His chin tilted up, "I'm hittin' the weed now but next year I'm going to be an electrician, and they make you take drug tests so this is my last year, word nigga, I got places to go." He gave the Dutch to Marcel, "This is just a seasonal thing."

Electrician, I thought and Sean Bell flashed in my mind. It was the field he trained for until the police shot him down the night before his marriage. The odd associations between them made me look at Vells and wonder if he would be killed too.

I leaned in, "Are you willing to write about your arrests?"

"Oh, fuck yeah," they said, "we got episodes, you don't even know." I got up and Marcel asked, "You want me to bring it to you." My nobility was wearing off. I didn't want them knocking on my door, "No, put it on the mailbox downstairs." They nodded but the smoke from the Dutch clouded their faces.

I pulled out a photo of a slave, hands bound, covered by a net as his eyes begged for rescue. It was the photo on my desk as I wrote my dissertation, the first book that set me free. After the work, slavery's reach into the present became visible and the need to act more imminent. "Vells, here," he took it and looked. I pointed at the net, "What we're caught in is not visible like it was back then but it's real." He looked up. "It's like an invisible net," I said and motioned like I was trying to pull it away.

"Is that why fish kick in the nets," he said, "they can't breathe here either." I was enjoying my words so much I almost didn't hear him say it. Startled by his raw honesty, I asked, "You feel like you can't breathe?" But he was already rolling a new blunt. "I'll get you that story," he husked and leaned into his lap, "it's all good. It's all good."

A week later, I asked about the stories. They mumbled, bobbed their heads like balloons. After a few weeks, I stopped asking. It was easy to slip back into my private world where I could be a witness but nothing more.

Marcel reappeared in the stairwell, smoke in his mouth like a fog. I scolded them, "You two were stopping to be electricians." Days later, I saw Vells leaning into a car window, passing money back and forth. The last time I saw him was at the bodega. He was high, eyes wet and red. Our hands slapped, gripped and broke apart. He opened his mouth but no sound came out, as if he couldn't breathe, like he was caught in a net.

Future Perfect — The Indypendent, November 2008

> "All that was beauty, all that was Love, all that was Truth, stood on the top of these mad mornings and sang with the stars. A great human sob shrieked in the wind, and tossed its tears upon the sea, – free, free, free."

— W. E. B. Du Bois from Black Reconstruction

"YES WE CAN," we sang it, chanted it, our voices unfurled like a flag blowing in the street. We raised the slogan to the sky as people with drums hammered new rhythms. We danced and faces blurred into a swirling kaleidoscope crowd. Our eyes reflected the same fiery brilliance.

A man pulled me into the circle where we writhed like human flames. Heat, unrelenting heat, carried us into a vortex of time. We sang sounds older than words. We felt some original human need that could not be named blast through us and when we used words again, it was the chant, "YES WE CAN!"

Dizzy, I staggered out of the circle and stood in the street. People flowed around me like a river. Arms on shoulders, they smiled, laughed and raised their hands and yelled. Every color, shape and shade of humanity moved in the same direction. "The future has arrived early," I said aloud. The sight of Rainbow America, more colored than not, was supposed to be visible after 2042 but here we were dancing in the street.

I looked around. New York is ahead of the nation by decades. Here, people come from the corners of the world. Here, we squeeze next to skyscrapers and the brutal motion rubs our illusions off. So it's natural we'd see the future here first but the charge in the air was more than the promise of power, it was beauty.

I spread my arms out wide as if to hold the people and this moment forever. "This is who we really are," I shouted. In order to survive, we build walls between each other and peek terrified through the peephole at who is outside.

But today, the wall fell. Under the pressure of millions of people, chipping one vote at a time, it fell beneath our feet, and we poured through. Obama promised us this moment and we believed him. He was more than a politician. He was our hope for redemption. Since the first slave was bound to the first master, our nation was divided by a line of power. Each generation, each immigrant group reinforced that line, built it higher until it became a wall too large to bring down. But tonight, we went into the voting booth and pulled Obama's name, we reached through the symbolic blackness layered on brown skin to the humanity of the man within.

Every time a lever was pulled or button pushed in his name, a brick came down and the world we wanted, a world seemingly exiled into a perpetual future, could arrive. But as we danced, red and blue lights spun through the crowd, police cars rolled through nudging us on the sidewalk.

Instead of cooling down, I hopped in a cab for Union Square. During the ride, I thought of earlier that morning, walking to a church near my home in Bed-Stuy, joining the line of people, seeing the warm joy in their faces. Older black folk, hobbling on canes, were led to the front. They went into the booth and came out smiling.

As the voting official looked for my name, an older woman teased me, "Who you voting for." I smiled and said "I've been waiting to vote for McCain since 2000," we laughed knowingly. I asked her how she felt. Her face opened and eyes watered, "Oh honey, you don't know how long I've waited to feel what I'm feeling right now." We hugged, swaying back and forth like a bell ringing.

I voted, left the church and saw the line went down the block and around the corner. Young men in bandannas, mothers sipping coffee, workers in hard-hats, hipsters nodding to I-pods were sharing the same sidewalk, the same goal, the same need to break the wall of color. *Four centuries*, I thought, *four centuries of slavery and terror and doubt*.

My eyes were hot and wet. I blinked and saw the cab had pulled up at Union Square. People swirled in circles around the tuba players and drummers. Jumping out, I ran to them as they chanted, "Yes we can!" Curious, I waited for the backbeat and yelled, "Stop the war!" The two chants went back and forth for a minute but no one took up my call.

I dashed to my friend's house and he took out two huge ecstasy pills. "God, those fucking things look like UFO's," I said. He smiled and said, "Want to beam up?" He tossed me one and we gulped them down with a swig of water and ran back outside, buoyant energy spreading through our bodies that felt like balloons floating through the street. I bought incense, lit it and walked to Tompkins Square Park, smoke curled behind me like a vanishing tail.

Along St. Mark's, hundreds milled around. Some danced to Bob Marley anthems that poured out of the top window like a waterfall of music. Some waved the flag and sang the *Star Spangled Banner*. Some kissed strangers. At the end of the street, police stood grim-faced with an unrolled orange net. We wanted the park. The cops gripped the orange net. The silent lightning of challenge flashed between us and police. We stood there, our eyes in friction with their eyes.

But a new chant rose, "Dance, cops, dance," we yelled, "dance, cops, dance!" They didn't but we spun in our center of gravity and the police stood there, holding a net that only they were trapped inside of. Blue light ascended the sky. I stumbled home and slept in my clothes.

Days later, I play my phone messages from election night to feel rapture again. In the last message, I heard my former lover as the crowd roared behind her, "History. This is history, this is such an incredible moment, I am without words but I just wanted to share my joy and hope."

The Abyss — Indypendent, January 2009

"Step up," the cop waved a metal-detector wand over me. I didn't bring weapons but thought about it. When I told friends my plan to sleep at a homeless shelter on Christmas Eve, they said simply – *do not do it*. Insane men lurk the halls. Your stuff will be stolen. Reverend Willie, who I met in New Orleans, said, "A guy just got raped in a shelter. Three dudes held him down and took turns." Laughing in the phone, I said "I guess you should pray for my asshole. It might need it."

Their warnings were a net thrown over me but I felt that safety was a betrayal of the people. Since the Wall Street financial crisis, each month, jobs, hundreds of thousands of jobs, are vanishing. Families are being squeezed out of their lives and drop like rocks into the shelters below. New York City has more homeless now than at any time since it began keeping records. Nearly 37,000 people have no home. To understand it, I decided to slip under the numbers and come to a shelter on Christmas Eve. Standing in line, I tossed my bag on the conveyor belt while the guard talked on the phone, not even looking at the x-ray. How many knives have slipped under his careless eyes?

The 30th street intake shelter was like a prison with hard concrete walls and floors, meal schedules tacked on boards, and hallways that smell of sweat and panic. Guards laughed as one said, "Yo, give me three months and I'll be able to rip a nigger's head off," and flexed a large bicep. I winced and looked around for the desk. Above it, on a doorframe, someone wrote – God Hates Africans – Africans Are Cursed.

"Is this your first time?" the Nigerian secretary asked. I nodded. "Go down the first stairs on your left." As I walked, eyes flashed like cameras. They sized me up and I did the same, measuring each shadow sleeping on the floor. In the waiting room, men dozed on chairs like puppets with their strings cut. No one was at the desk. I sat and the guys woke up, saw my glasses, dreads and decided I was not a threat and nodded off. No one really sleeps, I thought. We're too afraid. Fear tightens the body and we never descend too far, always ready to wake and grab our stuff before it's stolen. Then it struck me how easily I started to think "we."

Hours ago, I was in my warm home emptying my wallet of cards, a metropass, video, library, Trader Joe's and school ID. The only things left were a driver's license and loose change. Shaking it out was a purging of what connected me to the bourgeoisie. It is the "we" that I belonged to and it had money, had home, had safety. We also have a mythology that justified our comfort. So when "we" walked by homeless, the old stories surfaced. They're junkies. They're criminals. They're lazy.

It's only when our world collapses do we ask about the ones under us. My thoughts faded into wind blowing through the ice-lined streets. At the corner was a payphone. I called a shelter and put in my second to last quarter. No ring, no quarter and the last one shined in my palm. This is how close it gets. On the last try, it ringed and a secretary picked up and gave me directions.

First lesson: people don't give a flying shit. In the blustery night, my feet froze. Hot goo trickled out of my nose. Numbed, I reached the shelter. Jittery women scattered from me. *God, how open their wounds are* – I thought. The guard frowned, "I'm sorry, this here is a woman's shelter. Hold on, let me call, yeah, where is the men's shelter, okay, no, it's not cold out." She turned to me and said, "You have to go to 30th street intake on 1st Ave." I asked for a metropass, even just going one way. "No," she shook her head, "when it's not cold, clients have to walk."

Second lesson – New York is big. I didn't have a subway pass. While walking, the only thing to distract me were my thoughts. Time is as slow or fast as the conversation in my head. After arguing with the memory of a lover or re-living a childhood triumph, I looked up and wasn't half way across the Brooklyn Bridge.

Third lesson – freedom isn't free. Walking through downtown, I saw my reflection on the store windows. I had no money. If I never did again, I would not be welcome here. New York always seemed like a mountainous maze of interlocking rooms. Without money the city became an endless wall of store windows that, like one-way mirrors, you could see in but no one could see you.

I walked past Union Square, past 23rd street. A big man in a fur coat pawed through garbage bins, stuffing half-bitten burgers in a bag. I heard a mucusthick wheeze in his breathing and wondered how long until it clogged his lungs. Ahead a slim shadow of a man zigzagged across the sidewalk. Was he wearing a leotard?

He looked slim but when he passed under a streetlight, I saw he was naked save for rags tied around his loins. Loose babble frothed around his mouth,

"Change? Change?" His eyes bobbed like buoys in a storm. Mind sloshing out of his mouth, he waddled barefoot into the wintry night.

What kind of people cut the weak loose so that they walk wild through the streets, so numb with insanity they don't even know they're dying? I heard the arguments, "Some of them want to be homeless. It's a freedom from civilization." *Fuck you* – I thought. Anyone can see that pain has broken the homeless. The pressures that pound on us have hit hard enough to shatter their lives. Every step closer to the shelter felt like a descent into the city depths. The phantoms I ignored on the subway as they shook cups were now very real.

At 30th street, I saw men leaning on the fence. "Rasta, let me talk to you," one of them shouted. I hunched my shoulders. "Rasta, I just need some help," he shouted, voice like a cobweb, sticky but tearing as I went by. Finally he spat out, "Nigga, we got business!" Men squeezed by each other on a soggy wooden plank that led to the shelter where staff circled around cigarettes, measuring me as I went in. Once in line, a cop said, "Step up," and waved a magnetic wand over my body and later a Nigerian secretary pointed to a stairwell where I found this room of men stranded on the edge of sleep.

We waited. The room was like a cavern, every step echoed. Guards walked by as the guy beside me called, "Hey! When are we going to get rooms?" The guard barely shrugged, "She comes when she comes." The guy sucked his teeth and leaned back and said to me, low as if passing a secret. "They have to give us a room. It's the law."

"How you get out here?" I asked, chopping my grammar as if broken language reflected a broken life. "My father kicked me out," he fidgeted. "Been sleepin' on the subways but I can't do it anymore. I was here before. It's law. They have to give you a bed." He sounded schooled and he was more anxious than angry. The men further down were harder, spoke knuckle hard slang. One had been cut from temple to chin. Privately, I titled him Scarface. The one next to me kept repeating, "They have to give you a bed."

On the other side of me was the Chatterer, a man on the payphone who talked fast as if weaving words to the outside world. A guard came in with a black trash bag. "Here guys," he said and pulled out plastic wrapped meals. "Merry Christmas," he said and tossed them to us. I caught one and peered inside. "Can I have your cheese puffs?" the Chatterer leaned in over my lap.

"No, I'm hungry," I said. I wasn't but didn't want to give too much too quickly, it could brand me a weak pushover. So I waited, laughing, thinking what kind of Survivor shit is this? But it was. Here you build alliances with who won't attack you or steal your bag or bother you too much, who'll listen when you need to drop your secrets. After eating the sandwich, I held out my cheese-puffs, "You want?"

"Yo!" He grabbed the bag, "Thanks." Well at least my tikki torch would not be snuffed out by the Chatterer. The secretary came in yelling in a thick Nigerian accent as we got up, "You wait! I'll call you." I thought of the door-frame curse. Is this where immigrant employees get posted, the bottom of the bottom? An African sifting through fallen African-Americans, she took our names, scanned our fingerprints and sent us to another waiting room. As we left, I saw an old man, breathing heavy, balanced on a cane, his knee was stiff and he swung his leg like a pendulum at each step. "Need help," I asked. "No, it's okay," he muttered. I saw the heavy bag he carried. "Let me help with the bag," I said, "don't worry I'm not trying to run with it." He nodded, I lifted it and it hung like lead. "Man, what you got in here?" I joked. He swung his leg and said, "My life."

We slept on plastic chairs. Neon light buzzed. I studied the cracks in the floor, each like a lifeline written in city stone. How tangled and random we are. Many of my friends have been homeless, even if only for a brief time. A former lover escaped her abusive family trudging through a blizzard to a friend's house, bouncing on couches until she found an apartment. My girlfriend was kicked out at sixteen by her father and floated from San Francisco with a guitar, singing songs of exile. And everyone I knew who brushed homelessness came away with a desperate need to squeeze too hard whatever and whoever looked like home until they destroyed it. Even I, raised in an orphanage, was on the run. Maybe that's why I came here, to recreate the origin of my exile and heal it.

Another man came in, tall, long face, small dreads bouncing on his head. He waited a respectful moment then asked, "Has anyone been called yet?" I shook my head but watched him. His body was calm, hands folded between his knees, "What's your name?"

"Cadrell. Just came out of prison today." A string inside me pulled tight. "Hell of a Christmas gift," I said. "Not that Christ is Satan, I mean, fuck, what do I mean…"

He laughed, "Yes sir. Yes sir, it is a great gift." *Sir*, I thought, he called me *"sir"* and I knew that sometimes, in order to survive, a prisoner will lock himself inside a faith, any faith to protect the innocence they have left.

"Cadrell, I want to ask you something," I held my palms up. "If you don't want to answer, it's cool, but how long were you in prison?"

"Five years, sir."

"How'd you make it with your spirit intact?"

"Surround myself with positive people," he said, his hands circled his chest as showing me the invisible force field he lived within. "I stay right with God and God stays right by me," he said and held me in his gaze. "You don't believe in Him, do you?"

"Cadrell, I've killed God inside me so many times," I giggled bitterly, "so many times."

A staff guy came in and gave us room assignments. The old man and I shared a room. He was old, crippled and harmless and I fell on the cot, breathing slow, able to relax when Cadrell came in and asked, "Anyone need toothpaste?" I shrugged, "No, I'm good." Good prison etiquette, I thought. If I was in jail, Cadrell would be a solid cellmate. Then I realized the doors did not have locks. Anyone could come in at any time.

Should I move the cabinet in front of the door, I debated in my head. Suddenly my roommate said, "It's better here than the other shelters. Too many young boys there. They cut each other up." His voice rattled like a can, "I was here before, a year ago, they tried to get me to therapy but I'd be high, miss meetings back on the street. I stopped doing the drugs." He chuckled. "Man, let me stop lying, I stopped doing the heavy drugs. I still get high sometimes and drink some but I stopped the heavy stuff."

The light was off and in the dark room we were just voices floating around each other. I looked through the window and saw clouds molded by wind, driven, like us, by forces we can't see. My roommate began again, "Crazy how you get high, you forget to eat. At the end of the day, my stomach sucked itself in."

"Why stop?" I asked. He coughed, laid back in bed, "I just woke up one day, knew I lost three years of my life. Three years." He said it as if taking the full measure of his loss. "What happened to your knee?" I asked. His cot squeaked as he turned, "I twisted my knee but never got treatment. I was high so much I didn't even feel it. Now I can barely move it."

"It's Christmas, where's your family?"

"Where's yours?"

"Dead," not true, but it felt true.

"Oh, I'm sorry."

"Don't be, they weren't good people."

"Like that, huh."

"Like that."

"My son won't have nothin' to do with me," he sat up and began scratching his chest, his torso, his knee and his legs as if scraping the years off. "I should be at Christmas with my grandkids," he kept scratching and it sounded like sandpaper. "Instead I'm in this damn shelter," he snarled and scraped himself with his fingernails. I just sat there watching this man tear himself apart.

Panting, he laid back down. I wanted to ask why his son was mad but was tired, too tired to carry his story. Through the window I saw a building under construction, its walls like cards stacked on top of each other.

"I was born and raised in New York, seen it change," his voice trickled through memories. Finally, some odd whisper moved through me.

"Why can't you go home, brother?" I asked but either he didn't hear or didn't want to so I repeated, "Why can't I go home, brother?" It's not what I meant to say but I knew it was a question I haven't been able to answer for years.

I didn't sleep but grazed a thin darkness, thin enough that faint sunlight was enough to wake me. Morning glowed through the steel net window. Christmas Day and I was in a strange bed. The hallway was busy with men showering and going to breakfast.

"Merry Christmas," I waved to the servers handing out small plastic boxes with French toast over a meat patty. Men sullenly ate their food. I ripped the top off and took a few bites and spat it out. A brother, face pierced with rings and bolts, said, "They gave us the worst stock of meat." I nodded, surveyed the room. Men beaten by pride, beaten by sickness, by guilt, by dumb bad luck, by a system of power they refused to see or fight, such men ended here. So much pain and I had no power to heal, only to witness. Leave, I thought, leave what you can't fix.

Walking out of the shelter, arms upraised, I laughed, "Home is for losers," and reached into empty pockets. A woman in a fur coat stood on the corner waving a cab. "Excuse me miss," I gently poked her with my voice. She glanced, pulled her coat tight and it looked real warm. "Merry Christmas," I tried again.

And silence. "Could you spare change? I'm two dollars from home," I pleaded as she stepped back. Each heel clicked like a loud heartbeat. "Thank you anyway," I walked away fantasizing about ripping off her fur coat and taking it. A man sipped coffee on the corner. I stepped up slowly, hands out. "I'm just trying to get back to Brooklyn," I lowered my head, "could you spare change?" His mouth pulled tight, "Sorry…"

"I ain't tryin' to bother you," I spun my hands as if digging at a wall, "I'm just two dollars from home." He jogged to the other side of the street as I spread my arms. "Oh, you can't give a nigga some change," I snarled, "fuck Christmas!"

Warm wind billowed out of the subway entrance. I stepped down and walked to the booth. The MTA man studied me. I held up my palms, "I'm cold. I'm trying to get home." I raised my eyebrows, "You think you can let me through?" He nodded to the gate and buzzed it open. Aching, I leaned on a girder. The train came, I rushed in and collapsed on a seat. Head on the window, I tried to sleep but the tunnel lights flashed through my eyelids and with each flash I saw a face from the night: first the naked madman, then Cadrell, then the old man with the cane, next the Nigerian secretary, then the guy running away with his coffee, and then finally my own.

The Mountaintop

I sit between mom's knees and watch on TV a ragged Spaniard aiming his gun at hairless natives. Later, he holds a knife over his fiancé and brother, asleep after making love, and kills his brother. Guilt eats at him until a priest visits. Now the mercenary drags his armor, his sword and guns inside a balled net, tethered to his waist, up steep hills. He staggers across the land, hauling his violent past behind him as the priest follows. After climbing a waterfall, he falls on the muddy ground. Native people eye him, knowing he killed their families. One runs to him with a knife, yanks his head and levels the blade at the neck but then cuts the rope and rolls the bundled weapons into the ravine where they splash. The Spaniard weeps as the natives touch his beard and face. He cries thank you, cries for salvation, cries for the end of guilt. When the film is done, I look around and see mom and her friends openly weeping.

Night

"Tonight, I cut away fifteen years," I cradled my dreadlocks and stroked them, felt the years in their length. LED lantern in hand, I left my tent for a night black forest. Step by step, I began the climb to the top of the mountain where at sunrise I'll take scissors, wait for the first ray of light to hit my face, and cut, cut, cut.

Everything is loud at night. Boot crunched twigs are loud. Breath is loud but thoughts are louder. They seek the person who first spoke them and as I clambered over dew sparkled rocks, I heard everyone yelling in my head.

Are you going to cut us off with them? Why did it take you so long? You're not black. Do you speak for us? Don't go silent. You look like Jesus. Cut those ugly shit locks off.

The voices came from Eddie, the dead homeless man I saw floating in flooded New Orleans, the raped woman I interviewed in a refugee camp in Chad, random strangers who smiled and shook my hand or scowled in disgust. But mom's voice was the clearest. When I first locked my hair, she was afraid I exiled myself to the fringe of society where I would fall into drugs or crime or madness and take her with me. "You'll never get a job with those," she said, "they will see a Caribbean criminal stereotype and you won't even know that doors are closing to you."

Panting, I climbed the rocks and stood on a creaky wooden bridge, a moonlit white river foamed under me. Raising the lantern, I saw grey stones like broken steps ascending in a tunnel of gnarled trees that lead into darkness.

"You're going to get lost," she said to me years ago and I heard her again as if she was at me ear, scowling at my chin length dreads, "and no one is going to find you."

Conked

"Now this is going to burn," she gripped my head and rubbed hair straightening gel into my scalp. A tingling, needlelike heat lit my head.

"Mom," I splashed water over my face, "is my hair getting white?" "Hold on, it's cooking," she said and leaned over me in the bathtub, rubbing it in. Flames seemed to leap from my head. "Mom, I don't know about this," I began to fidget. But she had me in a cop chokehold, screaming, "Let it burn! Let it burn!"

I could not help but think of the Vietnam War photo of a young spindly girl running naked on the road, burning from napalm. "Mom, it's eating my brain," I shouted, squirmed loose and dunked my head in water gushing from the faucet. Sound blurred and oily rivulets coated my face.

"Let me see," she said and pulled me up, dappled my face with a towel and guided me blind to a mirror. "Oh, you are so handsome," she cooed. My nose, cheeks, eyelids were red. I opened one eye slowly, then the other. We both stood, amazed at the dark, limp, straight hair that swayed on my forehead. I pinched a thread of it and smiled with her, arm in arm, staring at her new son.

Vista

"Oh my god," I clutched my chest, staring at the moonlit trees that looked frosted by sugar. Above them, stars shined like chandeliers. Wind rustled in leaves, twigs snapped and in a passing moment of absolute silence, I felt my own heartbeat like an underwater drum.

I held my arms up, dark hands seeming to pinch the stars, "Why *don't* you exist?"

Roots

"Tell me about Great-Grandfather," I asked.

"Jose Castro," she said and turned the steering wheel, sun flashed over her face, "was a mean son of a bitch. Pop hardly talked about him. From what I remember, he was a soldier in the Spanish Army, switched sides when he saw the U.S. was going to win. He had a black woman in the countryside named Eleutaria, means liberty in Spanish. If that's not ironic, I don't know what is. She had his kids, one of which was my father, Emilio. From what I remember, Jose had a light-skinned mistress in San Juan, maybe had kids by her too. At that time men just dumped their sperm in any hole they could find."

"Anyway, I guess those African genes traveled through Pop to me because I was born dark, dark, dark. Remember that photo of me as a girl?" she prodded me with her eyes before looking at the road again. I rummaged through my memory and saw it, a fragile photo of her, very brown, in the park, already a questioning mood on her face.

"Yeah, I saw that one."

"Well," she snorted, "Grandma said I was too black to be her daughter."

The Dark

Steam spiraled off my skin like a comet's tail as I hiked up the dark mountain. I was a small man climbing upward in the night with a swaying lantern.

I held the light over a puddle and saw my silhouette, looked up and saw craggy trees near my arms, cobwebs glistening like diamond nets slung over branches, looked down at rocks and the faint shape of the trail in the dim hall of lantern light. But beyond the egg-shaped glow, blackness was thick as a theater curtain.

Clicking off the lantern, I soaked the dark into my eyes, saw rocks as grey, trees as dark lines and starlit puddles as if someone had sprinkled glitter on the mountain to lead me on. Pulling off my last shirt, I hooked the lantern on my belt and climbed through the night, trusting my feet, hands, eyes.

Afros

The memory is old, so old their voices are washed out and it runs in my head like a silent movie. I was digging in mom's closet and hauled out a heavy family photo album, blew the dust off, carefully flipped the pages so the pictures wouldn't slip around but some did anyway and one showed my mom and uncle with huge glistening afros.

"Your hair," I looked at her as she sashayed back and forth in the kitchen, "mom, your hair."

"What," she said, "what about my hair? Hey, that's the family photo album." Leaning over, her one sauce covered finger touched her image with the afro. "Oh Jesus, I haven't seen that in a while," she said. "In those days, all the Puerto Rican kids wore dresses and got their hair straightened, danced in heels at the balls. But I hung out in the Village watching Allen Ginsberg write poems at cafes and then perform them right there. It was a whole different world. Natural hair and jeans, bohemian styles, and so I showed up at the Puerto Rican dance looking like a hippie, afro, jeans and some hot Leftist rhetoric. They were freaked out. They did not know what to do with me but a year later they all looked like hippies too." Her eyes glowed as if a giant light bulb had been turned on.

"And Uncle Junior," I asked pointing to his pride filled face and huge round afro.

"He was into it too," she said, "everyone was. It was the Movement that made us beautiful again."

Wind

Blasts of cool air whipped and roared around me. Up here, trees are thin and sparse. The trail narrowed into wedges between hip, high rock. On either side was a plummeting green pine valley and looking up, I saw a purple horizon.

"So close," I muttered, "so close." A great wave of wind splashed against the mountain and I gripped the shrub brush and pushed ahead.

Revenge

"This might hurt," they said and tugged, twisted my hair into little knots.

"Keep going," I squinted in the mirror, watched my two friends comb back my hair into nubs and rub it with bees wax. "Would Bob Marley be cool with two white kids dread-locking a black man?" Erica asked as she chopped the comb into my hair. I glanced back at her, "Reparations?"

We laughed and then back to dreading my hair. "But seriously," Ted asked, "why are you doing this?"

I pointed to the Bob Marley poster, "I need a father and since he's dead, he can only tell me what I want to hear."

Afterwards, I paraded my dreads in the dorm halls, blowing huge clouds of marijuana smoke. I began selling it and people lined up Friday nights in my room to buy a dime bag, a twenty or a full ounce. I gave a Hershey chocolate with each bag. After friends smelled the weed, they rolled a joint and turned up my radio which played a Malcolm X or Ram Das speech. The white kids who were into Wicca used tape to make a pentagram on my floor, put the Koran and Bob Marley cassettes inside it, lit sage and scooped incense on my body as if bathing me.

I named my bong Allah and when people came I said, "Take a hit from Allah," and we'd laugh. Eventually I read the Koran and Karl Marx and semiotics and began spreading the wisdom I was quickly learning to recite from my radical theory books.

When my mom came to visit, she walked into the dorm halls with a smile that twisted like a coat hanger when she saw my hair. Her eyes were red lasers that seemed to cut the small bouncy dreads off in puffs of smoke.

"Why did you fuck up your hair," she huffed, "and what's with the incense?"

"I'm going natural," I stiffened my legs as if standing on steel beams. "I don't want the white man in my head or on it. We have to free ourselves from this colonial ideology that's been on us for four hundred years."

"Fine, don't have the white man in your head," she pointed a finger at my hip, "but keep him in your wallet. You think anyone's going to hire you looking like that?"

"I don't want a job working for Babylon," I smirked while saying this and still am surprised she didn't slap the shit of me. "Jobs are slave collars."

"I took out student loans for you to tell me this shit," she hollered, "I pay for you to go into poverty. Well, take care of it yourself if you know so fucking much." And she stomped out leaving a wake of faces with raised eyebrows.

"I guess I'm too black to be your son," I yelled down the hall. As she left, Ted and Erica came by, "Hey man, are you okay? Should we take the dreads out?"

New Orleans

The helicopter made a tornado of trash and debris. I covered the kids who grabbed my shirt, my arms and dreads. We made a knot as it flew up and when it was gone, they clung to me shaking in fear until their parents came.

"Thank you," they shouted as they took the children, "thank you for looking out for them." We were on a crowded street in New Orleans, hundreds of families waded out of the flood to dry land, carrying babies, the elderly, food and clothes. Reverend Walker and Willie and I shuttled the sick to hospitals, the lost to checkpoints, handed out supplies. When night came, I walked to a campfire at a building where families slept on the sidewalk. One child entwined his hands in my hair as I gave his mother tampons and bandages. She watched him play with my dreads, "He likes your hair."

Smiling weakly, she reached out, held my locks and asked if I would pray with her. I said yes. She closed her eyes, "Dear Lord, thank you for sending us help, thank you for moving the hearts of people like this man here to come and help us," she gripped them tighter, "dear Lord, please deliver us and please, please, please guard my baby girl." She sobbed and bright tears streamed down her face, "Tell her that momma is looking for her, I'm going to find her."

I felt her vibrating with fear, agony and hope. Finally, we let go and she said, "Thank you. Thank you for praying with me." She dried her face, took her son back into her arms.

Over the course of days, we waded in flood waters. I doled out the supplies I brought and at night sat on the porch of Reverend Walker's church, smoked a joint and stared at the cemetery across the street as a dark river flowed through the city.

Days later, I was back in New York and Mom called, scared and angry that I had gone without telling anyone. We met at a diner and she gave me a long hug as if putting me back together again.

"How was it?" she asked.

I looked at her and silently shook my head. We sat, the waiter came, took our order and afterwards Mom reached across the table to me, "Hey, I'm proud of you for going. Just let us know next time, okay."

I nodded, swallowing memories back down my throat when the dank smell of the flood wafted by. Following its scent, I lifted the tips of my dreadlocks and inhaled.

Blue

I could see the summit, the place of cutting and letting go, and slipping my backpack off, I gulped some water, forearmed sweat from my face. Panting for air, I looked up and saw a faint blue line on the horizon and felt how close the shearing of the dreads was. A surge of grief, joy, nostalgia shot through my chest into my throat and eyes. Face twisting in tears, I felt everyone who had held my dreads in love, in fear, in lust, in hope, were hanging from them now and waiting.

Blue light washed the purple from the sky, stars vanished and yellow seeped up from the horizon. I grabbed my bag and dashed for the summit.

The Whip

A year after New Orleans, I was hired as a professor. During my lectures, artsy students drew me and gave me their portraits after class so that by year two my desk drawer was full of Rasta Professor Powers art.

But a coal of rage smoked in me. Teaching Black literature, I lit every racist lie on fire, showed white supremacist ideology at work on how we love, hate, hope, live and die. I saw my students in peril of rising self-doubt, rising cost-of-living, rising unemployment as the American empire collapsed and these ideas could be their lifejackets.

During class, I began to have flashbacks of flooded New Orleans that seemed like someone waved photos in my face. Ending class early, I took the train home and I saw all over again homes on fire, families crying in the street, dead bodies floating downtown. And what had been done to stop this from happening again? Not one fucking thing. I wrote a story that few people read and that was the extent of my good work. Taking my dreads, I began whipping my back saying, "Do you think dead Eddie floating in the streets could be saved by damn literature?"

I whipped harder and harder until a man came up to me and stayed my hand, "Brother, please."

Mom's Return

Mom was moving from Boston and I went up there to help. A few blocks away from the house, she called me.

"Hurry, I have a surprise for you," she said. "I'm down the street," I saw her on the front lawn, wearing the sweater from her trip to Alaska. It had indigenous designs on it that made her look all native. When she got back, she showed me the pictures of the immense snowy mountains, elk and rustic wooden stores. "They told me I look Eskimo," she lifted her chin as if finding out she had been adopted by a crazy family and now was claimed by her real one.

I jogged the last block and saw that she looked new. She turned to me, her smile was like wrinkled lace. "My hair," she fluffed it and I reached out, touched her natural tight curly swirls and gave her a huge unending hug.

"Mom, you look beautiful," I said.

"Really?" she asked. "Really?"

The Summit

Running between trees, I leapt on the stone summit ledge and saw the great expanse of a green valley. Sucking in such a large breath I wanted to drain the sky of air, I held it until my lungs throbbed and yelled, "FREEDOM!"

The echo traveled across the horizon. I threw my bag down, got my scissors and eyed the tree line. A spout of red light gushed out like volcanic steam and hardened into a beam. Hair in hand, I felt my pulse hammer and my skin was like a blanket about to fly away. I held the blade over them, my dreads, my roots, my anchor, my life-weight that kept me balanced with the unseen lives of others and then a red drop of sun broke.

I cut them, sawing through thick hair that was like arteries gushing me out on the earth. Another cut and they tugged loose, a final snip and the front locks fell like dark ropes on the summit.

I grabbed more dreads and cut, cut, cut, screaming as the sun filled my eyes, my skull, obliterating thought – just hands cutting weight from me.

Panting, I stopped. My dreads were on the ground. I ran a hand through my rough, tangled hair and felt wind on scalp. Sunlight bathed me. And I danced in a circle, I sang a native song, the one native to my body, the one shaped in my belly and blasted through my voice across the valley in sounds carrying my inside-self up to the sky.

Sweating, I took cell phone photos, shaved the hair down to the skin with an electric razor, bundled my dreadlocks into a bag and began the descent down the mountain.

Epilogue

Stumbling back into the tent, I kept stroking my bald head in wonder. Collapsing inside, I pulled the poncho over me and sank to the bottom of sleep where tides of slow beta waves washed the self away.

Dream light flickered. I saw a TV, on it, a Twilight Zone episode but Uncle Junior was the host. Face on my hands, I lay in a room and turned from the TV to see Mom and my Aunt Mona on stools debating about my name. Looking again at the TV, I saw myself on screen stepping into a shower and shortly after Uncle Junior, in a wig, stepping in after me. I screamed for Mom to stop talking and help but she couldn't hear me nor could Aunt Mona. Finally my uncle stepped out of the shower and said we would cut to a commercial. Yelling at Mom, I asked, "Why didn't you protect me!"

Waking up, I heard my dream-self yelling in my ears like someone screaming from a passing car. My hands shook as I wiped my face. So there it was, so there it was.

Invisible Man

Looking at my bald head in the bus window's reflection, I felt my face with my fingertips as if my sight had just returned. Thumb on chin, palm on scalp, I seemed to sculpt myself out of the fifteen year memory of who I was with dread-locks.

When I focused my vision on the road, I saw the skyscrapers of New York like giant stalagmites. What would my neighbors say? Would they think I betrayed them? Would their eyes wince when they saw me? Would they believe I cut my dreads to be a part of Babylon? The bus pulled into Port Authority and I warily stepped by a Rastafari who worked the halls but who looked through me as if I was invisible.

No one saw me. The side glances, the stares, and sometimes tourists asking for photos, were gone. The somber head nods, the furtive Rasta fists to heart gestures were gone. The cops eyeing me were gone. No one saw me.

I felt weightless, a phantom slipping through the crowd with no one to answer to but my own voice. I could eat pork or junk food if I wanted and not feel a stare. I could disappear into a whole other life and no one would know what I was before. I was not owned by history.

Lugging my backpack past store windows, I stopped in front of a row of mannequins wearing suits. Angling my reflection on the store window, I seemed to being wearing one. Who was I free to be now?

I felt how much I didn't want the weight of testimony as my life's work anymore. Going into the subway, I worried at seeing the disappointment in everyone's eyes. When I got out, Tony the neighborhood DJ, broke a smile and hugged me. "Man," he said, "I almost didn't recognize you."

Walter, the local Rasta troubadour, came up and gave me a hug, "Dread man." I must have had a sheepish look because he pointed at my chest. "Rasta is not in the hair, it's in the heart. No man is one thing. Your dreads are still growing."

I shook my head, dazed, smiling and as I left Tony shouted, "Don't worry, we still know who you are if you forget!"

Walking to my building, Dolores, an older next door lady who I always talked to came out. She kissed her hands, rubbed my bald scalp and said, "Now that you climbed that mountain, go find another one."

The Red Star of Bethlehem — The Indyblog, July 2009

"A Christian and Commie sitting in a tree K-I-S-S-I-N-G," I sang my ditty into Aaron Davis Hall where Harvard preacher Cornel West and Communist Carl Dix would talk about Obama. After getting my ticket, I saw the audience was mostly young, mostly of color, hair twisted into dreadlocks or picked into halo-like afros. Some had Pan-African dyes while others had Che staring from their chests.

I sat down and smirked at the event title: *The Ascendancy of Obama and the Continued Need for Resistance and Liberation*, which felt like a lot of syllables. When Obama won, even cynical Leftists danced in the streets, carried by the flood of joy. But six months later, the change we can believe in has not. So we came to Aaron Davis Hall to hear two elder black men of the Left say yes, it's time to bring Obama to measure.

Waiting offstage is Professor Cornel West and Carl Dix, of the Revolutionary Communist Party, which hosted the event but really we came to see West. He plays Leftist rhetoric like a saxophone, blowing it to a trembling point and then lets it cascade. And he loves to love, a rare thing on a Left that prides itself on splintering into sharp ideological points. Dix, on the other hand, well, I saw him on YouTube "inviting" people to the event by accusing the viewer of not wanting "straight talk" and warned them to "stay their asses home" if they can't deal with his truth. Weird, like watching an uncle talk to himself.

After opening remarks by R.C.P. member Sunsara Taylor and journalist Herbert Boyd, West came in clasping Carl Dix as if shouldering shared weight. Dix began with the euphoria of election night, standing over it like a judge and said, as an older black man, he saw it as misguided passion. The audience tensed but Dix won us back with a childhood story. On a family trip, the car broke down and his father, panicked at being stranded in the Upper South, called a tow truck. A white youth came, fixed it but called his father "boy." Afraid for his family, the older man kept quiet as his young son looked on in disbelief. The anger and shame in Dix's voice rippled through the rows.

After that he told us not to get caught up with Obama being at the top but to look between the lines. He told us the same war, the same torture and the same detentions are going on under Obama. He told us in the end it's not about any one man but a system that cannot be fixed, only overthrown.

Dix mapped the erosion of faith for those who believed in Obama. He talked of Sean Bell and I remembered seeing the young man in a coffin. I went to his funeral where his mother sagged in the pew, wrung out by despair. His family lowered his body into the ground without hope for justice. Bell's life was laid briefly on the scales of justice before the police badge tipped the balance. Three years later, his death has sunk beneath the stone pillars of the state into the silent depths of the people who see more lives snuffed out by war or poverty drifting down like ash.

I snapped out of it and heard Dix saying, "Obama's problem is that the system is in trouble and his mission is to save that system. Our problem is this system. We don't need to see it saved. We need to see it ended through revolution." Many people clapped but I didn't. He told us we can bring "revolutionary institutions of power into being." He talked to us of the Chinese Revolution because he is a Maoist. During Mao's rule, Dix says, drugs and prostitution were ended and equality brought to the people. Heaven on earth can happen again with Bob Avakian, the Chairman of the R.C.P., who will guide us further. Again I didn't clap. No one did. It sounded too easy, too antiseptic, as if millions of human lives weren't used as cement for the new paradise.

He told us the youth have to be transformed "by fighting the system." He's right but fighting who and how? Is it with guns? If so, how will that power, bought with violence, be different from the one we have now? He said it won't happen by lectures from Cosby or Obama or by giving our lives to Jesus. And he's right, lectures don't work, including his because his words feel imported from some fantastic world where we harmoniously erect the pillars of the new state. But to get to his utopia, we must wage war against this world. I suspected that we didn't clap loudly because enough of us have felt violence and know that once set in motion it doesn't end with victory but becomes the language we use to answer questions, replace doubt and end debate.

Dix finished and we were hopeless. West hobbled to the podium. He parsed the air with his hands and said we must "create space for principled criticism of the Obama administration." And he did what Dix could not. He let us keep the euphoria, saying it was real, the glass ceiling of white supremacy was shattered. But he warned us not to overlook the poor as we gaze at the black man in the white house.

He swung his voice above Obama to a historical peak where we saw the lives and deaths that made him possible. West grabbed the podium and brought down his five decades of living, "We know defeat. When Martin was shot down like a dog, it killed something inside us." Some ageless raw ache jutted from his voice. I studied his lined face, his sagging body and oiled gestures and saw a man thrashing in the nightmare of history.

He pumped his speech into hot seething rage at the first Obama betrayal of bringing in the same Neo-Liberal economists who ruined the economy to fix it. "What's the angle of vision," he hacked at Obama, "they send money to London and France but when poor people ask for help they're told, pick yourself up by the bootstraps." His Harvard pedigree and Civil Rights era authority allowed him to reach up and down the class hierarchy and pull everyone onto the level field of humanism. Standing there he attacked the hypocrisy of the elite but I wondered why is he not talking about ours?

In college, I listened to Malcolm X tapes and saw *All the King's Men* by Robert Penn Warren and both had an intimate critique of the hypocrisy of the poor by someone who once was poor. In the movie, Willie Stark yells at share-croppers that "you're hicks and nobody ever helped a hick but a hick." Malcolm X viciously dogged the way black folk clutched at status like life preservers. Instead of getting him booed, people laughed and roared. They felt released from the effort of erasing themselves or the shame of not being able to. Self-lacerating laughter creates solidarity. But West doesn't dig into our shadows. Instead, he unifies us through shared indignity. I always sensed it was his major fault. He says we're better than the ruling elite but we aren't. We don't just love, we also hate and desire and collaborate.

He lamented the government's infiltration of the Movement and shouted, "We know the CIA and FBI are here and we welcome them." The hall rocked with laughter. Were we praising ourselves for courage in the face of surveillance or did we need to believe we were being watched to feel important?

West ended with a call for action, with a call to the youth to take his place but by this time I was listening to him more as music. We applauded. The moderators asked them questions as microphone stands were set up in the aisles. Soon the Great Howling began. It's a ritual at Leftist events to honor democracy and open the floor but, as always, the ranters grabbed the mic' and made long soliloquies as the rest of us trickled out.

Outside Aaron Davis Hall, I called my friend LeRonn. He gave me directions to a bar. While walking, I remembered when I first met the R.C.P. while in graduate school. After the Twin Towers fell, I like everyone was numb with terror. In a daze, I found Revolution Books and read the history of U.S. Middle East policy, the regimes we propped up and armed, the money flushed into Mujahideen hands. And to their credit, the R.C.P. predicted the wars, the police state, the fear to come and they yelled in bold print not to give in. I wanted to be brave like them just not with them.

After a few meetings, I realized the R.C.P. was a pyramid-scheme, one that constantly sought new recruits to seek new recruits so the base would expand under the shining eye of the all-knowing genius of Chairman Bob Avakian. Every time I hung out, they offered Bob Avakian pamphlets, Bob Avakian CDs, Bob Avakian books, Bob Avakian DVDs, Bob Avakian condoms, Bob Avakian tote-bags. His memoir was stacked at the window. On the cover was Bob as a pale cherubic teen before he became the grizzly bear-like man of the R.CP. Bob is always intensely staring above a clenched jaw as his eyes grind illusions to glitter.

More irritating than the cult-like aura was the way the R.C.P. leveraged their moral claim against you, as if to keep a good self-image you must buy their newspaper, open it like a window to a hidden world of misery and shocked by it, go and proselytize to the blind, opening their eyes until Bob leads us to utopia. Humanity will be forever free and we'll shine in history as the last saints who delivered heaven on earth.

It's a compelling story because there is real, brutal suffering and none of us have the power alone to stop it. We endure experiences we can't name or that warp our lives into unrecognizable shape. Their grand-narrative promises an end to pain, and redemption through revolution.

But I wondered, what if the global crisis deepened and hundreds of thousands of people flooded progressive parties like the R.C.P., how would that small circle hold against such tidal force without splintering into factions? Isn't that the very history of the group itself? How can we trust their promises about tomorrow when in a revolution those who first made them might be replaced by hungry ambitious newcomers?

If the global crisis deepened and the state was weak enough to attack, how would the R.C.P. deal with violence? Once used, it becomes addictive. Violence creates a climate of fear that leaders mistake for legitimacy. But these are laughable questions. The R.C.P. is not and will not be anytime soon a threat to the state. They are more of a threat to the Left because they build a dream on a shaky assumption of human nature.

They hold an image of humanity as a victim of a small parasitical class and if we kill that class, install new modes of production and social relations, we will shed our alienation and be free. But we've had revolutions in America and France, Haiti, Russia and Cuba. Each of these freed some but not all and not forever.

What if it's because war cannot create peace? What if the ruling elite are not aliens but people, like us, who are caught in roles they didn't create? What if Plato's Noble Lies, the famous girders in the architecture of oppression, are not driven into us by the state but emerge from us because we are innately divided between who we are, how we see ourselves, and the emotions we sense but are too faint or too fast to be named? What if the first casualty of truth is war?

I don't know and may never know but ahead was the bar with my friend waving. We hugged. I asked if he heard the event. LeRonn grinned, "Yeah, on WBAI. Cornel just outmaneuvered him in every way. He went there for street-cred and they got to bask in his light. They used each other."

"I thought there might be some sparks but…" I shrugged.

LeRonn shook his head, "You can't rhetorically wrestle Cornel, he just slips out, kisses you and steals your girl."

"He stole the audience."

"Put them in his pocket."

We chortled and ordered drinks. "What you think of Dix?" I asked.

LeRonn squinted, "When he said that story of his father, I heard how trau-matized he was by it, you know, deeply wounded. So he's coming from that space and things like that mark a man, some never get beyond it."

I sighed into my hands, "Are we trapped in those moments?"

"If we stay in them," LeRonn slid a beer to me, "but as long as we're alive, we get new moments. We have choice. We are free whether we know it or not, whether we want it or not."

The Holy Man — The Indyblog, September 2009

Our seven days of dancing, ass-slapping, body-painting, yoga-bending, Tantric touching, Kabbalah meditating, nude New Age revelry in the fire-blasted Nevada desert was coming to an end. It was the last day of Burning Man. On Sunday, I walked across the city sighing at its dismantling. Domes that pulsed with light and music the night before now lay flat, half rolled up. Soon this ephemeral utopia will vanish with little evidence that it ever existed.

I walked to Center Camp, a large circular tent with flags fluttering in the grainy dust storm. Inside, sand-coated burners lounged on pillows, faces alert, listening to a rolling sermon. I turned and saw Reverend Billy, a performance activist from New York who is campaigning for mayor. He paced the stage, blond hair bobbing as he ducked and weaved and shouted. His white suit blazed in the sunlight, a black microphone coiled around his arm as he exhorted the audience, "Changeallujah!"

I watched them bask in his fervor. "Children," he rolled his voice into a preacher's rhythm, "we know the wonders of Burning Man. Here we see things seen nowhere else. Here the sun and moon set at the same time." Voices whooped as he leaned in, "I know you want to take this fire into the world of big box stores. But children, without social change, we support the American military culture whose statement is, 'If you threaten me, I will kill you.' We support this with our taxes. We do most of our shopping, as Americans, not at Wal-Mart but at the Pentagon!"

People nodded as if his words were weights tipping scales in their minds. His hands jumped around the air, "We need to be radical Americans, like we've been before, in the Labor Movement, in the Civil Rights Movement, in the Women's Movement." He dabbed his face with a sweat rag, "The earth is sending us messages. We see it in the typhoons that rip our coastal cities. We see it in the floods that sweep away towns and the earth is saying, we must be like the typhoons, we must be like the flood."

Eyes lit up. His mythic words opened a door into a world of primal forces that washed away our numbness. "All the life that is not human is calling us to join it in a duet of activism," he crooned. "Children," his voice darkened as he stopped and held out his hand as if gently parting a veil, "some of us are going to have to die. In every great movement our freedom was earned by those who died, and there is life in death…"

A strange light glowed on their faces. He made visible a terrible truth that promised us a reality more powerful than our lives. I've heard preachers my whole life and many have said the same thing but I read about Reverend Billy and know that his campaign for mayor has taken a toll on his body. Recently his heart skipped and jumped. He missed campaign events until medicine thinned his blood, now he's back on stage inviting the silent anxiety of people to shake him until these prophecies cascade out and the audience can see their dreams again.

"Gradualism has taken over the world of social activism," he yelled in a fluid melody of passion. "There isn't a '60s movement that hasn't become a Starbucks flavor. The earth is saying join in, join in your survival by participating in the survival of the earth. Change-a-lujah!"

"Amen," someone shouted. The brunette woman next to me said to her friend, "That's exactly what I needed to hear before going back out to the world." Reverend Billy ambled off stage into the pews, he reached for hands, pulled people up and embraced them, taking care of their need for faith. The circle of fans tightened around him and I waited at the edge, looking in, wanting to interview him. I asked his handlers for a moment, they agreed but cautiously, he was wrung out but squeezing more for the audience. Also, I write for the Indypendent and it published a piece asking if his surrealist candidacy has hit the hard wall of real politick.

Reverend Billy glided from admirer to admirer. They slowly peeled away to five then two then he felt the pull of my stare, sat down and I told him who I write for, he nodded, and I asked him what instrument he played. "You seem to have a musical bent," I said. He grinned and said the cello, and mimed playing it on his raised forearm.

"Why did you choose the televangelist persona?" I began.

"The Right had been looting our icons for years and distorting them. So I took one of theirs, the 80s TV evangelist," he said, hands shaping the scene. "It was a figure who was punishing and victimizing people through religion and I turned it around, made it a parody."

"When did it stop being a parody?" I hold out my hands as if balancing a wobbly weight, "You aren't just entertaining but strongly attacking capitalism." The question hung in the air.

"9/11," he said.

I searched his face but he was inside himself, maybe seeing the smoke wafting over the New York skyline or remembering the chalk-paste smell that settled in the hair or the terror spilling out of open mouths. I had the same memories.

"9/11," I prodded.

He shifted his weight. "The parody was cleansed. We wanted fellowship, even if many of us had walked away from religion. We wanted to be in a room holding hands. At that time I was reading in the Gnostic tradition and developed a faith that was less parody."

I paused before asking the next question, "Reverend, you said the earth is sending us messages, through the typhoons and floods, to be powerful and unstoppable but if we extend that analogy, doesn't nature kill, and is that saying that we, like nature, should destroy anyone who stands in our way?" His forehead creased. Maybe he saw the direction each answer would take him or was calculating how it would play off his image.

"Non-violence can be middle-class affectation but I respectfully disagree with anyone planning violence." He leaned on his hands that were clamped on his knees, "I'm in the Gandhi, King, and Tolstoy tradition." He raised his finger, "But the most effective movements have been when those who struggle non-violently and those willing to use violence work together in a duet."

I saw his handlers waiting for him and closed my notebook. Every interview has a natural arc when questions and answers climax to a point of illumination. He rose, offered me his hand, we shook and I wandered through Center Camp hoping his words could change the life outside of this vanishing city.

Later, as I walked across the dusty streets to my camp, I saw a man waving at me. It was the Reverend. He was in a casual jacket and jeans. I trotted over, "Man, I almost didn't see you." We stared at the desert for a moment. I turned to him. "How do you survive being a human lightning rod for people's emotions?" He thought for a moment, "Walks in the woods. I have to be healthy on purpose."

"Your heart?"

"I've had heart troubles," he said, "we've missed a few events but we keep going."

Between his words, I saw his shyness. It's as if his public persona is so important to so many people that he lived within it, warily watching it grow, knowing each new believer adds more weight to a performance his body is being worn down by.

His wife, Savitri D, came by and he introduced us. Another woman, young and giddy, bounded up and showed off her costume. He took off his jacket and offered it to her. She refused at first but the sun had set and the desert chills quickly. Already, cool winds blew from the dark side of the sky. She put it on like a daughter given her father's oversized coat. She looked happy, safe, loved. It's a small gesture but I trust those more than the large theatrical ones which are meant for an audience.

We said goodbye and promised to e-mail when we returned to New York. I walked through dusty streets to my rental car and rolled up my tent, packed bags, separated trash into recyclables. In an hour it was black night. Throngs of people went to the Temple, flashlights swaying in hands, sending beams crisscrossing in bright circles that slipped over the dark desert floor.

Every year at Burning Man, a Temple is built and on its wooden timbers people write goodbyes to loved ones who died that year. Sometimes it's a memory, sometimes it's a belated forgiveness, sometimes it's angry grief at being left alone but all the messages, whether printed, taped or scrawled in black marker are how we let go of those taken from us. It is a Temple soaked in grief. I went there this year and said goodbye to an old version of myself and to the many mistakes he made.

Thousands of us gathered around it and watched the fire sprout and curl around the Temple, engulfing it. We were so silent, I heard the wood crackle. People wept openly as the flames incinerated our goodbyes, our attachments. When the last of the Temple crashed in a spray of orange sparks, we rose and walked toward it. Some sang, some chanted, some drummed as we danced like shadows around a primal light. As I circled the inferno, I saw Reverend Billy, closer to it than anyone, smiling serenely as if he saw the beauty of the fire and was at peace with feeding his life to it. Over the shoulders of the people, I touched him briefly, this holy man with a skipping heart who reaches between its faltering beats for a truth we can believe in.

There Is a Light that Never Goes Out — The Indyblog, September 2009

The drizzle on my face tingles and beads into drops that roll down my shoulders. The whole sky sweeps around me until I look at the city and then memories pour back in.

I'm in Brooklyn, on my roof, on the eighth anniversary of 9/11 and across the skyline of thick clouds, I see the beams from the Tribute of Light shooting up from Ground Zero. I hook thumbs into my pockets and study it. Churning clouds smother the illumination, causing it to look like sulfur-fire, as if downtown was still burning, as if it was the first night of the attack and steel was melting into orange liquid, trickling in the wreckage, searing a hole between life and death. Every year after it, Ground Zero was cleared, the city sent two towers of light into the sky and from a distance it looks like souls fleeing the pain below.

I step back and think of funerals with candles glowing around coffins. We use light to peer into death, to glimpse loved ones, to make loss visible. The Tribute of Light is that act magnified by money and technology. The immensity of the tragedy demands it but what of others? I peer over the roof and down to my building's doorway, a neighbor's son was shot there and I imagine a light shining where he died. I look down the street and imagine more light rays, one for each boy killed during the summer by a hail of bullets. I look up and see the city brighten like sunrise as each death breaks its silence.

What would we see about ourselves in that brilliance? Would drivers stop by bridges and pray at the place where the unseen poor froze like stones? Would satellites see the glow of the thousands dying each day from dirty water?

What if the endless death and pain glittering across the globe fused into one bright glow? I saw the earth for what it truly is: a second sun that irradiates space with our sorrow.

The Event — The Indyblog, February 2010

4:53:09 PM, Tuesday, January 12th was the last moment of Old Haiti. The nearly 300,000 people who were going to die in the next few seconds were still breathing, still talking. In Port au Prince, in a cool office, sat an American-born Haitian named Lesley, called Big Zoe by his friends. He read a paper, swatted at flies. Across the sun baked city, Ilonese Julot arranged pots in her home to cook and sell food by the road. In the town of Carrefour, Margaret Jean-Louise was heavy-eyed and sleepy but a strange unease kept her awake and she went to the porch to sit.

4:53:09 PM, life was still forgettable. It was a man turning a page at his desk, a mother sloshing rice inside a pot, a woman rubbing her feet in the sun. Miles under them, deep in the earth, tectonic plates on hot fluid rock had been grinding edges for decades, building pressure until at this moment those plates slipped. Shockwaves zigzagged to the surface with the power of thirty two Little Boy atomic bombs. When it hit, those forgettable gestures of reading a paper, scooping rice into a bowl, dozing on a chair would be cast in the after-light of catastrophe.

4:53:10 PM, Margaret felt sand tickle her face. The ground heaved and swayed. She ran to the street as people screamed and tucked heads under arms to shield them from falling stone. In Port au Prince, Big Zoe's desk rattled, he looked up as the building next door crashed toward him and thought, "I'm going to die." Seconds later, he stumbled through dust following the yells of his friends into the sunlight. Across town, Ilonese felt her legs sway under her as pots rolled away. She panicked but her daughter hurried her to the park where people screamed at the sky, some holding their heads in numb shock, some dusted white as blood dripped down their faces. Evening fell and neighbors frantically dug through rubble by candlelight, bodies half-crushed were pulled out and a great wail of pain rang through the night as they cried, "Jesus, save us! Jesus, save us!"

The horror of that night was like a silent exploding star. It wasn't seen but felt in the sudden silence of cut-off phone calls, e-mails unreturned. It left an eerie quiet traveling the great distance between the Third and First Worlds. By the time the initial reports creased the brows of newscasters and photos were seen in the glittering capitals of the world, already in Haiti the shock had become grief and weary-panicked digging to rescue those buried alive.

New York to Haiti

I was walking home balancing grocery bags and saw my neighbor Tony smoking on the steps. We knocked fists, said what's up but he had a faraway look. "You know the sister on the third floor," he asked and I nodded. "Heard her crying," he said, "I think she lost people in the earthquake."

My throat tightened. It was Francesca, a small, thin, deep brown woman, always a new hairstyle, always modeling or taking photos with her door open and a woman posed under a bright umbrella of light. She had an ambitious energy that tired me when we talked. I went upstairs, stopped at her door and raised my hand to knock but lowered it and kept going. In my apartment, the computer was still on and I searched the internet for reports. It was bad. Haitians pled at the cameras. Buildings leaned so far to the side it seemed they should fall. People scrambled over piles of stone as a hand reached out from the rubble and men circled it and pulled the survivor out.

It was bad but where most people felt pity I felt fear because I could go and help. I'd been in New York during 9/11, had flown to New Orleans when the flood drowned the city, had flown to the far edge of Chad to interview the war-scarred people, had shared Christmas Eve with troubled bed-turning homeless men of New York. I knew I could go. I had the money. I had the experience. But I was tired.

Each trip from the glowing wealth of my world to the invisible world of ugly poverty ended in failure. The stories were published, a few people read them and soon the articles were forgotten as the crisis ended. My stories of Going-to-the-Heart-of-Darkness were ugly souvenirs that I showed off at parties. I could talk intimately of disasters they only read about. In their eyes I seemed to glow with some holy light. One time I joked, "If you want to touch the cuff of my pant leg, it'll heal your food allergies." And then I made the sign of the Cross.

When I looked at the pictures from Haiti, pity outweighed fear because I was not going. Instead, I'd give long distance sympathy but then I saw a photo of a girl standing on rubble looking into the camera, not with hope, anger or sadness, just resignation as if not expecting help. I felt "It" happen.

"It" is that unpredictable lightning deep in the mind that sparks a decision long before I can consciously know it. *Who was helping her?* I wondered. Sadness and anger floated inside me, touched and exploded into a brightness that left me dizzy. Walking around my apartment in circles, I ran hands through my hair because the fear was real. Since childhood, I've seen an ideal version of myself that lives in the future and always I try to catch up to him. He goes places I don't want to go but if I lose him, a cold fog will envelop me. He is my ideal self and now he ran into the photo and was in Haiti, helping the girl, finding people, giving out food and I was afraid he was going to get me killed.

I began to pack. At first I didn't tell many people but the more friends I told, the more praise and fear and wonder surrounded me. They crowned me with "good-lucks" and "I can't believe you're going" and "stay safe." They hugged me hard as if imprinting me on their bodies in case I did not return. My ideal-self began to glow in the distance like a saint. I believed if I caught up to him that I'd shine forever, that I'd be invited to TV shows like *Democracy Now* or *Real Time with Bill Maher* and become the new poetic Leftist loud mouth. The promise of permanent goodness was so blinding that fear was overtaken by ambition. I didn't see the girl in the photo anymore standing on the rubble staring into the camera but me posing against the backdrop of disaster.

I called Willie, a photographer I met in New Orleans in 2005. We worked for the weekly newspaper the *Village Voice* and days after the flood hit, met at Baton Rouge airport and drove his parents van to the drowned city. Sloshing in dark toxic waters, we interviewed people weeping openly in the streets. At night we sat in the front seats, threading our life stories through the narrow of sleep-heavy eyes. He told me about overdosing on drugs. I told him about the agonizing confusion that drove me. We came back, published our stories and photos but kept talking, bonding over the smell of death and the sight of destruction that seemed to us more real than the world we lived in.

"Do you want to go to Haiti?" I asked him. By now it was an adventure not a rescue mission. He agreed. We bought airplane tickets. Within two days, my friend Tanya filled a duffle bag and suitcase with toys, gauze, medicine and power-bars. We'd leave Sunday night, land in Santo Domingo and figure out the rest on the ground. The night before I left, I knocked on Francesca's door and she opened it, new braids swayed in front of her almond-shaped eyes like a curtain of beads. I told her I was going to Port au Prince and, if she had family, I'd deliver a message. She touched her chest, thanked me and gave me a thick envelope. It had their address in Carrefour, photos of her niece, sister and grandfather, a letter and two hundred dollars. I went back upstairs, spread the photos on the bed and studied them. An old man sitting in the pew of his wife's funeral, eyes tight to keep the grief from exploding, a young girl leaning awkwardly on one foot, smiling a coy smile, and a woman, eyes closed, face tilted to the sun, arms over her head as a bright orange cloth spilled around her like a flame. Inside me, sadness and anger floated, touched, sparked.

Santo Domingo

Five days after the earthquake, Willie and I arrived at Santo Domingo airport. It was eerily quiet. The uncle of his Dominican friend picked us up and drove us to the hotel. I expected rumbling lines of aid-trucks but the highway was empty. The night was moist and salt-scented. Palm trees bent in the breeze and beyond them was the dark ocean with moonlit waves rolling towards shore.

"Tu habla Espanol," Willie's friend asked me. "No," I answered, "me Español es muy pequeño." He was a tall big-shouldered man who worked as a cop, which made me feel safe. If we took the bus to Haiti, I worried about the crowds trying to crush into one door or thieves buzzing near our bags knowing they were packed with supplies. He would scare them away because Third World police don't play, they will disappear your ass. I smiled at the cold math of survival. In the States, I was a Fuck-the-Police kind of guy but that pose was dropped when I felt my bulging money-belt itch and saw the crumbling cement homes on the roadsides with the hungry poor walking the night looking, looking, looking... It's dangerously naïve to think people are going to help you help others when they are slowly starving to death.

He dropped us off at the hotel. We checked in, collapsed on the beds and watched CNN reports of Haiti. It looked bad. Children were being pulled out of wreckage. Helicopters threw food at the crowds that swirled below. News anchors were amazed there was no violence and I thought there was guilt in their amazement.

I paced the room, the halls, feeling trapped in the hotel. I went downstairs and smelling money, a driver walked up to me, offering to take us to Port au Prince but for five hundred dollars. I handed him photos of Francesca's family, the awkward smiling girl, the elderly man and young woman. "I have a Haitian friend in New York, these are her family," I said. "She's worried about them and I'm trying to find them so I can't pay you that much because they need that money. Everyone in Haiti needs that money more than you or I do." He studied the photos and his shoulders sank as if feeling the weight of crisis but shook his head no. Walking back to the room, I looked at the photos. They felt heavier then when I first got them.

I sat on the bed and studied the photos wondering how we'd find her family in the chaos. Maybe they had to leave? Maybe I was too scared to do anything useful?

We woke early, packed and waited in the lobby for a driver to take us downtown where public buses traveled to Port au Prince each day. It would be hot, crowded, and we had luggage stuffed with supplies that might be stolen. I saw a bus parked by the curb and a slender man directing work. I told him who we were, he said the bus was chartered by the Swiss embassy and we could ride with him to Port au Prince.

We drove to the Swiss ambassador's home and helped roll clear jugs of water into the cargo. After loading, we drove out of Santo Domingo. The city shrank from tall buildings to small homes to a countryside of wind tussled palm trees, leaf thatched roofs and people playing cards in the shade. We drove around large hills, into the loud din at the border where vans, buses, cars, military vehicles, bulldozers nudged around each other spewing dark smoke, heaving through mud holes. At the border, the Swiss aid worker asked us if we had any contraband, we said no and then he talked with the guards, who sent us through.

The border was a line not just between nations but wealth and poverty. Half crumbled homes and children in rags darted around the streets of Port au Prince. Large crowds watched the jugs of water jostling in the window. Women with scraped faces hobbled on broken limbs. The driver parked in front of the Swiss embassy and workers quickly emptied the bus. Willie and I got out, stacked our bags, and a tall Frenchman named Christian who, like Satre, had one eye askew, began telling us of the dangers of Haiti. Don't go out alone or at night or with money. It was the *Night of the Living Dead* storyline, as if he was extending the border between nations into our minds.

I wandered past the gate where the guard held a shotgun and I stepped into the street. An invisible circle of status surrounded the bus, and young men stood at the edge, hungrily watching us. One tapped me on the shoulder and motioned for food but I held up empty palms. I walked out and they followed me.

Standing outside the embassy, vulnerable in the street, I felt that fear of being exposed to people's hunger, worrying they might cross the line from asking to taking. I stretched out my arms like antenna, soaking my body in their world and, after a few breaths, the blur of people on the street became focused. I saw a mother with a bag balancing on her head as children bumped around her legs, a man carrying an elderly woman, families huddled by a fire, a baby being rocked in a man's lap and the invisible rebuilding of Haiti in the way people looked at each other as if each gaze was a girder to support the wavering spirit.

I shook my head that was filling with rage. They were people, just people who for generations were forced to survive the stupidity, hate, greed and fear of the West. My own fear that seemed so real a few seconds ago now had a bitter aftertaste. "Fear," I said aloud and knew it was the ink the elite used to draw lines, and sadly, the poor used to draw distinctions among each other. I turned and saw the men who followed me. They must have thought me strange, standing there with my arms out. I waved and went back inside the embassy.

Christian had a driver drop us at the airport. Young men quickly circled us, clamoring to drive us anywhere, translate anything. "Mister! We need work! We have families! Give us job," they shouted over each other. I stopped and stared, feeling the wild desperation in their stares. They were young like my students at college. "I'm not looking for help tonight," I said, "but if I see you tomorrow." We looked at each other and they nodded, still asking but letting go. We walked in, showed our passports to the guard, and lugged the bags through a corridor that was cracked from the earthquake. We walked out on the tarmac where huge planes shook the air and left our ears ringing to the field where green U.S. army tents looked like giant caterpillars. We pitched the tent and slept a deep dreamless sleep that was the last rest we would get for days.

In the morning, we woke, ate and talked to two photographers, a scruffy San Franciscan named Michael and a tall lanky Czech. We left the airport, hired men to drive us to a cemetery where nameless bodies were dumped in a mass grave. Old men with creased faces watched us arrive. A solemn air blew through the arch as the four of us walked in, cameras aimed, pens angled. A woman's body was being nibbled by flies. Over the face, someone lifted her shirt as a makeshift veil.

She is what death has become in Port au Prince, meat rotting in the street that leaves a sickly sweet smell. Death cannot be wrapped in prayer or made into memory. Instead it's quickly dumped or burned. If not, the festering will kill the living. As the photographers shot, I asked the cemetery chief, a weary calculating man, what will happen to the corpse.

"Someone will take it soon."

"Do you know who she was?"

"No no no. They leave many bodies here. I don't know her."

"Did you lose anyone in the earthquake?"

"My daughter was killed."

I went quiet. As we walked, the photographers trailed behind us. They leaned over a skull in the street or the ashy black soot left of a sidewalk cremation and cut the image from time with a click. And then loud yells erupted behind us. We turned and saw four men lifting the corpse on to a gurney, haul it up and carry it quickly through the tombstones.

We followed them as they turned, leapt and climbed mausoleums while keeping the gurney balanced. The cemetery chief pointed directions and the men angled her above a crack and slipped her in. They left. Panting hard, we lowered our pads and pens and cameras.

We asked him to show us the pit where the people are dumped. The cemetery chief said yes but asked for a donation, "Maybe you can help me out?" The tall Czech photographer yelled, "We aren't paying for that, this is a public place." We stared at the cemetery chief who shrugged and said, "You must leave now. We have work. If you want to see the bodies, pay me ten dollars for the time away from work."

They sulked back but I pulled him to the side, "Look, we're not aid workers. We don't have resources. We are journalists. We write the stories so that others can see what's happening here and keep helping."

He smiled, "Okay, pay me five dollars."

"Two hundred pesos," I held it between us, "it's what I got." He took it and whistled to the others who trotted back. We followed him between tombstones to the edge of a large ditch. Rising from the pit was the sweet smell of rotting bodies. I clenched my feeling into a ball as we looked inside the ditch. Six entangled corpses lay in a pile. One had a broken arm, bent like a stick of wood snapped in play. Some were nude. Flies crawled over their anuses. One had a black swollen face like a baby's pout. Stiff and still they gripped each other.

We circled them, I wrote as they shot photos. I wondered what more images of death would do. How will they be read back home? Who were these people, what did they believe in, how did they love and hate? Until even those basic questions are answered, all the corpses in Haiti will be defined by the spectacular rarity of their death. I worry about this because until the invisible are loved not as symbols but as people, they will not be protected from the disaster of history.

The cemetery chief looked at me, "Would you like me to sing?"

I scrunched my eyes, not understanding him, "Sing a song for the dead?"

"Yes," he said, "for a small donation." I rolled my eyes. We left the cemetery. Outside, Haitians milled around aimlessly, stunned with horror. They stared at a rescue team strapping on equipment. When we emerged into the street, they stared at us. They begged for money, yelled offers to translate, to work. Others stood silent watching people being pulled out, covered in white dust, bright red blood crowning their heads. The feeling in the air was like gasoline jelly, thick and flammable and sparks flew out of everyone's eyes. We got in the car and left for the U.N. compound.

The talk in the car turned to the cemetery chief and how everyone raised the price of everything. It was hard to work when no one was trustworthy. Nothing said will stay firm but I knew this culture of lying and haggling is based on living with the broken promises of the West. Promises were made from the Haitian Revolution to the election of Aristide, one atop the other until the earth shook and the centuries of lies collapsed on them.

The U.N. is a Disaster Hotel

Michael and I were at the U.N. cafeteria, guzzling cold apple juice, ripping sandwiches apart and organizing our stories. I renamed the U.N. compound Hotel Disaster and laughed at my own joke until the floor wobbled and walls swayed. We silently listened, watched and waited. The aftershock ended and slowly voices picked up and forks and knives scraped on plates again.

Each day, we make the pilgrimage from our tents on the field of Toussaint Louverture Airport to the U.N. compound. Each day, it gets harder as more soldiers with nothing to do man the pathways asking for I.D. Arriving back at our tents, we crashed on the soft grass and watched the jets roar upwards. Planning the next day's outing meant weighing personal risk against the value of the story.

Out of nowhere, we saw a group of people in bright yellow shirts erecting a large tent. We looked at each other, got up and went over. The closer we got, the more in focus their shirts became and we read: Scientology Volunteer Ministry.

"This isn't real," I said to myself as one of the men shouted hello and came to us with his hand dangling like a bear trap. "We just arrived and look forward to helping." He looked at me and Michael who were a hot mess. His eyes squinted with suspicion as he said, "What have you guys been up to?"

The next day, I rolled my suitcase full of tampons, aspirin and juice to the medical center. In a frenzy of compassion, my friend Tanya bought supplies and stuffed individual bags which I showed the medical staff. The nurses looked at them and gave me the green light. I went from one gauze wrapped body to another and gave them each a bag. I watched as Haitian women opened them, saw the tampons, smiled and waved at each other and pointed to me. Some were groggy from surgery. Some wept as they saw the stumps of their amputated legs or arms. Some stared blankly at the ceiling.

A doctor invited me into the operating room. He said people should know how bad it was. I saw a man's leg bolted to a metal clamp to keep his broken bone straight but it kept oozing blood that no amount of wiping could stop. On another table, a woman lay on her side as they cut slabs of skin off her thigh to get inside. Weary of the carnage, I left and saw a nurse cradling an abandoned baby and weeping. She held the child like a mother who knew the hopeless future it had ahead. So many abandoned children sat on cots, bored and scared.

And then blackness fell. Yells rose from the staff as they dashed to the generator to rev it up again before the people in surgery died. In the chaos, I took out a blue L.E.D. light from my pocket and turned it on, swirling it around the children's faces like a wild glowing star. They giggled and grabbed for it but I spiraled it up, out of reach. They loved not catching the light. They loved leaping for the sake of wonder.

The Rubble

The next day, Michael and I hired drivers to take us to downtown Port au Prince. Glass crunched underfoot. It was a jagged valley of collapsed stone. Walls had split from buildings and had fallen to the street. People scampered in and out of stores. Electric cables swayed near us like giant cobwebs.

I hired a young, skittish "fixer" named Bretin to guide me in as we followed the Haitians who climbed rubble and crawled into nooks to find shoes or clothing or electronics to sell. Slipping around a boulder, we saw a cop waving a gun at two teenagers, a boy and girl, laying face down on the street. He yelled and they lifted their shirts to show they had no stolen goods on them. He told the girl to leave first and said, "Can't believe I caught a girl stealing." People laughed and then, as if hearing a silent alarm, moved quickly down the street.

The photographers angled around the crowd. I pushed Bretin to ask what was happening, where, who and how. Like many people here he promised more than he could deliver in order to make money and buy certainty in the chaos. I watched him and grimaced. He circled me like a shadow, a gentle touch to warn me of a rushing car, a grasp when gunfire boomed.

Michael slung his camera, looked at me and shot a glance at Bretin, "He's fucking useless." I studied the young man as he blankly stared at the swirling crowd. "The fixer I had before was an ex-boxer, spoke perfect English, was on point with it," Michael husked, "this guy's a fucking pussy. Whoever's with you has to be able to tell you what the crowd is saying, to tell them to back off and be heard, you know. This guy…" He blew through the corner of his mouth.

I knew where he was coming from. Just yesterday, while he was shooting photos in these ruined streets, police found looters clearing out a store. Some fled across a roof, the police fired and a girl, paintings in her hands, was hit in the head. Blood spilled from her shattered skull. Friends lifted her body and took it home to her parents who saw their daughter and wept bitterly. When Michael told me the story, I saw fear and anger and sadness mix like paint in his voice.

He needed to feel safe. Bretin needed to feed his family. We had to conserve money. Everyone was colliding in the pressure cooker of a destroyed city. But as Michael slipped between the cop and a boy who he dragged by the collar down the sidewalk, and as I glided in the crevices of the crowd without being grabbed, it hit me that we were "white," if not by skin color then by wealth and nationality. A shield of privilege surrounded us. If we were hurt, if our bodies were seen on TV, lifeless and limp as dolls, the image of Haitians would have gone from victims of a natural disaster to terrifying wild black people. They knew this and they let us know they knew it. When I followed looters, pen and pad ready, a man yelled by my ear in English, "This is what you came for, isn't it?"

I wanted to say fuck-off because without the media no one would give a shit about your death. But the sharp crack of gunfire and the heavy chug of a shotgun yanked our eyes upward. Two police were on the roof, the same one the girl was shot on yesterday, firing at looters. We climbed it quickly and orbited the police with cameras and writing until they lowered their aim and fired at the looter's feet to scare them. Two dark young men, glistening in the sun, stared at the police.

The cops yelled. Bretin, who scrambled with us, translated, "If you don't step down, I'm going to shoot you!" The men stopped and one of them held his arms out and shouted. Bretin didn't translate but I heard challenging sarcasm in the man's voice. He was saying, "Are you going to really shoot me over this shit I'm stealing when I have nothing." He shrugged loudly and left. The cop didn't shoot but aimed his shotgun at the other man, barely a teen really and yelled, "I'm going to kill you. Get down! Get down!" His face lit up with terror and he got sucked into the gestures of obedience. Bowing his head, the teen lifted his shirt to show his naked belly and empty waist belt, then raised his hands and crossed the craggy rubble strewn roof. The cop grabbed him, forced him down and kicked his legs apart.

If we weren't here, would the cops have shot them dead like they did the girl? As we scrambled down the building, people watched us briefly and then ran into the collapsed stores. Dust rose around the large rumbling supply trucks that passed close enough to graze our faces. Haitians dashed in and out of the broken stores carrying shoes, carrying clothes, carrying appliances with dangling electric cords that I knew would find no socket in their tent cities. Why were they taking them? A motorcycle zoomed by and the driver's face was scraped raw pink as he clutched a stolen fan under his arm. I walked around two boys laying face down on the ground as a police officer stood over them swinging his gun from one head to the other. Before I could ask their names, I jogged out of the way of a truck, a car and then another truck as people ran in the street. Someone tugged my arm, I turned and a young man circled his hands between us as if trying to dig through a wall, "You American?"

I shook my head yes.

"You listen to me! You take down my voice!"

I held my pad and nodded. "Terrible happening here," he yelled, "MY BABY KILLED! MY DADDY KILLED!" He hit his palm with his hand like a hammer, "My HOUSE is broken." I asked his name. Bretin tried to spell it for me but the man waved him away. "Saint Vin. Last name. M-A-C-E-L-Y-N. Macelyn," he jutted his finger at each letter and said, "I have nothing left in life! Tell Americans, I have nothing left in life."

In the evening, we returned to the U.N. compound, hunched over laptops, typed our stories and arranged our photos. I reread my article, knowing my friends in the Left back home were going to hate it. It was too raw, too graphic and not ideological enough. And for a moment, I hesitated, thinking maybe I should put an explicit political message in it.

But I saw them in my mind's eye, sitting at home as they read up on distant wars or disasters from the safety of their couch, drinking wine, eating good food and inflating their egos on righteousness. "Fuck you all," I muttered and hit send on the keyboard. Leaning back, I imagined the story zipping through the sky on the digital web that connected the world and how it would grate against their need for heroic victims.

My friend called me over to see a photo of the dead woman we first saw. "Look at the tag on her toe," he said. It read, "Roseline Dey." Studying the picture was the first time I stopped moving or thinking and just breathed. When I did, the smell of her death filled my nose, I looked down and found it on my hands.

Francesca's Letter

The next morning, Michael called Big Zoe, a Haitian-American deportee who taught English in Port au Prince and now worked as a "fixer." We saw him in the throng outside the airport. He was tall with an ex-boxer's grace and a jack o' lantern grin. His friend Nat, a smaller man with quick radar eyes and raspy voice, was behind the wheel of a battered truck, one of his students, James, crammed with us in the back.

As we drove, I saw the windshield was smashed. It looked like a crystal spider web.

"Nat, what happened to your window?" I asked.

"A building fell on it," he said and everyone laughed. "Are you serious?" I asked. He nodded and pointed up and around, "Man, my building fell on my truck. I'm homeless. I sleep in the back, take showers in the back."

Twisting around, I saw big jugs of water. "Everyone got turned out," he said and as he drove the smashed window sparkled in the sun.

"The way you guys talk, I feel like I'm in New York," I said.

"You from New York?" he asked.

"Brooklyn, Nostrand Avenue," I said, "off Quincy Street."

"Yo, I grew up on Lexington," Nat said, "I got family there." He did jail time, they discovered he was born in Haiti and deported him. Big Zoe said the same. His parents are Haitian, he was born in the Bahamas and they moved to Miami when he was young. While in New York, he committed a robbery and did prison time. Soon the authorities traced his birth to the Bahamas and deported him. "What's it like to be a deportee?" I asked.

"You're the lowest of the low," Big Zoe said, "Haitians assume every deportee is Hannibal Lector." Nat laughed bitterly behind the wheel, nodding and laughing.

"They think America is paradise and you were stupid for getting kicked out," Big Zoe continued. "When I got here, the girls were lined up to be with me. They thought I was going to take them back. After a few years, they saw I was still here and they were like, 'Oh, you just Haitian.'" He and Nat laughed again but it was a rough laughter like a scab over a wound.

I asked them what vision they had of Haiti, what new nation did they want to rise from the rubble? "I got married, my wife and I have a daughter," Big Zoe said, "I want her to grow up with lights in the street, to be able to go out at night without danger. I want schools, universities, movie theaters, nice shiny stores." From the front seat, Nat chimed in, "Haiti is real young, a lot of kids. They should have parks."

Next to me, James nodded yes, yes. Finally he said, "I'd like that instead of this…" and looked out of the side-window. We followed his gaze and surveyed the ruins as the imagery of New Haiti hung in our minds like a stained glass window.

"James," I called his name.

"My friends call me Ranks and we're friends," he said. I asked him about his family. He said his sister and mother were living in tents. I asked to interview them. He agreed and Nat drove us to Champs de Mars, a park turned into a sprawling camp. Ranks guided me through the bustle to a makeshift tent of bed-sheets tied to poles. He introduced me to his mother, Ilonese, who kissed him and held my hand. We squatted. I asked her where her family came from and what she did.

"We lived at Avenue Poupelard. It's gone now. Everything's gone. Before James was born, I lived in the countryside raising corn, millet, coconut with my brothers and uncles. It was too difficult. We were hungry," she said holding her belly, "I moved here to survive. I used to sell food by the road." I asked her about the earthquake. Ranks scooted nearer as if to protect her from the memory. "We thought it was the end of the world. I was preparing to cook when the walls began shaking," she said. "We screamed for Jesus to save us. I saw a boy hit on the head by rock. He bled all over the street. His uncle carried him here."

Her eyes filled with scenes and she blinked fast as if to wipe them away. Ranks leaned in to steady her but she stiffened up. I asked her how often the aid comes. "Haven't seen it," she said. "I don't eat so others can." I saw a baby crawling nearby and understood. "A brick fell on my back and I feel pain there," she touched her side. "We have been through a lot of bad things. God is getting mad at Haitians."

I asked why God was mad at Haitians. "For killing babies for Vodou sacrifices," she said. "We need to get down on our knees and ask God for forgiveness," she said and I winced because it sounded like what Christian fundamentalist Pat Robertson said on his show the 700 Club. He pronounced that God had punished Haitians for making a pact with the devil. Of course liberals and even mainstream reporters slammed him but what could I say to her, what questions could I ask, except the ones I quietly repeated to myself?

Five years ago, I heard the same from Reverend Willy who I met in New Orleans during the flood. While wading in the black water, he announced, "God was punishing us." Was this the last way for a powerless people to control chaos, blame themselves for letting it loose and thereby create the illusion it was in their power to stop it?

Her daughter Gladina came in and sat down. A pensive steady-eyed woman, she told me when the earthquake hit that "everyone was losing control" and circled her hands around her head. "I put my feelings aside to help others." She offered me water. I thanked her, gulped it down and asked what happened after the earthquake. "Dead people in the street," she looked down then away, "I can't say anything about that." I asked her what change must come out of this disaster. "I want the government to enforce a construction code," she grinded the words. I prodded, "How long has Haiti's government been a problem?" She laughed, "I'm not old enough to remember that far."

As we rose, people came over to me. Ranks interpreted. A red-eyed woman asked for Neosporin for an oozing gash on her leg. Others told me that yesterday a local group pulled up with a truck filled with food and tents. Everyone asked for help. The police came, beat people back and left with the truck. Now the food and tents were being sold in the market.

A crowd of people followed us to the Ministry of Culture, a gated building where an aid truck came to deliver food. "How often do they come?" I asked and Big Zoe interpreted for me, his voice rising and falling with mine. The people had bleak, haggard faces, some with broken noses and everyone's eyes boiled with hunger and rage, yelling, "Once a day!" I asked how many people get food and how much is it. A scarred man waved his arm, "One third gets to eat and everyone else hungry." He pointed at a boy who stared wide-eyed at us yelling, our voices shot like lighting above him. "This boy gets one meal a day! ONE MEAL," he shouted. They surged forward holding cupped palms, "This is how much we eat a day."

I saw their hands filled with nothing, jabbing the air and I wanted to pour the wealth of the world into them. Closing my notebook, I said, "I'm not speaking as a journalist now. Don't let them steal from you." Ranks and Nat sat nearby watching us. Big Zoe was in sync with me and a silence fell around us. It was like walking on a tightrope of stares.

"They've been stealing from you for decades. The French stole from you. America stole from you. Papa Doc stole from you. Baby Doc stole from you and that's why the city fell and your families are dead in the rubble," I was hollering, the rage at seeing their helplessness was an open flame in my mouth. "We will follow this story about police theft but a story won't solve the problem," I held my hands out to them. "Only you can. Do want your ancestors did. Revolt. Take the country back. There has to be a New Haiti."

They began to nod. "A New Haiti," they repeated, the words floated around like pollen, "a New Haiti." I asked where tents were being sold and they said Petionville. As we climbed back in the truck, I saw Big Zoe talking to a boy. "He's scared," Big Zoe said, "he says the police will kill us if we try anything." Zoe had his hand on the young man's shoulder like a father as the boy's face brimmed with fear and hope. "We can't keep living like this," Big Zoe said, "we need a

New Haiti." He got into the truck, drove up the hills to the middle-class neighborhood of Petionville. One blue tent stood in the street. We asked how they got it and a well-dressed woman said it came from a "friend" in the government.

On our way back to the airport, I told them of Francesca's family in Carrefour and passed around the photos. They said it would be almost impossible to find them but we would try. Evening fell quick as a black curtain across the sky. Motorcycles revved and zipped through the streets, their headlights looked like runaway stars roaring by. Nat parked, ordered some by-the-road food and Prestige beer. As we ate, he lit up a joint and I took it, sucked in a lungful and held it until my head felt like it was floating away. He laughed. I passed it to the others but they waved it off.

We sat in the front seats of his truck, the orange glow of a joint bobbing between us. He told me of growing up in Brooklyn. As he talked, I felt him uncoil. "I was in jail twelve years, Nick. Stuck people with knives, shot them, I was doin' all kinds of dirty but when they deported me here – the police held me for a few days and said to me, 'Do what you got to do to survive, just don't make us kill you,' and as soon as I got out, niggas was offering me gun-work," he turned to me, his eyes spilling apologies. "I don't want to do that anymore. It did nothing for me except kill my heart."

I pointed to the city around us. "Everything can grow back, a heart, a nation. Imagine if Haitians took some rubble and built statues of Queen Anacaona and Toussaint L'Ouverture, tall statues that people can gather under just so Haitians can see the history of their freedom."

"Man, you puttin' images in my head," he passed the joint. "Today, man, you was out there with the people. In the middle of it and you weren't scared."

"People are people," I said, "just defend their freedom to choose and they'll surprise you. Look how beautiful everyone's being, no riots, no murdering, I mean, a few knuckleheads of course but in the tent cities, folks helping each other out."

"No doubt," he said, "the people are beautiful." Zoe and Ranks squeezed back in and we drove to the airport. I told them of my luggage filled with supplies and for them to take it back to Champs de Mars.

"Ranks, come with me," I said as they dropped us off at the U.N. gate. We walked to the entrance where guards stood. I drank my Prestige beer and fumbled out my passport. The soldiers looked at me with scrunched eyes. I said

Ranks was my translator and took him with me into the airport field. We found my tent and I laid out the sweater, stacked on it a pile of Neosporin, sanitary napkins and alcohol swabs. Ranks fingered the sweater, "To wrap the baby in," he said.

The next morning, Big Zoe, Nat, Ranks and I drove into Carrefour, halting, holding out the photos of Francesca's family to strangers, asking if they knew them and where they lived. We were pointed in one direction then another and then back to the same one. The sun was rising and the day was boiling. "I don't know about this, Nick," Big Zoe said, "they may be gone. The neighbors may be gone." We stopped an older man and he pointed at a door we'd passed by two times. We got out. I knocked. A young man with bouncy, nervous energy appeared and led us in. I showed him the photos and as he looked the gate opened and an elderly white-haired man with almond-shaped eyes came in. It was her grandfather and next to him was the small girl from the photo. Ranks, Big Zoe and I rocked each other's shoulders and whooped as the family looked at us strangely.

I told them through Ranks that Francesca lived in my building and handed them her letter and money. Her mother Margaret, her uncle Louis, and sister came in and the family circled it. They held the letter as gently as they would her hand. They showed us the crater-sized hole in the living room wall as Margaret told me of the funny feeling she had before the earthquake. She was tired and going to lay down inside but a quiet nervousness kept her up. She sat on the chair, closed her eyes and was startled by sand falling on her face. Bolting up, she saw the world shaking itself apart.

I handed them a video camera and told them Francesca would be able to see them. The grandfather was short and stoic. The sister looked to it and said, "I'm scared." She talked like a river flowing into a small door. The mother comforted Francesca. The uncle assured her they were fine and the little niece playfully waved. After everyone had given her their love, they handed it back and we said goodbye.

On the drive home, we saw an angry crowd in front of the school, Bon Samaritan. We parked, got out and instantly people circled us. Ranks held his hands out like stop signs. He translated for me. "How long have you been out here?" I asked. "Six hours! Six hours and no aid, only water, they keep the food and sell it in the market." Their eyes sizzled with anger as they pleaded for help.

"The police are taking the food and selling it," a woman yelled and pointed at cops who stood grim-faced, hands on their guns. A police officer walked to his car with a mattress on his shoulder and a crate of food swinging from his hand. I watched him open his car, stack his goods inside, close it and turn to see me writing his every action down. His face went slack and he just stood there staring blankly and then drove away.

A truck rumbled in through the gates, on it a sign saying "Vendre" was taped to the side. "What does that sign say?" I asked. Ranks held his hand over his eyes to block the glare, "For Sale." Inside the gate, men loaded it with food, water and drove it away even as people pulled on the sides. It rolled on, tearing loose from their hands.

As we drove away, Ranks said, "Do you see it?"

"See what?" I asked.

"Everywhere the same," he grimaced, "skinny kids, fat cops." I looked out the window and he was right. Cops had plump faces, guts over bellies. When we were stuck in traffic, skull-faced children tapped on our window for food. "If I didn't know English," Ranks said, "that would be me."

The last day, we were downtown again. The photographers took pictures as Big Zoe and I strolled. "It's your birthday tomorrow?" I asked. He nodded ruefully and said, "Thirty-two years old." His jack o' lantern grin flashed then faded.

"Wish we could get you back in the U.S.," I said. He wiped his face and agreed but his voice was heavy like syrup. I asked him how long he was here before picking up Creole. He looked up for a second, "Three years." I asked if he felt like he was in exile. "I feel resentment, you know, I'm as American as apple pie but they used a technicality to kick me out. My parents are Haitian, I was born in the Bahamas but raised in America. I want to go back home. I have a wife and a daughter here. If I can get my papers straight, I can bring them back. I don't want her growing up…" he waved his hands at the ruins.

We walked past a throng of men and women who yelled their shoe sizes to boys on a crumbling roof top, who in turn threw boxes back to the crowd. Two guys who grabbed at the falling sneakers wore white doctors' gowns they must have stolen from an aid truck. Blazing in the sun like criminal angels, they jumped higher and higher.

We strolled further into the broken city of Port au Prince, leaning against walls. When a black van with masked men pointed guns out of the window, we took a turn to another street and suddenly saw curvy blue shapes emerge out of the sunlit dust. Two long-legged, beautiful Haitian women, in bright new dresses boosted from a store, walked the street like a fashion runway. Men stopped their yelling, heaving, digging and we turned our heads, following their saunter, hips swaying like bells in front of us as they walked down the street, blurring into the dust and disappearing. Everyone bent back to work, yelling, heaving, and digging.

We stopped to rest in the shade of a building. I leaned on a wooden crate until an old woman tapped my shoulder. Standing up as she hauled it away, I looked at Big Zoe with a question in my eyes. "Fire wood," he said.

Shots rang out. We ducked. The people scattered and we backed up. A dust covered man stumbled out of the dust, his face slack, eyes glazed as blood trickled from a bullet wound in his chest. Men hovered around him, catching him as he began to fall. "We got to get him to the hospital," Big Zoe said and we called two men on motorcycles. They rolled up, I helped the wounded man on, sat behind him to keep him from fainting and falling off and the driver shot us through the streets. We rode over fallen cables, zipped between buses, as I held the man who moaned in pain, his blood leaking over my hands. We turned into the hospital where an American soldier stiffened up. I shouted in dollar-crisp English, "Gunshot wound." The soldier wheeled around, pushed open the gates and we sped in. A team of paramedics laid the man down and began to cut off his shirt.

Big Zoe and Michael pulled up in a motorcycle, got off and we started walking back downtown. "Jesus Christ," Big Zoe said and tugged me off the sidewalk. I looked back and saw the upper half of a crispy burned body on the ground. We walked further up the street. I pointed at a small leather ball. "You play soccer," I teased Michael and Big Zoe. A little closer we saw it had clothes. Closer, we saw it was a baby's corpse. We circled it, studied its hard leathery skin ripping around the eye sockets. Numb with shock, I turned to Big Zoe, "I'm going to go home now."

Big Zoe got us a bus to the airport and I pulled out the last of my dollars. He said, "You don't have to pay me." I told him as long as I don't need money to leave, I don't need to leave with money. When we got to the airport, the line was there again guarded by bureaucrats and soldiers. We got Big Zoe in through a side gate and soon he was standing by our tent looking at the planes taking off. "You're a short ride away from home," I said as he stared at the planes taking off. I brought him to the medical tents so he could translate between the American doctors and Haitian patients and maybe find a way onto a flight. I left to get on a military evacuation line and the last image I have of Big Zoe is a man staring at planes.

When I returned to my apartment in Brooklyn, I went downstairs and gave Francesca the video camera. She cradled it, thumbed play and saw her family, their home, the hole in the wall, the rubble-strewn living room. "Take your time with it," I said. Hours later, I heard a knock on the door. I opened it and saw Francesca standing with wet eyes, "Thank you so much. I didn't know when I would see them again."

The Black Hole

It felt like someone was sitting on my chest. Slipping a hand under my shirt, I rubbed at the tightness. At the airport bar, I watched a businessman flicking his newspaper, scanning the zigzagging stock market reports, thumbing the rowdy sports photos but he skipped the news on Haiti.

Glancing away, I blinked memories of Haiti out of my vision but kept seeing the burnt corpse Big Zoe pointed out, black and crispy like a giant lamb shank. Then I saw the woman eaten by flies, the baby whose skin was torn leather flaps and the bodies in a ditch melting under the sun as the sweet rot stink buffeted on the breeze. No, Mr. Fucking Businessman doesn't want to see that before his next big deal. Blowing a hard sigh, I let my body unravel. But still, a clenching darkness lingered in my chest.

My phone rang, "Hello."

"Hey, we were worried about you," Arun, my editor said. "I just got back from Port au Prince," I swigged the beer, "drinking at the airport bar, you know, numbing the numbness."

He was oddly quiet.

"Thanks," I said, "for getting the articles on the website so quick."

"Yeah, there was some talk about them," his voice was like the hem of a dress pulled before walking through a puddle.

"Obviously not enough talk," I chided, "I'm still not famous."

"People said it was war porn," he barked. "It was too graphic and you called people looters which played into conservative ideology. It showed you don't know Haiti's history."

"War porn? Did you guys jerk off when you read it?" I slurred, "Because I got off to it, hell, I stood over the corpses and rubbed one out and when my jizz hit a dead man on the forehead, he opened his eyes and said, 'spit or swallow?'"

"Look, none of us downplay that you went but it's about ideology. It's not just that you were there but how you interpret it and you called them looters and that plays into a racist narrative," he charged ahead, his words like a bulldozer.

"Heroic victims," I aimed my voice like a spear, "you fuckers want heroic victims. Well not everyone was a victim or a hero. Life does not fit into ideology, brother, ideology sets up a central thesis which pushes anything that doesn't fit into it to the margins where it becomes the repressed part of the text," I took a shot of rum and felt it hit like fire in my belly, "but a real writer reports from the margins. By the way, did you know what I just did, it's called deconstruction. And how did I do that? I have a Ph.D. in literary theory."

"You're angry at us, aren't you?" he pulled back.

"Fucking cowards," I felt heat in my throat, "you professional moralizers, sitting on soft couches in front of desks, telling me what's real and what's not. Go fuck yourselves. I'm the one who went. I'm the one who sees this shit when I sleep and I can tell you that your ideology is another way to kill them."

Event Horizon

Rocking in sleep, I heard a metallic jingle and opened my eyes to a tall man in military uniform standing at the bathroom. He took a step and faced me. It was Toussaint L'Ouverture, the Haitian general from the revolution, his gaunt, near skeletal face was like chiseled stone and his dark eyes ablaze with grief.

He put a finger to his mouth and said, "Remember," then left in a heel heavy walk, medals jingling. I woke up again, panting, blinking the dream from my eyes.

This Little Light

The New Orleans Superdome was peeled by wind, metal roof flapping like a toupee. The ceiling projector lit the screen. I saw students grip their desks and lean forward, sucking up the scenes from *When the Levees Broke*. We watched mothers cradling babies through black water, elderly dying in their wheelchairs and men with burning eyes staring at the camera. I wiped my face with my hands because I had been there and, years later, the sights and smells and sounds of flooded New Orleans were still in my body and could rise to my throat if I let them.

On screen was a bald brother, "We had this big man named Radio, spiritual man, and he started clapping it up, warming it up, it was just this spirit, this big spirit, it was one of the proud moments for us because as he started clapping it up, people just started shouting out praises, we had to do something." The scene cut to a line of black women, babies hoisted on shoulders, singing through the trash strewn hallways of the Superdome, "This little light of mine, I'm going to let it shine. Everywhere I go, I'm going to let it shine." They put hands in the air as if receiving signals from the divine. It cut to the bald brother saying, "It was powerful because it was a sad time, you didn't know what was going to happen but you had to have faith in God. After we marched around the dome and people was joining in, after we marched around one time we go on the outside and, at that time, I felt the movement, the Civil Rights Movement, after that things kind of settled down."

I paused the video and on the screen a woman held her hands up in praise, "When pressure threatens to destroy not just your body but the most precious thing about you, the quality that you hold close, people will rise up to protect their spirit even at the risk of death because to live without it is to live in death, to go numb and exist in a limbo of nothingness."

"I think this is one of the key elements to understand about religion and Black America. Of course at its worst, it can lead to sexual bigotry and ignorance. At its best, it secures for people who have little else, a sense of self-worth, a great joyful connection to life that they will rise up to protect. The question I ask you is: what is sacred in your life, what is within you that is your source of power and that you'd risk everything to protect?"

They sat for a minute as the images, the music and the question fell into place inside them. Finally chairs scraped as they put books in bags and left. When the last student was gone, I clutched my chest, feeling the black hole from Haiti that pulled me into numbness slowly unravel.

Replaying the scene, I heard the women in the Superdome again and stepped in front of the projector's beam. Lifting my hands in praise, I saw my shadow on screen, its arms out as people marched into my darkness singing of God, bringing light.

The Vortex

"It's the Law of Attraction at work so if you clearly see what you want in your mind and focus…"

"The Law of what?" I cut in.

"The Law of Attraction teaches that we create our own reality by manifesting our desire in the physical plane," her voice was like a flag waved over a conquered hill. "We pull into this reality what we set our minds to and if we align our thoughts to a positive frequency, our true lives will emerge."

I shook the phone as if getting dirt out. Hypatia was silent, waiting for me to respond. We had been in love for years but could scream for hours over religion or what I called 'magical thinking.' I was atheist, she a New Age Christian. The words between us were less debate than my endless cascade of judgment and her swimming against it.

"That sounds like bullshit," I said.

"What?" her voice winced.

"That sounds like bullshit," I repeated, "it justifies oppression. So we 'manifest' our reality by thinking about it. Well, I'm sure the Haitians being killed in the earthquake were really thinking about being saved but they fucking died anyway. I guess they didn't believe in the Vortex. But middle class white people watching Oprah can get new cars if they just really put their minds to it."

She was quiet.

"No, I'm serious," my voice a tank pushing through walls, "this way of thinking blinds people to how systems work and their role within them. Instead, they blame themselves for not believing hard enough. It takes American individualism and turns it into the psychological prison of spiritual narcissism."

She wearily chuckled, "Is there any magic in your world?"

When I went to her apartment, I saw the book *The Vortex: Where the Law of Attraction Assembles All Cooperative Relationships* near her bed. On the cover was a spiral galaxy. I opened it and read a few lines. Her face brightened as if I saw the truth. I put it down and slipped my hands under her bathrobe, her skin was steaming from the hot bath she just took. We fell into bed, filled silence with kissing and stroking. While inside her, I reached over her head and started reading from the book as she got close to orgasm, "Your Source, no matter how extreme the situation will never draw its love and attention from you."

Manifesting Crisis

Glancing over my shoulder, I stepped into the aisle where copies of *The Vortex* lined the shelf. Taking each one down, I inserted inside a photo of the dead bodies I saw in Haiti. The pictures showed the bloated bodies and puss streaming over faces. Typed on each one was the line, "Your Source, no matter how extreme the situation will never draw its love and attention from you."

Working my way up and down the New Age Self Help section, I stuffed each book with the morbid photos. Finishing up, I waited downstairs near the Customer Service. A couple strode quickly to the counter, he was red faced and she was in near tears as they flung the photo on the counter. The staff stammered their apologies and jogged upstairs.

I left, cackling out loud and called my girlfriend, "Today I was in total alignment. The universe gave me exactly what I wanted."

Big Zoe

"You've got H.B.O.," Big Zoe said in mock child's voice. I scrunched my eyebrows and asked, "H.B.O., what does that mean?"

"Haitian Body Odor," he half grimaced, half smiled, "that's how the kids teased me in school, my odor, my blazer that had holes in it. Mom said we had to save money."

Big Zoe paused, lifted his eyes to stare at a memory that was coming from a great distance in him. I sipped at the coffee and looked through the window to the Haitian street. Every wall blazed with sun and a morning haze rose as vehicles jangled on dirt roads. Rubble lay everywhere. Two months after the earthquake, I came back during Spring Break to report on Haiti's recovery, see Big Zoe and extend the stories of people beyond the brief window they had in the U.S. media.

Big Zoe hosted me. I camped in the lawn, enclosed by cement walls with jagged glass wedged on top to cut the hands or feet of thieves who tried to break in. Everyone knew Zoe had a gun so no one tried. The first day, I was awakened by the chickens and goats baying in the morning. When the animals shouted glory to the new day, I stumbled out of my tent, half asleep and chased them, telling them to shut up. Big Zoe sat on the porch laughing, "Welcome to Haiti!"

"Fuck Haiti," I yelled and crawled back into bed. Later we went to a local eatery, sat down and I asked him his life story and the first words he said were, "Bucket showers."

"We couldn't take baths," Big Zoe said and his eyes lit up, "we lived in Tampa, Florida. Mom cleaned hotels. I loved taking long showers until she showed me the water bill, the electric bill, and said we couldn't be wasteful. So we had a bucket in the bathtub and I took bucket showers damn near my whole life."

"And your dad?" I asked.

"Love my dad but as a man he lacked a lot," Big Zoe's face pulled tight. "My brother Joseph, he was my real father figure. I wore his clothes even if they were too big for me," he rolled his shoulders. "I want my child to know she has a father. I want her to wake up and see that I'm there."

"How did it shape you," I pointed to his head, "when you saw your mom struggle to pay bills and your father was in…?"

"Miami."

"Yes, Miami." I said.

"I thought, why bother with petty shit," Big Zoe's eyes hardened into obsidian, "got some crack and cut it up and sold it after my shift at McDonalds. Imagine me standing there in my oily apron on the street corner with hundreds of dollars of crack in my bag. The police came and the other dealers scattered like pigeons but not me, I stood there real cool with marijuana in my soda cup and a grin. 'What you doing out here?' the cop asked me but I was like, 'Officer, I just came from work.'"

"At McDonalds, I'd clear like $600 a week, but selling rock, I could clear $2400 in a few hours. I gave my mom my McDonald's check but never dirty drug money. I didn't want it to touch her but after a while I liked the cash so much I forgot why I started selling in the first place. Instead of taking a load off my mom's back, I put a load on it."

"You got busted?" I asked.

"Not then, not right away," Big Zoe said, "but I got into the life and in 1999 I was busted and went to prison. When I was on the bus to Florida, I saw black dudes in fields picking white plants, I was like what the hell and the guard said, 'That's a cotton field, boy!' Oh my god, I thought. Oh my fucking god."

"I entered a prison of convicted felons, some serving thirty-year sentences. My game plan was not to get caught up into cliques. In prison that will get you killed. And in prison if you have a drug habit that also will get you killed. If you want marijuana or crack, you'll sell your ass. The strong prey on the weak, they have loan sharks who'll give you the money for drugs but if you don't pay up, they will kill you. I knew a lot of people who died."

"Dudes would hop in front of you in the food line just to fuck with your head and guys put locks in socks to swing at your face or would shank you. What saved me was bodybuilding and the Bible. I don't even remember the second year. I just knew the number – 60 months, 5 years. And then I get a call over the intercom, 'You're going to get deported!' I blanked out. How am I going to get deported? I'm American!"

"So what was the loophole?" I prodded.

"My parents are from Haiti and I was born in the Bahamas before I was brought to the U.S. They followed my paper trail and found out." Big Zoe leaned back in his chair, "The first time I was on a plane was when I was being deported to Haiti. I had a window seat and looked down at the tin roof homes, cars, bare treeless hills. The other Haitians on the plane are happy they are coming back. I'm like FUCK! What am I going to do in Haiti? The plane landed and everyone got off but I was shackled to my seat. The air marshal turned to me and said, 'You're in your country, buddy.' "

I spent two months in a Haitian prison. My family came and did a lot of negotiation with the officers and they let me out. I'm there in the street after being in the U.S. and now I have to survive and stay out of the police's way."

"At first, my family here treated me like a king because I was being sent money but when it didn't come anymore, they began to treat me like a peasant. It hit the fan when my cousin accused me of stealing. I yelled back at him, 'How am I going to steal when I'm working? I don't need your money.'"

Big Zoe's face twisted as if he was in the moment again and I felt for a second how nothing ever disappears, how the past stays inside us.

"He began to try to punch me," Big Zoe went on, "he yelled, 'Fuck your mother.' You don't tell a Haitian anything about his mom so I snapped and hit him with a right jab. In prison I learned how to box and nailed him and ran as he bent over coughing. I moved in with my brother Joseph."

"And now," I said, "you have a family of your own." A wide smile opened his face, "Lescinda. We fit together like hand and glove. She understands me. I understand her. One day, my family sent $100 dollars and I said let's go get dressed, see a movie, and she took my money and said, 'Let's put this money in the bank because one day your family will stop sending you money.' I was like wow, I'm going to have to wife this one."

"And now you have a little girl," I said "and you're a much better father to her than yours was to you."

"Yeah, I told Lescinda when she was pregnant. She didn't tell me," he put his hands behind his head, "I control her menstrual cycle. I know when it comes and when it goes."

"That is an amazing superpower, Mr. Menstrual," I said. "How the world would change if all men had such gifts." He tore a bit of bread and ate, smiling. "She likes it when I say funny, crazy shit. As a man, you have to have game to get past their pain. God knows we cause most of it."

Finally, I felt we trusted each other and words could go straight to the feeling without shame or pride sending them into a long wild orbit away from the body. I took a step to the last part of his story, "And what happened during the earthquake?"

His eyes squinted and his chest rose and fell, "The earthquake?" Slowly his hands spun as if weaving thread, "After the shaking stopped, I was shocked at seeing buildings gone and was saying to myself, fuck, I got to get home. I'm trying to call home but I can't get through, there's no public transport and the skyline wasn't there, just a white fog. People were yelling, 'This is the End of the World. Repent! Repent!'"

"I saw a woman stumbling out with a red gash that showed her bone and a girl cried, 'Help me! Help me get my aunt!' That's when I remembered my wife wouldn't be at home or work, she gets off at 4pm and may be in a bus which scared me more because the buildings fell on cars. I ran home to my daughter, I just sprinted, I didn't get tired, just ran. One way was blocked off so I turned and found myself in front of the National Palace that was split like an egg.

"I ran for two hours, when I looked around, I saw the cathedrals had collapsed, people lifted concrete to get family out," he blew a long sad breath, "my only regret is that I didn't help anyone else along the way."

"And when you got home," I asked, "what did you see?"

He was a dam breaking and pouring out memories. "In my mind," he rubbed his arms and shook his head, "in my mind, I thought they were dead. 'Please God, don't let them be dead,' I kept saying over and over. I sprinted, ran, sprinted more and ran. When I got to the neighbor's house, I almost ran into him, I'm looking at him and he patted me on the back and said, 'They're okay, your family's okay, your wife and daughter are there.'"

"I believed him but I didn't believe him so I sprinted down the street and by now my legs are burning, my lungs are burning. I see people at my house, the gate is open and people are in the yard. I yelled and saw my wife, my daughter, and we fell on each other and hugged saying, 'Thank God. Thank God.'"

"Later," he knuckled tears from his eyes, "we checked on others and a block of stone fell from a church wall and ripped a neighbor in two. We covered her body."

Epilogue

Big Zoe hired motorcyclists to zip us around Port au Prince. We got to high ground outside of Port au Prince and stood at the rim of the valley.

Hills flashed with hundreds of zinc roof homes. They looked as thin as cardboard boxes and they were built on near treeless hills. One hard storm and the dirt will become streaming mud. And those homes will tumble into the ravine and anyone living inside will die.

I saw an old man sitting on rubble. He rose, shook our hands as Big Zoe translated my questions. His son has been buried under the rubble since the earthquake and he piled debris to keep dogs from eating his child. Breathing hard, he forearmed sweat from his eyes, pointed to a mummy-like face in the dark crevice. As I kneeled, the driver sucked his teeth and left.

Notebook open, I wrote, "dead three months, prune dry skin ripped to skull, face of petrified agony."

I asked him who his son was. The father told us, "His name was Jean, he had a learning disorder and always he was embarrassed that his younger brother was smarter and took the lead but Jean loved to eat rice and le gume. The day he died, we made his favorite meal. I asked him, 'Why are you smiling?' He said, 'Today my belly will be full and…'" he paused to breathe, "the earthquake hit."

We stood in the bright heat staring at the face of Jean who died screaming. The father begged neighbors for help since they knew his son as a boy but they wanted money to dig. "Even after death, he is suffering," he said and placed stones back over Jean who remains sealed in the darkness with countless other souls thrashing in our memory, pleading for rescue so loudly because for them the earthquake never ended.

Forget
For Jorge Luis Borges

"Like you, I too have struggled with all my might not to forget. Like you, I forgot. Like you, I longed for a memory beyond consolation, a memory of shadows and stone. I struggled everyday with all my might against the horror of not understanding, like you I forgot."

— from *Hiroshima Mon Amour*

There is an earthquake in me. If I hold still, my hands will tremor. Each day and night adds distance to the sight of a dead son buried in rubble or people in Port au Prince waking up with amputated stumps. The moaning of survivors is covered by other days, a memory under memories.

But inside sleep, beneath thought, the tremors continue. When I walk by an abandoned building, I see bodies sandwiched by stone. A week ago, I sat on a friend's couch as she asked me about Haiti's earthquake. Jutting my finger like a saber, I cut into U.S. foreign policy until suddenly my eyes stung with tears. She reached out and held my arms, massaging them until my breath slowed down to a whisper.

Talking to a photographer I met in Haiti, we stopped mid-sentence and swayed from the screams blowing through open memory. Our minds cracked like hard earth split by a geyser's steam. Again I felt the distance between our most vivid truth and the mask we wear in the mirror of the other.

What else do we carry in silence? We have a short time to answer before our body takes our memory with it. Generations born later will know the disasters I witnessed – 9/11, flooded New Orleans, the Darfur Genocide and Haiti's earthquake from news footage researched for school assignments. But the ringing terror of it will end with some last person.

At some unknown moment, when some unknown man or woman dies then the tremors will stop, evaporated, as all history is, with the body. And a new terror will take its place. Another city will shake, another day will turn black. And who will remember that terror and when will it be forgotten? Is this why history moves in an endless cycle, because at its hub is a body that speaks but is never heard?

One

My neighbor, Castle, stands out in the street holding a radio. The U2 song "One" blares its bitter lyrics, urging us to carry each other but to let go if pain is the only reward for love. He plays rock and roll in a neighborhood of Rap, Rap and more Rap. When I asked him why, he joked, "That ain't real music. This is the real stuff." And then he turns up ZZ Top or AC/DC while everyone shakes their head.

But now "One" plays as cars with bass heavy reggae pass by. Leaning out of my window, I watch him hold the radio on his shoulder as families laugh on the stoop and drink beer. Young men lounge on the corner boasting about shit. It's an ideal moment but I know later, when drunk, they will challenge each other until dizzy with recklessness, and fight.

I've been here for years but it's just an address, not my home. I smile, say hello. They nod and respect me. But I haven't eaten at their homes or gotten involved in their lives because I don't have enough to give them. And they always want something. I hear them fight over money, over respect, over love, over drugs until everyone walks away with less than they had before. When I had long dreadlocks, I was camouflaged but now I am just another gentrifying neighbor. I want to leave and I have the money but I haven't yet.

I could float to another neighborhood where these lives are distant headlines of crime and sorrow. But I am afraid of losing the role of the witness, the one act that gives my life meaning. And life without destiny terrifies me. So I listen to the song blaring from Castle's radio. As it ends, the DJ says, "And that was U2. Bono just recently got an award for humanitarian work in Africa…"

Alienation

I wore an astronaut helmet and white jump suit through my street. Men stopped talking and lowered their beers to eye my one-way visor, trying to read me. Was I crazy? Was I gunman from a rival gang coming to shoot one of them and run?

After I passed by, I smiled inside the helmet at their fear. How many times have these same men harassed women? Or crowd the corner in order to force everyone around them just to prove their power? How many times did they shoot their guns into the night, waking up the neighborhood in a cold sweat? So I took it slow, stared at their frozen eyes and reached into my bag as they held their breath.

Behind me, they yelled that it wasn't Halloween yet or astronauts need to go back to their fucking white neighborhoods because they don't play that in Brooklyn. I laughed, I had my own oxygen. I had my own money and my own thoughts. I was a visitor in their world studying how they lived and how they died. I saw their future in the wars and flooded cities of the world, in funerals of men killed by police and in the dead souls staring at walls in jails. They saw it too but they did not care enough about their lives to organize and fight the system. Instead, they fought each other and spilled blood in the street. My job was to write reports to the college-educated ruling class who paid me to give portraits of this broken world. I was tired of it.

I found the building on my Google directions, showed my ticket and entered into a large dance club. Reddish silhouettes overlapped in the smoky hall. It was a space-themed party and everyone wore costumes. Aliens, astronauts, and topless women in green body paint with sizzling plastic ray guns, all rode their hips on the same beat.

"Where have you been?" a man who wore silver robot latex and a blinking helmet leaned into my ear. He opened his visor and I saw it was someone I knew, someone I danced and smoked with but whose name slipped from me.

"Earth," I shouted.

"Oh, I heard about that place," he yelled above the music, "how is it going there?"

"Their problems look really small," I said, "from a hundred miles away."

The Tin-Foil Hat Crowd — The Indyblog, August 2010

The panelists talked about U.F.O. wreckage and aliens fusing a human head on a cow. I looked at the audience, assuming they weren't buying it until a woman asked, "Who here has had contact with U.F.O's?" Everyone raised their arms. Faces shined with bright defiance. Near the back wall, a man in a bright psychedelic shirt waved both hands and danced. I laid my head down, thinking: *I'm in a room of crazy people.*

I was at the event, "Aliens Amongst Us," organized by the Evolver Movement, a neo-Hippie social network whose website promotes the "transformation of humanity" but those who came were not activists but devotees. They wore dreadlocks, hemp necklaces, "energy" channeling crystals and many had a faraway look as if they left some part of themselves in their last acid trip.

They were the New Lost Generation, folks who'd fallen through the cracks of our crumbling empire and found this mystery cult with its promises of secret knowledge and chemical salvation. At its top stood lanky, sandy-haired Daniel Pinchbeck who years ago was an editor of *Open City*. After a friend overdosed on heroin, Pinchbeck fled to the Amazon to drink potions from shamans to cure himself of nihilism before he died like his friend. Those dizzy vomit-soaked trips became his book *Breaking Open the Head* which made him a counter-culture guru. Now he hosts Evolver events, circled by mostly white, well-off audiences who look to him for meaning. And he gives it to them: shaman drug rituals, Mayan prophecies and a suspicion of reality that adds up to escapism. Our world *is* a wreck but Pinchbeck has them look outside of it for a truth that can heal it and the crazier that truth the better.

But the Crazy was hidden until the woman asked who had contact with aliens. The hands-in-the-air-salute exposed the insanity and none of the panelists said a thing. Sitting on the couches were Bill Birnes, a raspy wrinkled salesman of the otherworldly who headed History Channel's *U.F.O. Hunters,* therapist William Gibbs, a slow, bloated man who treated victims of "alien abduction," and a dark-suited U.F.O. historian, Richard Dolan who wore a confident smile.

Pinchbeck pointed to an older woman who talked of life-changing wounds left in the wake of starships. She screamed, "People who have been abducted have increased paranormal abilities." He called on a young Brit who yelled, "I've seen the labs," her hands clenched into fists, "they are making human alien hybrids and people must be told!"

I've seen this defiance against reality years ago at Nation of Islam meetings. In the late 90s, my mom lived in Hartford and during my visits she showed me closed schools and corners where shootings stained the sidewalk red. The streets were filled with pain and people looking for answers. They packed the mosques to listen to dark-suited men preaching how the white man invented AIDS or Jews controlled the media or that every president is a Mason or that the Illuminati controlled us. Sitting there, I sensed that proof wasn't needed, what mattered was belief. If we could name evil, give it a face, then we could fight it.

But when we left those halls, we didn't see Jews or Masons or the Illuminati. We saw the same people we always saw, the mother who slapped her child in the street, men fighting on trash-strewn corners, the homeless guy lying on the street as dark urine trickled from his pants. We learned in the mosque not to understand but to pity them as puppet-like victims, manipulated by mysterious others only the Nation of Islam could see. Our job was to cut the strings, no alcohol, no pork, no Jesus, no "Jewish" media, just submit to Allah and become purified.

Some joined but most didn't, held back by hopelessness or the shame of showing raw need in public or the sense that one could not survive the world by retreating from it. The few who joined the mosque shouted with bright defiant faces. The world-government wasn't going to keep the truth from them anymore because we had a Messenger. I remember Farrakhan at the podium announcing the Million Man March. We were Fallen, he said, but could be saved if we submitted to Allah. The plan was to gather in D.C. and show our strength. His call and our response got louder until we spoke as one man and in that sublime moment our power was revealed. Afterward, dizzy with adrenaline, we bought tapes and newspapers and "cures" for ailments of the soul.

Years before the mosque, I felt that awe as a child. Dozing in my grandma's home in Puerto Rico, I lay in a mosquito net shrouded bed, reading a science-fiction book when her boyfriend Daniel yelled for me. I dashed to the balcony and saw a twisting line of smoke in the sky. "It was U.F.O.," he said. The book I'd been reading in bed was the story of a young boy planet hopping in a spaceship through the star-speckled void of space being, of course, chased by aliens. Grandma said it was the Devil's writing but when I jumped out of bed and ran to Daniel's side, both of us pointing to the sky in wonder, I was also pointing to the images the book left in my mind. But what kind of spaceship leaves a trail of smoke? Does it run on diesel? More likely, it was a jet or meteor but Daniel's wonder at seeing a "U.F.O." was as real as our joy at Farrakhan's vision of a re-deemed Black People. Both were glimpses of a world beyond this one.

The wonder of transcendent visions comes from our real need for whole-ness. Being divided against ourselves is part of the human condition, one seen as far back as the ancient plays of Sophocles, where King Oedipus is divided by fate and hubris. In the tragic vision of Modernity, we are divided from the ex-panse of eternity by the smallness of our bodies and from life by the language that describes it. Living divided means the need to be part of a larger reality is cen-tral to us. Yet our need for transcendence is always defined by history.

As a boy in Catholic Church, I was divided from my body by the concept of sin, transcendence was floating as a spirit in Heaven. As a teen, I was divided from myself by racism and transcendence was the Nation of Islam's vision of a black-ruled world. Raised in an orphanage, I was divided from my family by class, transcendence was the Communist prophecy of an equal world. As a man divided by bitterness, transcendence was the euphoria of the Obama campaign.

Whether it's one's body, color or place in society, transcendence is reclaim-ing what was lost and faith is the first step. Whether it's a messiah stepping down from Heaven in glory or a U.F.O. streaking through the sky or a media haloed politician saying, "Yes we can!" we are trained to reach for lights in the sky.

And for the sake of that faith, people close their eyes and reach for the dream. The more they're told it's not real, the harder they hold it. I came to "Aliens Amongst Us" to see how certain and how reckless they'd be in their per-secuted truth. Ufology shares with the Nation of Islam a vision of hidden truths censored by invisible forces but at the mosque it resonates with the real violence of our racist history. What did Ufologists lose that they search for it so fervently in the sky?

When I first arrived at the Commons, a woman in the front row dropped her marbles. "Wow," I muttered, "she lost her marbles. It's a good sign." I chat-ted with the man next to me. He had a weathered face, kind and shy. "What do you think about this?" I asked.

"Well, if aliens really came all this way for us," he said, "I think they'd say Hi." We laughed as Pinchbeck began, "I'm glad to see a packed room of people.

My concern was that Evolver is trying to build credibility and I was afraid we'd lose it. But it's important to see Gnostic Theology, the Truth of native cultures, aliens and spirits as all part of the same continuum."

He introduced Bill Birnes, the host of History Channel's *U.F.O. Hunters*. The wrinkled raspy man began his gothic tale, "There's a veil of fear. If you dare mention U.F.O.'s, you are marginalized. No one will deal with you." But he is brave and tells us that U.F.O. wreckage has been turned into modern technology like F-16 jets using "cloaking devices" to disappear. He just flows with Crazy, telling us about Pentagon conspiracies, men screaming in secret mountain labs as aliens attacked and then fused human heads on cows.

The air tingled. Wow, the Truth is Out There. Pinchbeck turned to a bloated man next to him, William Gibbs, a therapist who treated "alien abductees." He had a wisp of a smile, "I've always asked big questions and U.F.O.'s are an anomaly that defies scientific categories. I've been a psychologist for a group who were convinced they'd been abducted..."

His voice receded and I stared around at people held rapt, barely blinking. I wondered, *What if they're aliens?* I imagined them pulling off their human skin, reptile faces glistening, long forked tongues flickering as they sipped their Starbucks chai-tea lattes. After draining the last drop and still thirsty, they'd grab my arms and pull me apart. I'd be alive just long enough to see my hand being swallowed down an alien throat.

I snapped out of my daydream to U.F.O. historian Richard Dolan's earnest monologue. He spoke in a soft velvety tone, "Jets chasing discs that out-flew them. We have more than 100 reports. Our military was asking, 'Whose flying these things, the Soviets?' But why are aliens contacting us? We are the greatest show in this quadrant. We changed our civilization in the blink of a cosmic eye. There are aliens living amongst us."

"Are they benevolent?" asked Pinchbeck. "People think in terms of Good Aliens or Bad Aliens. Is that helpful? Are we being controlled?"

Dolan rubbed his hands, "All I can say is that we are part of a larger narrative." Numb at this point, my pen twitched but it felt like someone else was writing. Dolan said aliens had created a hybrid race to take over the world and his words struck something in me. Were some people on this planet less human than others? Snarling, I wondered what would he have us do to find this hybrid race? Should we force people to get DNA testing? Wear arm-bands with a blue star? Experiment on them or put them in alien ghettos and maybe gas them?

Afterwards, I asked Dolan if his vision of "aliens amongst us" doesn't parallel the language of racism in making a hierarchy of humanity. He said he doesn't promote violence but that aliens are on earth manipulating us. Of course he'd never personally incite violence, it would be a career killer. If people took his paranoid vision of the world seriously, what else would they do but round up aliens? Hell, we already round up undocumented workers like animals. His voice left oil in my ears.

Dolan's vision of a mongrel species threatening our purity is as old as the Civil War when racists stoked fears of black people mixing with whites. It's as old as Nazi Germany's Nuremberg Laws. The terror of miscegenation rises when people lose their power and status. U.F.O.'s are blank screens to project cultural anxieties. As I left, Dolan told people huddled around him, "When Obama met the Bilderberg Group, who is deeply involved in this cover-up…" What next, I thought, the New World Order, 9/11 Truth, the Masons, Illuminati or the Elders of Zion?

I confronted Pinchbeck, "I think what you're doing here is dangerous." He squinted for a second. I said U.F.O.'s were people's projections onto explainable natural phenomena. He said that was a dualist way of thinking, reality was more interrelated. I said that was slippery Hegel. We went outside, I borrowed a cigarette and we stood there blowing smoke.

"What you're doing is dangerous," I pointed at him. "You're spreading false hope and escapism."

"You keep using that word dangerous…"

"It is," I flapped my hands, "we have real problems on the planet and telling people to do drugs or waste time searching for aliens is a distraction. I mean, look, I defend your freedom of speech but that doesn't mean it's worth saying. This isn't real. Hunger is real. Poverty is real."

His eyes searched for an escape, "These states of consciousness are real. I've experienced telekinesis, making things appear and disappear through alternate dimensions, telepathy…"

I studied his face. My lips squeezed like a zip-lock bag and I quietly shook my head. It felt cheap to bring in miracles to a debate.

Sensing my frustration, he told me to read *The Structures of Consciousness* by Jean Gebser. He talked of indigenous cultures and that our modern rationality is destroying the planet because we are disconnected from the larger holistic reality. I looked away from him and remembered the woodcut drawings of Tainos being hacked apart by Spanish soldiers. "If they had the power of telekinesis or talking to plants or being in touch with galactic intelligences," I countered, "then why not do some Avatar shit and defend themselves against the Conquistadores?"

"The European consciousness was something they never dealt with before," he calmly explained, "it's why one soldier could kill so many native warriors."

"Daniel," I spread my hands to let go of the conversation, "maybe it was the smallpox and horses and armor and swords." I paused. More smoke. We were both exhausted and he said, "Read my books and e-mail me."

We shook hands and I left, head reeling, running my hands over my face as if wiping away his words. Crazy.

The End Times

"Do you want to kiss Jesus?" the nun asked as behind her a long-haired man wearing a crown of thorns, a loin cloth with vodka on his breath, stumbled up to me.

"You want to kiss me," he slurred.

"Sure, Jesus, but can I get you a little more drunk?" I held up a jug of honey and a bottle of rum. He got on his knees and gripped the back of my legs, tilted back and opened his mouth.

"Jesus, you don't even know me," I shot a look at the nun who shrugged. Climbing out of an art mobile was the Pope who yelled, "He's never sober after noontime. And there are too many souls to save out here."

I squirted honey on his lips and shot liquor down his throat. He stood up, reset his crown of thorns and brought me in for a deep kiss. Our beards tangled. Our chests scraped.

Pulling away, I reached into my bag, held up nipple clamps and locked them on him so that he looked like he was getting a jumpstart from a car battery. Moaning, Jesus walked in drunken zigzag steps to the disco camp behind us where a dozen people roller-skated or bladed in circles on a 100-foot wide wood dance floor as Donna Summer's *Love to Love You Baby* boomed from the dust-coated speakers.

"So, how was kissing Jesus?" the nun asked.

"Well, it's the first time I ever kissed a man," I laughed, "and the last but I'm glad it was Him. I grew up Catholic and it's healing to be tongued down by a drunken messiah."

"He sure is a drunk fuck," she pointed and we saw him leaning back and roaring in pleasure as a woman grinded her ass on his crotch. She was wearing his crown of thorns as he yanked her hair and slammed himself on her. The nun, the Pope and I looked at each other with smiling eyes.

"Burning Man," I laughed and shook my head.

"Burning Man," they agreed.

In the Dark

"Like the end of the world," I whispered into a black desert night. Again I was at Black Rock City. It has become, over the years, a sort of church for me. The day was a blur of dancing, art car hopping, drinking and smoking with campmates as The Man stood in the Playa like a giant pharaoh. But at night, I felt the emptiness of the horizon tug on me and I walked to the city's edge. Hopping over the pink trash fence, I studied the stars above me that glinted like faraway diamonds.

The LSD I swallowed washed me in cascades of color, unraveling thought. When a cool wind blew, it carried me away like a kite on a string until my heartbeat reeled me in.

Faces and voices surged up into my head. I saw Big Zoe, the fixer who I met while reporting in post-earthquake Haiti. He guided me around the dried corpses in the street to the survivors choking on the names of lost loved ones. He almost took shape in the dark. *You didn't forget about us, did you? No, you wouldn't do that.* As he waited for my answer, behind him, next to him, others took their place, familiar faces but like silhouettes crisscrossing each other in the blackness.

It was my absent father, my uncle, my work-tired mother, Hypatia whose heart I broke into bitterness, a refugee I met in U.N. camps who had been gang raped, another who was a child dying of hunger, a face, a skull tightly wrapped in skin, random faces who I almost knew, passed around me in the night.

Can you give me everything? I gave it to you. Who are you fucking now, if it's not me? Are you happy that I left? No one listens to us here, no one will be there at the end to know who we were because everything fades into nothingness before the next beginning. It's hot inside stars, too hot for memory. Whose calling you so late at night? Are you still angry? Are you going to watch me die alone?

"I hate all of you," I said and reached out to them as if these phantoms were real. A dark tide of despair rose and brimmed over my body. Somehow I wasn't surprised when everyone I loved, everyone I betrayed, touched my face, wiped the dust from my eyelids and embraced me.

Exodus

"Today we analyze Exodus and its relationship to Black American literature," I held up the photocopied handout. Eyes rolled and sighs steamed out of their mouths as they took copies from their folders. It was the start of the semester and in the classroom I was in a tug of war with my students who did not want to be dragged into the past.

"I know, I know," my sarcasm hacked at their apathy, "reading the Bible with the atheist professor is so fun. African-Americans used this myth to visualize freedom. We can't read black literature with depth if we don't know the mythology that gave it shape. But first, how are we going to read Exodus? In this class, it will be a secular reading that interprets its imagery for meaning. And that stands opposed to fundamentalist reading which looks at holy texts as if they literally happened."

"Well, that's how I read the Bible," one student, young, black, female, hollered without waiting to be called, "Jesus Christ is my Lord and Savior."

"And Zeus is mine," I said flatly. Everyone's foreheads creased. I gestured to the young woman, "If you lived twenty five hundred years ago, before Christianity, do you think you would believe in the Gods of your family and village?"

She squirmed a little, "I guess."

"Well then, saying you believe in a religion doesn't prove its reality," I spread my hands as if springing a jack in the box, "it just means you're a product of history."

"OH SNAP," a red-haired student laughed. I held up my hands, "No, no snapping on the believers." Another hand shot up, it was Ms. Mini-Me, a female student who was always trying to catch my eyes.

"Well, I don't believe in God," she cut a look at the Christian.

"You don't have to believe in God to read Exodus," I said. "Just believe in metaphors." They chuckled and opened the photocopies. I read each of the plagues that God struck upon Egypt, the water turning into blood, frogs leaping from the river, soot from the furnace causing boils on the Egyptians.

"Look at the water turning to blood," I leaned on the scripture, "if you read it as a symbol rather than a historical reality, what could be the meaning?" Heads bowed, I studied their silence. As a professor you become attuned to the quality of quiet. Is it filled with brains buzzing or is it a retreat from the page?

"Write the word blood and meditate on the associations around it," I scrawled the word on the blackboard. "Write the word water and the associations around it, whatever comes to your mind and then draw lines between them. Now keep in mind the core conflict driving Exodus, slaves rebelling against their masters." They saw me making a web that linked water and blood, slavery and freedom.

Hands began to flutter on the desk like pigeons waking up and finally three or four flew. "You," I called on the quietest one who sat near the back, face hidden under a baseball cap.

"Is it that God is making the Egyptians drink the blood of the Hebrews," she tiptoed her idea out, "after the slave owners whipped them bloody, it's like revenge or punishment for what they did?"

"I was going to say that," Ms. Mini Me shouted and people rolled their eyes. But a few others nodded and said that it made sense. A buzz was in the air.

"So now we get it," I stepped from behind the desk. "Analyze each of the plagues and write down what the allegorical meaning is and then what the overall theme is."

They bowed their heads, glancing back and forth from text to page, pens twitching. After ten minutes, eyes shot up sizzling with answers.

"God, I mean whoever wrote this is forcing the Egyptians to deal with the pain they put on the Hebrews," a snappy voiced student said, "so like they toss the soot into the air and it's an image of the work the slaves did but now on the wind it burns their masters with guilt."

"And everything is out of place, frogs jump out of the river," the red-haired male in the front row said. "Nothing stays still and slaves are supposed to stay in their place because everyone else is on top of them."

"The locusts eating the Egyptian crops is like the Egyptians eating the food the slaves made," the Jesus Is My Savior student offered. "Now they get to know what it's like to be hungry but it goes deeper. It's saying the rich act like locusts eating everyone else's food."

I held my hands, "Now you get why interpretation is powerful. The lesson is that real revolutions happen when people leave their social roles, and the violence that's been done to the poor or slaves or minorities is turned back around on the ruling class. And this is why Paul Robeson sang *Go, Down Moses* or…" I pulled down the screen, turned on the projector which beamed an image of Bob Marley standing large in front of us.

"It's why he sang *Exodus*," I pressed play and the march-like beat pulsed in the room. Onscreen, Bob Marley held out his hand as if catching lightning. A young Jamaican woman, half dancing in her seat, said, "This song is making me feel mad Hebrew."

Occupy Wall Street

"Did you hear what's going on?" Arun said over the phone as I stirred the pasta in the bowl. "No, what's up?"

"People are sleeping in Zuccotti Park," his voice an orange spark snaking up gunpowder. "The protest on Wall Street got pummeled but folks started camping out at a nearby park and the police can't kick them out because it's half private, half public and open twenty four hours. Get your ass down here."

An hour later, I walked up Chambers street gazing up at a half built Freedom Tower. It looked like a giant crystal. Cops stood in a line on the street as protesters filled Zuccotti Park. The glances between them created static electricity in the air. Anarchists in dreadlocks painted the blank sides of torn apart pizza boxes and handed out freshly made placards. A roving circle held the signs to the media cameras and the slogan "We are the 99%!" was beamed around the world. People lay on mats, sleeping bags and mattresses as if the thousands of foreclosed homes around the nation threw their beds into this small granite park between the financial towers of Wall Street.

"Hey man," Arun called, I turned, saw him and we hugged. "Pretty amazing," he said with a blissful voice. We walked between the circles of people planning marches on banks, sit-ins and outreach. A voltage illuminated them. Using laptops and cameras, a media team connected Zuccotti Park to the Occupy sites blossoming in other cities like wild flowers cracking open the sidewalk. People zigzagged from place to place, hugging and breaking bread with strangers. I studied the TV anchors telling cameramen to aim their lenses at this or that protester whose faces shined with hope. An inspiring joy and defiance spilled into millions of TVs or computer screens.

"And the water turned to blood," I said, "and all of Egypt could not drink without tasting the bitterness of the slaves they once had lashed."

"What did you say?" Arun asked.

9/11 Memorial

"Bag on the conveyer belt. Step through please," the guard waved me in. Twenty of us walked through the maze-like lines, turned a corner and entered the 9/11 Memorial Park. Somberness hung in the air like a damp cloth. I took off my shoes and walked to the roar of water.

Stepping closer my breath felt heavier. Where a skyscraper filled with people once stood now was a large deep hole with water falling into it. It was a symbol of those who died and the hole they made in our lives. But as I ran my fingers along the names engraved on the dark stone that rimmed the reflecting pools, I whispered the names of the innocents killed by our army in the Iraqi city of Haditha.

"Khamisa Tuma Ali, Abdul Hamid Hassan Ali, Rashid Abdul Hamid, Abdul Hamid Hassan," I recited the name of everyone who had been killed and included them, if only for me, on the roster of those killed by 9/11.

After the last name, I sat on a bench and pulled out my visitor's pass but two came out. One had been for Hypatia, my ex-fiancé. We broke up weeks ago and evidence of her popped up all the time. A memory of us talking in bed overwhelmed me. She demanded to be let into the corners of my life where I brooded alone, met friends alone, drank alone. It was an interior world I created after New Orleans and deepened with visits to Darfur, Sean Bell's funeral and post-earthquake Haiti. I never did let her in. I didn't think she wanted to see the man she counted on was, at times, near suicide with hopeless grief. And here I was at its origin. My need to be in the center of crisis, soak my body in the terror in order to translate it into stories began on 9/11.

When I said, "No," to Hypatia, it was to keep the nihilism, the black hole spinning inside me to myself because I did not believe she could carry me over it. Now, I rubbed my feet in soft grass at Ground Zero, heard the manmade waterfalls and said aloud to no one, to everyone, "It is over. For me, it is finally over."

The distance between First and Third Worlds, the death and ruin I witnessed to frame 9/11 in its true context seemed too high a price. I had gone numb along the way. I hurt people even while trying to alleviate the pain in the world. They all flashed inside me but Hypatia's face stayed the longest. Finally, I got up, ran my fingers on the names engraved in stone and said her name too.

Epilogue

The police captain yelled at us to catch the terrorists before they blew up the buildings. My partner and I nodded at each other and instantly a funky 1970s theme song played as we turned and ran out of the precinct to the helicopter.

We got in and, under the loud chops of the blades, I pointed at the Twin Towers below us.

"Is that where they are supposed to strike?" I asked my partner, a big afro-wearing man who looked familiar. But he didn't answer. We landed the helicopter on the roof of the North Tower and went downstairs into a half-finished office and used the kitchen to cook dinner. I kept looking inside the freezer but it was filled with my dreadlocks that crumbled to ice when I touched them.

I turned to him, "It's so fucking sad that they're going to be destroyed in thirty years."

"Yeah," he said and picked out his afro, "but it's definitely going to happen no matter what we do. It's almost sunrise. Ever see the sun come up from the top floor?"

We jogged up the stairs and stood in front of large windows as a rainbow of color filled the sky. The sun, painfully bright, cracked the horizon. Quietly awestruck, tears streamed down our faces. My partner gripped my shoulder and said, "Come on, let's go catch these bad guys."

I woke up from my dream, tears in my eyes and tightness in my chest. Was this how far I was from my real self? Must everything that's true, everything that matters most to me, wait for a dream to speak its name?

Utopia Now — The Indypendent, November 2011

"Who is ready to defend our park?" the speaker shouted. It was 6 a.m. and thousands of us filled the Occupy Wall Street camp under a pre-dawn sky. The day before, Mayor Bloomberg threatened to evict us. So we came prepared to lock arms in a human chain. We knew cops could scald our eyes with pepper spray. But we were ready to defend a vision and raised our hands and yelled like a loud crack of thunder.

"We are the 99 percent!"

Bloomberg backed down and utopia, an ideal society, an imaginary island, a word that in Greek means "no-place," was left to flourish just up the street from the New York Stock Exchange. Like dreams that vanish in the morning, utopia cannot survive reality. Yet here at Liberty Park a flawed but working utopia has appeared. In one square block, the Left has made a site of transformation that frees people from a commodified life to one of wild defiant joy.

No one is paid but we work. Few can buy food but no one goes hungry. We march with signs that shout for change but have made in miniature an example of the world we want. In Liberty Park is a glimpse of life beyond capitalism.

Utopian sites like Liberty Park or Tahrir Square or the long ago Paris Commune are geysers shooting desire into daylight. They transform our consciousness through solidarity. They provide the euphoria of fighting a common enemy — the 1 percent whose wealth and power we have come to reclaim. But at the core is an experience of democratic values. Until we speak of that vision, we will target Wall Street and not see the new world rising from its ruins.

Chaos at the Center

"I feel like a weight has been lifted from me," my friend Danny said as around us tired marchers cuddled in a pile and people lined up for free food. "It wasn't the ideology that brought me here but the openness," he said. "The left was separated like drops of wax and now this heat melts it together."

We talk of how ideology divides the Left but here empathy overtakes ideas. Fighting over abstractions seems silly when we sleep on cold cement together. Out of need, we help each other and find meaning no book or leader can offer.

In these new values a collective vision takes shape. In the donating of sleeping bags is the value of gifting. In the beautiful art, radical self-expression. In the weary nomads laden with backpacks, we see radical inclusiveness. In the feeding and healing of each other, we see interdependence. In the general assemblies, we experience direct democracy.

Weeks ago, I spent my first night at Liberty Park and watched protesters snoring in sleeping bags like large caterpillars. It was 3 a.m. A thin cold rain fell.

I met Tony, a young man from upstate New York. "I've looked for work for months but there's nothing," he said, "not in the classifieds, not through word of mouth." Before coming he left a note with his parents saying he was joining the occupation. "Mom said, 'You're doing the right thing.' And she's right. I don't feel helpless anymore," he said.

A few hours later, buses and taxis blared their horns in the morning rush. The 99'ers rose, shook puddles out of blue tarp. Their faces were strained from the cold and rain, hunger and fear. But whether it was greeting newcomers, sweeping trash into bags, or scooping food on plates, I saw a sense of purpose that illuminated each gesture with glory. I felt that elusive utopia where the spirit moves through the dark corridors of history to a light that answers every question.

Burning Man

The other utopia I have experienced with the same energy as Occupy Wall Street is Burning Man. Each August, thousands of people gather in the Black Rock Desert of Nevada to haul tons of metal, tools, fabric and generators, and build an ephemeral city. Rising from the bright white desert is the Man, a tall figure of wood and steel. For a week, we circle him.

At Burning Man, nearly everyone is joyful and open. And it heals. After interviewing refugees in Darfur or victims of flooded New Orleans or broken people in Haiti, it is a place where my soul unfolds into a new shape. You can dance or be spanked, fed, liquored up, massaged or loved, and laugh hysterically. You can weep for the dead at the Temple or pour nightmares into the desert and walk away whole. Burning Man is a site of transformation with the same values of Occupy Wall Street; in it we experience radical self-expression, gifting, inclusiveness, immediacy, self-reliance, de-commodification and civic responsibility. On the last day of the festival, the Man burns in a geyser of flame and crashes. We dance around his ashes to celebrate the sacred euphoria of our self-creation.

Blurry Lines

Every utopia has extreme behavior that is a symptom of its values. Horizontal groups bring in energy but suffer from "blurry lines." Into Liberty Park have come homeless street youth, drug addicts and alcoholics.

During one sleepover, I saw a jittery circle at the far end of Liberty Plaza. I jogged over and heard an Occupy Wall Street security man yelling at a bleary-eyed vagabond to take his beer away before the cops came in. The next day a spiky-haired youth offered to sell me marijuana and later that night another Occupy Wall Street security man shouted at a thief who "borrowed and lost" an I-phone.

And there are creepers, men who take advantage of the open atmosphere to grope women. Ai, a young activist said, "I was sexually assaulted at Liberty Park. I had to fight this guy's hands off me the whole night. At first I thought I was alone but other women said the same thing."

But when she gathered women together, one said, "Please don't bring this up and divide the movement. I've waited 32 years for this to happen." Ai shook her head, "What kind of movement is this if women have to sacrifice their safety?"

Of course, radical self-expression brings out the crazies. A tall, bearded man just loves to walk around with anti-Semitic signs. One time a group of us surrounded him and sang, "Kum Ba Yah. We love Jews, oh Lord, we love Jews." And then we hugged a gangly Jewish man with a big afro until he was dizzy with touch.

Beyond Wall Street

Thomas More was right to use Greek words "not" and "place" because utopia is "no place." It is the repressed part of selves that has no place in society and yet, miraculously, it surfaces again and again.

Utopia is real because society is not. Under civilization is the building pressure of discontent and it steams through the cracks of crime and art and radical politics.

Burning Man and Occupy Wall Street are two utopias. The former, isolated in the desert, is reachable only by those with money. It changes lives but not society. The latter sprouts in the heart of capitalism like a fountain of youth in a dead city. From here march union members to picket Sotheby's art auction house on the Upper East Side, to protest its attack on workers' rights, while others journey uptown to protest "stop-and-frisk" abuses outside a police station in Harlem.

On the surface, Occupy Wall Street is an oppositional utopia based on a common enemy. But at its core it shares with Burning Man the experience of creating a new world – which means as we march, we must see beyond Wall Street and point to the city flashing in the future and say its name before it vanishes.

Occupy Memory

16

"We found her sprawled on the bed, covered in vomit. The kids were eating trash," she said in flat monotone. Her face tightened around the eyes as if she stared at a distant image. She etched each detail – her mother's shit on the walls, the heap of empty pill bottles and promises of 'never again.'

I massaged her neck like a blocked pipe, "Did you want her to die?" She smiled, bit her lip as her eyes watered. "God yes, I wish that bitch had died." Crazy, bitter laughter spilled from her.

15

A loud noise woke me. I turned and saw her cursing in her sleep, kicking the comforter off the bed onto the floor where it looked like a pile of snow. "No, no Jesus belt," she murmured. Circling her navel with one hand, I kissed her neck. Her breath slowed. I slid a hand between her thighs to the moistness from our sex before sleep and slipped myself inside. My hot thighs slapped her ass, my nose dug into her scented afro and I stroked her arms. We turned like a wheel in bed, limbs rising and falling. I fucked her to nail her sorrow to my body. I fucked her to incinerate memory.

14

While walking to the subway, I felt my cell phone buzz and saw a strange number, "Hello," her voice cackled, "is there a cop in your head?"

It was Crazy Girl, my nickname for Roma, a young woman I met at Occupy Wall Street. During our walks in Manhattan, she told me of her mother beating her, then begging her for forgiveness. She told me of grandparents who loved Jesus more than her, of running from city to city, making bouquets of money as a sex-worker. And then she told me of being raped and staying in bed for days unable to talk. And she told me of living without hearing the word "love." But she never told me her address or number.

"I didn't think I'd hear from you," I said. She repeated, "Is there a cop in your head?" My eyebrows raised and I looked around the street, "Who am I talking to? Wait, you don't even have a phone, Ms. Ninety-Nine Percent."

She snorted, "I've got One-Percent friends. And if I don't call you, you become an insecure little bitch." I shook the phone as if her voice was water to pour out of it. "It's taken only a few moments and already I hate you a little," I said. "How have you become so important to me? It's like my heart is an African capital under siege."

"I am the Lord's Resistance Army. My guns are blazing. I took your diamonds," she half laughed, half said, "I took your women and I took you. I'm going to sell everyone."

"What are you going to buy with it," I joked, "your freedom? We lost that in the Middle Passage. Besides you don't even date really black men."

She giggled, "Once raped, twice shy." Bitter laughter erupted from us. "Why do we say such awful shit?" I massaged my temples and studied my neighborhood. The everyday life of work rose from the morning. Men drank coffee on the corner as trucks rattled in front of stores. Parents walked their kids to school. In their numb gait, sagging shoulders and hard voices, I sensed the invisible weight that molded life here. It cascaded down from police stares, unpaid bills and fear that the person next to you will take what little you have. And hearing her laughter on the phone, I felt that humor was how she shattered the terror.

"I'm saying, we're black and we're proud, we're lack and we're loud, we're cracked and we're Mua Mua. Come on semi-colored man, sing with me," she ordered.

"I'm not going to betray the race for the sake of a joke," I backed off.

"We are a joke," she said. "Ha ha ha! I'm laughing at myself right now," she paused, "am I self-hating?"

"Either we hate ourselves or the world that created us," I said.

"No," she said cheerily, "I'll kill myself eventually."

My teeth grinded, "It fucking pisses me off when you say that. It's selfish. I mean, I know you're carrying pain but you advertise it like a neon sign."

"Yes, a neon sign in front of a brothel."

"What did you fucking say?" I yelled, "Stop mumbling."

"Maybe I'm dead already. Maybe you're talking to a ghost. Just let me disappear," her voice shot up like a wild rocket, "I'm good at vanishing. You'll never have to hear from me again."

My chest sank and I blew out sad breath of surrender, "Hey, I'm sorry." But the call was dropped.

13

I came home and saw her on my bed, sitting cross-legged, her face glowing from the laptop. She knew I was there but didn't look up. Silently, I asked why did I give this vagabond woman my keys? Why did I let her in my home, in my mind so much that I walked through the bustling streets, seeing no one but her floating in front of me?

I stared at her obsidian black eyes in a bright yellow face haloed by a dark afro. Headphones wrapped her head and a wire spooled to the computer. She looked like a spy listening for a secret. She typed furiously, ignoring me. I took out my cell phone and dialed up my first photo of her at Occupy Wall Street. Holding it up, I saw on screen her sitting in a tangle of plastic sheets writing a poem. I looked up and saw her in the same squat, staring the same stare, searching for the same answer.

She swiped off her headphones and glared at me, "Don't take a picture of me. I look awful."

Holding the phone, I held the tiny photo as she stood up on the bed to snatch it out of my hands. "You feel awful," I said, "but you look beautiful. It's why no one understands you."

12

I kicked the box into the room, grabbed her things and threw them in. Socks, hair extensions for that "island girl" look, and a shirt that left her scent on my hands. I took her Juicy shorts off the bathroom towel bar, untangled a zebra bra from the chair and flung it in. It had been three days since I saw or heard from her.

She vanished. I didn't blame her. What twenty-something, slam-poet woman wants to date a thirty-something professor? Does she have a fetish for NPR? I grabbed my cock and balls and shouted, "She doesn't want you."

The light went out. I walked to the wall switch, flicked it up and down. Nothing. I lit a candle and, in its wobbly light, the charcoal drawings she drew on the wall were like black cave paintings. As if in an archeological site, I stepped around my own apartment seeing the images she left. Near my bed, I saw a pregnant goddess holding her belly. Kneeling in front of it, I recalled her face pinched in focus as she drew it. Some emotional plug inside of me popped and my anger drained away. I reached out to the goddess, pressed a thumb to her and rubbed a black mark on my forehead.

11

On the train, people pointed at my black smudge. They mimed rubbing it off by motioning their sleeves above their eyebrows. Some were shy but kind. Some panicked that I might embarrass myself and roughly jabbed my shoulder then pointed at my black mark as if it was acid.

When I told them I knew it was there, they shook their heads, angry that they had wasted their compassion. But it wasn't wasted. Every reminder added to its weight until it felt like an anchor stapled to my head. I was trying to atone for the sin of losing love and I wanted my shame to be seen.

The A train whooshed into Chambers street and I bounded up the stairs to the light drizzle spiraling down like glitter. It was past midnight and the streets were quiet. I walked to Liberty Park where the Occupy Wall Street camp had been before the police, in a night of violence, swept the tents and protesters into one screaming heap.

As I got near, my throat tightened like a wet sock, and at the corner, I was stunned by the empty park boxed in with steel barricades as burly security men stood at the exits. Exhausted with sorrow, I sat down and stared at the dark granite floor lit by strips of light. And the memory of Occupy Wall Street filled my eyes. I saw blue tarp tents jutting like hills behind hills. I remembered radiant protesters manning welcome stations, passing out leaflets and people smiling and sharing stories from the open road. I saw drummers pounding wild rhythms as barefoot dancers leapt about, seemingly carried by wind. And then I bowed my head, angry and hurt that this beauty was destroyed by the state.

10

I took my cell phone, dialed up the image of Roma sitting inside billowing plastic like an art statue forgotten in a move between museums. At the time, I just studied the blurry image, curious but wanting to be in limbo, not knowing who or what was inside the wind-whipped plastic.

I looked at her on screen, put the phone away and remembered walking up to her and peeking under the plastic. She was writing in a notebook but stared at me with hope, defiance, loneliness and coyness. Every question was answered in the flash of us seeing each other.

"Are you a poet?" I asked.

"Yes."

"So am I," theatrically I looked around, "and this place is a poem."

She patted the ground next to her and scooted over. I sat, wrapped my arms around my knees as she licked her thumb and rubbed the black mark from my forehead.

"You won't need that yet," she smiled.

"Wait, this is only a memory. You can't touch what hasn't happened yet," I held my hands up but she intertwined her fingers with mine.

"You think you are writing a story," she said, "but this story is writing us."

9

Where are we?

In a poem. Inside revolution, inside love falling through words. Ask yourself about me. I'm a woman pulling crucifixes from her skeleton. Every highway I've walked is on fire. My mother, her voice chokes goodbye into a mirror facing a mirror, and I'm leaping from one to the other. My father? To him, I'm a bar of soap to rub on sin until my voice is clean. It's why I can't become a name until I know whose coming. And you?

My turn? I am caught on the eternal wheel of language that for centuries flattens whispers and caresses into a yellow brick road leading to an empty throne. Or maybe this is just the bitter ranting of an abandoned sun that is too bright to be inside a uterus with no address, but my screaming is a ladder between worlds, please climb it.

See how easy it is to be beyond time, beyond narrative. Now, strange man, I am your woman. Tell me your name.

8

In the cold plastic sheets, we looked like twin embryos taking shape inside a transparent egg. We free-styled poetry for hours, speaking sounds that flashed with images like diamonds stirred into yolk. Leaning shoulder to shoulder to share heat, we watched silhouettes stride by until one tapped us. Peeling back the plastic sheet, the stranger smiled as he handed us two steamy cups of tea. We thanked him, closed the plastic tarp back around us and held the hot drinks, throbbing like hearts beating before birth.

7

"Thought I'd never see you again," she husked close to my ear. Her hot breath tickled my lobes and I closed my eyes to feel it like a sexual Morse Code. "A bunch of Occupiers told me to meet them at the Gandhi statue but none showed up," she said, "I was wandering around and there you were. My strange man."

"I knew you were there," I squirmed closer to her mouth. "I hired the C.I.A. to find you."

"The C.I.A.?"

"I want my tax dollars to do some good," I stroked her thigh.

She turned her head away, "No one loves me enough to find me." I got on my elbow and looked down at her, "What did you say?" Her mouth moved into a grimace and she vomited a stream of clear gooey liquid on the floor.

"Sorry," she mumbled, wiping her mouth. Long strings of saliva looped like a spider web on her fingers.

"Jesus. It's the third time," I got a rag and wiped the vomit up. "Can we please take you to a hospital," I said but she waved me away and laid back in bed. Dark rings circled her eyes. "I'm getting better," she said in a numb, whispery voice.

I sat next to her, rubbed her belly, "At Slut March, when you popped out of the crowd, I was so happy to see you." Her eyes made half-moons as she smiled, "Really? Little old rape survivor me?" We giggled and I nudged her, "Aren't you too sick to be laughing at trauma?" Her eyes narrowed into slits, "I'm too sick not to."

She got up on an elbow, fluffed the pillow, "It was easy to tell you though.

I didn't know how badly I needed to do that. After being raped the whole night by a man I knew and staying in that bed for days, slowly starving to death..."

"It broke me to hear that," I shook my head. "Here we were, you know, in a river of thousands of women marching and chanting against the terror, and I just wanted to cradle you."

"I think you tried."

"I did but you shrugged me off," a crooked embarrassment twisted my mouth. She squinted one of her eyes as if looking through a telescope, "You wanted to have sex with me at that moment. Didn't you?"

My mouth puckered, I didn't know what to say and the barely conscious feeling was tart like a lemon, "Well, yes, I did."

"Why," she demanded.

"I, um, I, well," my mouth opened, "I wanted to un-rape you."

Time froze and then she began a wild hiccupping laughter. I broke into loud guffaws and together we slapped the sheets and swayed blindly back and forth.

"Un-rape me," she coughed and laughed as tears popped from the corners of our eyes. She snuggled into me, "I remember when you first looked at me with real love." I watched her flex her toes. "It was at the Polish restaurant. I had told you about my crazy fucking Christian family, my former pimp turned pastor grandfather, my pill-popping mom who drove the car with my brothers and sister into a pond to drown them," she rolled her eyes. "Running everywhere, Pittsburgh, Florida, seeing my father for the first time and then him kicking me out, and then sleeping on trains, and then New York, and then you."

"Me?"

"Yes, you," she elbowed me, "do you know how long I've waited to see someone look at me with love?"

6

Three days after she vanished, a strange number flashed on my phone. I called it back, "Hello, who called me?" An amber toned female voice answered, "I'm a friend of…"

I cut her off, "Where is she? Is she okay? Does she need anything?"

I thought I heard her take a breath. "She's at Roosevelt Hospital. She tried to commit suicide."

My heart, my heart, I repeated silently and gripped the desk.

5

We sat in the waiting room watching the clock hands. "What time did they say?" I muttered. "Six, right?" Roma's friends had called from Florida and New York but one lived in the Bronx and she met me at the hospital. She had quick, alert eyes that scanned everyone like radar dishes and a sad, quiet weariness. We small-talked for an hour but her voice drove towards me in larger and larger waves until she opened her laptop, turned on Facebook and showed me messages Roma sent her.

- Dear G.

I took a bunch of pills at his place and just woke which wasn't part of the plan. But it's better this way. It would've been creepy for him to find me dead.

"CREEPY," I yelled. The stupid infantile word rang like a bell in my skull. "Yes, it would've been fucking creepy to find my lover dead and cold in my bed." Her friend looked at me, fatigue and shame glazed her eyes. We rose and took the elevator up to the seventh floor psyche-ward and each step felt heavy as rage sloshed in my throat.

I pressed the buzzer and as the nurse opened the door, we saw her waving and skipping around. She ran up and hugged us, kissed her friend, looked at me and said, "Uh oh, you're angry."

4

The next day, I returned to Roosevelt Hospital, to the same floor and buzzed the same door. While waiting, I swung the bouquet of roses like a baseball bat, "And the crowd goes wild." The nurse opened the door and I went in to the visiting area and sat down. At the next table, a young woman with dark wet hair slumped in the seat like a thrown away doll as her sister combed her scalp with gentle fingers. At another table sat a jittery thin man who clasped his knees and moved like a scared bird. Another man shuffled in a swollen-eyed drug haze.

She came skipping, "Hey, thanks," took the flowers and kissed me. While near my ear, she whispered, "I got to get out of this hospital jail. Everyone's crazy."

"Except you of course," I said through a tight mouth.

"Yeah, I'm just sad but these motherfuckers," her eyes flashed like razors. "Okay, we have Running Man who makes a dash for the doors every day and gets tackled to the ground. Then we have our lesbian Latina and former Wall Street Occupier Melissa who is super sweet but wants to fuck me."

I held her gaze as she made a TV sitcom out of the patients here but when she got lost in it, I glanced at the people she made into characters. Carefully, she filtered out their suffering to make them into caricature. At the next table, I saw a woman close her eyes, bite her lip and shake as her family held her.

"How are you feeling?" I asked her during a break in the story.

"Well, I don't want to kill myself but there's always tomorrow," she said. I leaned in, "Yes, there is tomorrow, tomorrow." We began to sing it together, "Tomorrow, Tomorrow, I love you, Tomorrow. You're always a day away." After the last note lifted to the ceiling, everyone clapped for us and threw invisible roses. "And the crowd goes wild," she said.

3

Afterwards, I imagined her face floating in front of me while walking through the holiday shopping crowd. It was as if her image, hovering ahead of me, was a magnifying glass which made visible the barely concealed despair of the people streaming by me.

"Is this the Ninety-Nine percent," I asked aloud, "when it forgets it's the Ninety-Nine percent?"

2

She left a message. They were releasing her in two days. "Come pick me up," her voice glowed, "and bring an extra bag."

1

Jumping with excitement, I buzzed the nurse to let me in but no one came. The psyche-ward was dark. I pushed the door open and hesitantly called her name but it echoed through the hall. Turning the corner, I saw her sitting in the visiting room at a table. She wore her pajamas and was barefoot, smiling and patting an empty seat.

"What's going on?" I asked. She reached out for my hands, folded them in hers and said, "I'm not going anywhere."

I jerked my hands but she held them. "Thank you for coming every day to see me. I love you for it. Now I have to tell you the truth. I did commit suicide that night and we both know you're writing this story to keep me alive but it has to end."

Tears puddled in my eyes. I asked her how she knew but she stroked my neck and kissed my eyelids. "It doesn't have to end," I pleaded, "I can keep writing."

But she pulled a plastic sheet over us as the room became black. Cold drizzle fell. Car horns blared and I looked up and realized we were at Occupy Wall Street. Silhouettes of people strode by as we held steaming cups of tea. Everything felt right, everything felt real.

"You think you are writing a story," she said, "but the story is writing us. And in this narrative, anything is possible, even memory."

The Last Horizon

"Can't see anything," I thrust my hands out into the swirling light that burned my thoughts.

"Hold on to me," a voice said but I was like a pile of crumbling sand. The ground spun until I screamed for rescue, screamed for my mind, screamed in terror and shattered into a million shards of glitter into the abyss.

Post Suicide-Try Hangover

Bright sunlight throbbed. The tent billowed like a giant lung. A woman lay on top of me, bronze limbs entangled in mine, her hand flinching, unconsciously on my chest. And then sleep pulled me in again.

Hours later, I stumbled out of the tent. *Oh fuck* – I palmed my head to stop the hammer-like pounding. On sun baked streets people rode their bicycles or couples walked to the giant 100 foot effigy called The Man. From a distance, it was a stick figure standing on a pyramid as around him, around us, swirled the ever present white dust clouds blowing through the vast carnival city of Burning Man 2012.

Last night was a black hole in my brain. Stepping underneath the parachute shade, I saw my campmates in chairs forking breakfast in their mouths but looking at me with alarm. The woman from my tent sat in a chair reading my journal. "You are a judgmental son of a bitch," she thumbed another page.

"What the fuck!" I shouted.

"Tonight I'll boil my brain in LSD," she read and stared at me, "or maybe I'll jump into the fire when The Man burns. I'm happy to leave life. The hardest part was returning to our gilded boredom. I can't live here anymore."

Her eyes punched holes in the silence between me and my campmates. Everyone saw my grief like ink spilling out of a broken pen.

"I'm leaving now," she stepped out of the shade and into the street, "and I'm taking this to read." I lunged at her but my nerves short circuited— it was like slipping on ice.

"I'll be at Center Camp. You can meet me there," she shouted. I finally gripped the chair and flung it at her but it fell short. "You throw like a girl," she cackled.

The Beginning of the End

I don't want him in the camp – if he stays, I'm leaving – Yo, that's fucked up – did he even wonder what his suicide would do to us – I don't want to be liable – what if the police come?

People whispered, glancing at me with arms crossed and worried faces. They were debating what to do about me, now unofficially nicknamed Mr. Suicide. After the nameless woman left with my journal, my friends walked me to their tent. It was intervention time.

"Were you trying to kill yourself?" they asked repeatedly. Their questions came like arrows that I dodged. "No, no, no," I shook my head, saying it was private journal fantasy, not a real plan. They put their hands on my shoulders and hummed 'Om' and I opened one eye, saw their dusty heads bowed toward me, trying to realign my chakras with prayer.

They told me last night I took too much LSD before performing at Center Camp stage. I lit poems on fire. The audience howled as I waved them like a torch. Grabbing the microphone, I let loose a bee swarm of prophecy, genital jokes and manifesto. But when I spoke of the rotting dead from earthquake Haiti, or spoke of Darfur and its many raped women who were raped again in nightmare sleep, or the drowned in New Orleans, soggy corpses crumbling like bread, some yelled at me to stop "bumming" their trip while others followed me out of Center Camp to the desert.

"Here," Tim showed me his cell phone, "you did amazing lyrics last night but we lost you." I saw myself on the tiny screen, eyes lit with holy fire, mouth flashing with images zigzagging between people like lightning bolts. Drummers and dancers passed in front of the lens. In a blur was a woman's face, I paused it – her, she was right behind me and carrying my bag. "There she is," I pointed. "That's the one from this morning."

Tim clicked the video off, "At the end, you were kneeling in the desert eating dust." He shook his head. "You were vomiting blood," he spoke slow, "and she stopped you and got you back to your tent."

"I don't remember any of it," I muttered, wiping shame and awe from my face. "I just remember being lost in light."

2012

Under a huge flaming asteroid, people danced to thumping house music, dust rising around their feet. Some were nude or in blinking fur coats but the fiercest was a group wearing white skeleton prints on black leotard. They moved like the dead striking poses of rage at the living. It was Camp Nibiru, named for the famous asteroid prophesized to smash the earth in 2012.

Apocalypse shtick was in. The official theme of Burning Man was fertility, the unofficial one was doomsday. Walking the rim of the city, it seemed Life and Death struggled for our faith. One camp named Zygote was a giant womb pulsing with music as couples writhed in love on red lit couches. Nearby was Galactic Plane, a black lit room that swirled with fluorescent paint, booming hard industrial music as the documentary *2012: Time for Change* lit the ceiling.

I peeked inside and saw projected above me Daniel Pinchbeck, the careerist New Ager loping from interview to interview peddling the future utopia. Goddamn it, he was fucking everywhere. He spoke at Burning Man, wrote on the internet, and his cascade of Crazy was trickling into my friends. Weeks ago, I was in Brooklyn drinking with a friend at a bar when she began reciting his ideas. It was like she took off her face and underneath was Pinchbeck, smiling, saying, "Believe me now?"

I left Galactic Plane wondering why I had a hard-on for this guy. "Oh yes," I knocked my forehead, "professional jealousy." Tall, lanky with hipster glasses, Pinchbeck sold a shitload of books. The last one told readers a new galactic alignment will put earth in the path of cosmic energy that would spark a global enlightenment. Meanwhile I couldn't sell shit. Even after going to New Orleans, Darfur, and Haiti, where kids were shot by cops, or skeletal families died in U.N. camps, no one read my articles. "Hey Pinchbeck," I said out loud, "imagine if after a dose of Ayahuasca, your famous tribal psychedelic, you saw that God was really a homeless war-orphan?" Laughing angrily, almost spitting, I yelled, "Like a Hindu God, it had a dozen prosthetic arms after the real ones where blown off by a land mine."

In Haiti, I saw people reach to the sky, begging Jesus to rescue them but no great hand ever descended from the clouds to lift the rubble or spark the dead back to life. No God came to those who deserved his miracles the most and against that evidence the selling of salvation, even the vague New Age type, seemed a grotesque business. At Burning Man, whether at *Discopocalypse* with Mayan chant flavored dance tracks, or Pinchbeck speaking to large wide-eyed crowds of the coming utopia, people swallowed the vision. As I walked to Center Camp, I rubbed my chest which felt like an open pit. The sight of privileged audiences shamelessly seeking escape carved a hole in me and at its bottom were faces I saw in the Third World, looking up, asking for help. But one face floated up into my heart. It was Roma.

After I came home from Haiti, I walked New York like a phantom. Hugs from friends slid off like watercolor. When Occupy Wall Street began, I reported on drum circles, workshops and tattered mattresses. One drizzly night, I saw a plastic sheet over what looked like a breathing statue. Pulling it off, I saw a baby-faced woman writing poetry, staring at me with joy. She patted the space next to her. I sat and we shared warmth and wove poetry like a web glistening around our secrets.

The next day at Slut March, one of the rivers of rage pouring from Occupy Wall Street, we met again. In the moving crowd of women shouting against male violence, she told me of being raped months ago. We hugged each other, arms like bandages on a wound. And the next night at the Occupy Camp, I asked her to come home with me.

For weeks we lay in bed, limbs knotted, laughing at the stupid apathy of the poor and the stupid greed of the rich. We watched Carl Sagan's *Cosmos* series, woke up, eyes sparkling with stars and dreams. After making love, we stared at the rainbow the sun made as it struck the compact discs on my bookcase and spread an arc of color on the ceiling. Wobbling on the bed, we kept jumping to touch it.

Her neediness and rage filled me like a sky. Weeks after she moved in, I found her crying in the bathtub. I held her as she told me that nightmares of her rape were too real to sleep through. She kept seeing her siblings, who she cared for that summer in an effort to steal them away from her pill-popping mother, when the guy she dated held her down and violated her all night. Curled up in the semen stained bed, she cried for days, her cheeks sunk, eyes caked with tear salt. She did not speak until a friend found her. Now the memory of rape floated in her body like one of those massive black holes we saw on *Cosmos*, tearing her apart and pulling her down, down, down.

Tired and aching with no sleep, I stroked her hair saying we'd get a therapist and she nodded. "I'm not going to let you go all Haiti on me," I said and we laughed and rubbed noses. Going to work, I felt my body was steel, I was going to pull us through – *I'm not going to lose her* – I raged in my head.

At work, I stared out of the office window and remembered the woman from Darfur who had been gang raped. I took her story and gave it to a First World audience that didn't give a fuck about doing anything other than demonstrating political sorrow. None of my writing did anything. It did nothing to help her, nothing to help the homeless in New Orleans, nothing to heal the broken bodies of people in Port au Prince. And here was a chance to actually save someone who was in my reach. I turned to my computer and researched crisis shelters, studied art therapy sites, and imagined what could be done.

Coming home, I saw her in bed, sat down and playfully poked her but she didn't poke back. Pulling the bed sheet down, I saw her face was a grey hard mask. I leaned over but no heat rose from her skin, no breath blew from her mouth, no blinking moved her eyes and I collapsed and screamed and screamed. Opening my eyes, I saw her stiff, claw-like hand and reached for it, held her and wept saying I was sorry, I was sorry.

When the police came, they were kind. I showed them her suicide note and empty pill bottle. We called her friends. They called her family. Wrapped in white, she was carried by paramedics down the stairs into the ambulance. My neighbors asked what happened and I told them, their eyes loomed like magnifying glasses inspecting me for guilt, for grief, for love. And bowing my head, I climbed up the eternal stairs to my room and slept on the floor.

Afterwards, the sound of the world seemed mute. Voices came to me muffled and from a distance. People were blurring into each other. The semester ended and I got tenure at my college. Friends took me out for a party and I kept going to the bathroom to send Roma texts saying how proud she would be of me. When I came back, an old friend, Brad, gave me a card and a studious quiet fell on the table as everyone stared at me. I opened it and pulled out a Burning Man ticket.

After the party, I woke up at home, groggy with drink and saw the familiar rainbow on the ceiling. I reached out to touch it when my phone beeped. I picked it up and saw a text from Roma, "I'll meet you in the desert, my love."

World War Three

The sun sank in a spill of color. Up ahead was Center Camp, a grand tent with bright flags, bicycles stacked in rows as people milled in and out. I weaved between couches where dust-coated Burners slept past a drum circle with Hindu painted musicians layering rhythms in closed eyed bliss. I cut through yogis who bent limbs into sinewy hieroglyphs of sacred knowledge to the stage where I saw her, the nameless woman who saved me last night. She sat on a stool, eyeing the crowd, her black hair spilling around her face as she strummed a guitar and touched my journal which lay in her lap.

"Thanks everyone," she smiled at me and I felt rage flush my cheeks, and my groin tighten. Gently stepping down, she passed by me and greeted people as I glared from the edge. When the last fan left, she smiled at me and I sat down.

"So," she said.

"So," I repeated.

"You probably want this back," she held the journal. I stared out as my hands balled into fists on my knees. She slowly lowered it but as I reached for it, she drew it back, "Roma wants you to live. You're here to make this a world where she and others like her don't kill themselves."

I swiped my hands over my face, "Please just give me back my journal so I can leave." She tossed the journal on my lap. I placed a hand on it.

"I was Roma once," she touched my knee, "I'm a very beautiful woman who had low self-esteem," she held up her forefinger and thumb then pinched the air, "which means I was this close to being in porn."

A chuckle burst out of me. I glanced at her thighs and she caught me. "Oh, the struggle," she scratched her cheek, stretched her legs. They were strange, nervous gestures.

"The struggle for what?" I asked.

Her mouth puckered, "I'm this hot, crazy bitch who raped your privacy and now you got nowhere to hide."

"Fuck you," I said turning to her, "you like to burn illusions until the mirror swallows every question." I circled my face with my finger, "We are the masks we wear."

"I was waiting for you to arrive," she nibbled her thumb, "that's who I read in your journal: a man haunted by a lost utopia of the transparent voice. So brilliant, so scared."

"No, I'm not that smart," I mumbled.

"You think you weren't smart enough to save her." She leaned over, "You got a poison dick? You have cyanide in your balls? Do you blame yourself for her absence?"

"Yes, how did you know," I asked in mock surprise, "it is the dick of death." Our braying laughter became panting. And then like a cup tilting over, hot tears filled my eyes. She pulled me in, "Feel better?" Smiling, I nodded and finally asked her her name, asked her why she followed me that night, why she slept in my tent, why she read my journal.

She placed her leg on mine, "Trust for once that you don't need to know me right away," pushing her hands like bulldozer scoopers, "we can live right now without past or future."

Over her shoulder, I saw a burly dreadlocked man in white overalls jogging up to the stage. He took the microphone as a crew of men and women in utility kilts unrolled a large blank projection screen. It rose behind him as he tapped the microphone, "Does this work? Okay, good. Hey people, I'm sorry to interrupt but we have some crazy news that we think you got to hear."

A projector beamed CNN on the screen. Black smoke rose over Tehran as a woman yelled for Allah. The newscaster stared grim-faced into the camera and pointed to jets fueling on aircraft carriers that heaved in the ocean, cutting white waves. Fast-moving type at the bottom read – *Israel Bombs Iranian Nuclear Facility* – *Iran Blocks the Straight of Hormuz* – *U.S. Navy Sails to Troubled Region.*

My heart clenched as her hand gripped mine. The big dreadlocked man gripped the microphone, "The sound feed isn't coming in but I think we can read the headlines." He stepped into the projector's beam and was lit up by bomb explosions and faces of men shaking guns. "I think World War Three just started."

The Hall of Mirrors

"What's your name?"

"Eury. Say it you-read but without the 'd.'"

"Well, Eury," I extended my hand in mock British tone, "it's good to make your acquaintance at the end of the world."

"And you too, my fine sir," she curtsied, "let it be better than the last apocalypse."

Behind us panicked people leapt on their bicycles and sped down the streets, carrying news of war to the camps, black flowers blooming in their skulls. Soon the whole city would be tossing worries, prophecies and panic from one camp to the next.

"How much time you think we have?" Eury squeezed my hand.

"Before Burning Man goes crazy about the war?" I studied the tight, scared faces of the people streaming out of Center Camp, "Early evening tomorrow. By then the city will be abuzz and some will make an early exodus out of here."

"And how much time do you think *we have*?" She moved her hand up and down my back.

"Forever," I smiled.

"Stop lying to me," her mouth made a tight line. "Even beautiful lies hurt."

"Eury, we won't last the night until you stop playing the mystery woman." I flashed my eyes, "These moments going by are dark and I'm filling them with the fake light of romanticism. You want to know how much time we have? Why do you care about this thing called *us*?"

She tucked loose hair behind her ear, "Do you know I've never been to Iran but I know what its beaches look like? My parents immigrated to the U.S. to make money, not that that worked out very well. Still, my cousins sent me photos and video over the years. And guess what? The fucking Islamic Republic puts a wall, get it, a wall on the beach between men and women. If you have ovaries and want to swim in a suit, behind the wall you go. Of course, my cousin Samina took pictures of her tits and sent them to her boyfriend on the other side of the wall, and he took pictures of his cock and sent it to her. They'd never go in the water, just text under their separate umbrellas."

"Those two, they loved each other. She wanted him to be her first. But in 2009, when everyone was in the streets trying to topple the regime, she was caught up in a mass arrest by the police and held in jail for like four weeks. Our relatives tried to bribe them, call in favors."

"Finally they let her out and she told us when the police looked in her phone and saw all these photos of cocks from the beach, they called her a whore and raped her."

Eury wiped tears from her face but didn't make a sound. Slowing down, I held her to me and we swayed together in the dark rage trembling in her like a motor.

"So when these hippies are like, 'Peace and love,'" her voice was a slashing sword, "I'm like, 'Fuck that. Bomb the leaders. Kill them.' But once war begins, my family will get blasted away by a fat forty year old drone pilot in Arizona," she let go and walked toward a glowing hall of mirrors in the darkening desert. Eury parted the bright L.E.D. vines twinkling like brain synapses and we entered the maze. On either side we saw our infinite reflections shrinking to a point that moved with us.

"I was so embarrassed about being Iranian," Eury said and a dozen images of her seemed to be a chorus, "At home, my whole world seemed a weird medieval sitcom. Mom cleaned and prayed and beat me when I was getting too American. Dad drove trucks across the state until she looked through his wallet and found pictures of another family he had out there but get this," Eury lifted her fists in the air, "she didn't even leave him. One night he drove his truck off and never came back. Her response to being left was to pray and clean and beat me if I was getting too American."

Eury laughed but it sounded like grinding glass, "She had no idea about anything. She'd put the shawl on me but at school I'd take it off and be Puerto Rican. At school, I wore doorknocker earrings, spoke Spanish. At home, I was a dutiful Muslim daughter. The only people who knew were my theater, geek friends, who were like, 'Write a play about it.'"

She bent over, fiddling with some cables on the ground and yanked them apart, blackness fell instantly. "Turn on your headlamp," she said and I did, sending a white beam ricocheting between mirrors like a comet.

"Oooh, that's nice," she cooed. "Anyway, long story short, I write a one-woman show outing my secret life to everyone at school. And they howled with laughter as I did imitations of my family but also of their stupid white American asses. It was going really good up to the climax where I read parts of the Koran and ripped out pages. Well, guess who comes storming up the aisle. My stupid immigrant family, cursing me to Hell, uncles who I had never seen, aunts who were only voices on the phone, and of course, my mom up front. The lights came up and the whole auditorium of my friends and teachers stared at them nearly spitting at me. So I went backstage, grabbed a lighter from one of my Marlboro friends, stomped back on stage and lit the Koran on fire."

"Eury," I said shaking my head.

"Yes, yes, I lit the Koran on fire and hollered to the very back row that 'Allah can eat my cunt,'" her voice boomed, "and threw it at them."

Silence tightened between us. I just stared ahead, seeing the holy book, the Koran, the one I used to pray to when I was a college Muslim, on fire, illuminating the faces of her shrieking family as it fell, slow motion to their feet. We laughed and laughed and laughed.

"Eury, that is some Salmon Rushdie shit," I chortled. We turned a corner and felt cool desert air blow into the Hall of Mirrors, heard blurred music echoing from a distance. We turned another corner and stood at the exit facing a vast, dark Burning Man where art cars blinked and shot fire into the night, sending orange light over the black silhouettes of people who danced around them like shadows in ecstasy.

"After all that went down," she said, "no more family for me. I slept on friends' couches, lived in their garages, finally graduated, left for Pittsburgh then New York, did some sex work to get cash for an apartment and college."

A hot flash ran through me, shame, disgust, desire in a tangled mix but I saw her look down awaiting judgment and remembered my shame over my uncle's sexual abuse of me and the years I lived in the currents of unnamed pain. Leaning over, I kissed her and said, "Forever."

Her eyes squeezed into a question. I stared at her face, smiled and said again, "Forever."

A large smile opened her face and she tied her arms around me, "I think I love you, Mr. Suicide."

"And I love you, Ms. Apostate."

Deep Playa

"So, this is my church," I said and pointed to the deep playa, black horizon of mountains against purple night and above us were stars glittering like a snowstorm frozen in time.

"I get you," she said staring up, "I'll grab some and make a necklace for you. But right now, keep me warm." Eury pressed herself to me and we kissed, hands riding up thighs, under shirts, peeling off clothes as the slap of our bodies ignited us. She jumped on my hips, I held her as she yanked my pants down and stroked me hard, aiming me into her and then she grabbed the back of my hair and slid down on me. Breath spilled out and our eyes were so close, our pupils like black caves with a single river flowing between them.

I held her as she bounced on my cock, we laughed and fucked, jumped and fucked, lay down and fucked, got up and fucked more, smiling, kissing, nibbling, spinning around until dizzy we fell on the desert floor, fucking until we came together in a giant spasm that tightened our grip on each other as the warm waves spread from our bodies and carried us out. Spent, panting, we curled into a tight knot of limbs and licked each other's lips, noses and chins, we fell asleep.

Hours later, I broke the surface of my dreams and opened my eyes. Something woke me. I scanned the night. Nothing. I covered Eury with my jacket and got up, walked out a few yards and saw, in the moonlight, skeletons running towards us, white skulls rushing in the dark, white bones in full sprint. Closer, I saw they were the troop of black leotard dancers with skeleton prints who danced near the flaming asteroid.

Their feet tread softly by and I heard the pant of their breath but they did not say a word. They just ran by like death in the darkness. A deep growl rumbled in the shadows. I turned on my headlamp and its white beam shot out like a stage light on a dreadlocked man dressed as a satyr, the top of him was human but the bottom was like a goat, his legs on hoof-like stilts.

Is he high? Is he caught on some acid trip and thinks he's a real monster?

The satyr scraped the earth with his hoof and bellowed at me a loud, cracked roar. I reached into my bag, pulled out my silver writer's pen and howled back. His shaggy head swayed and then slowly he slinked into the desert.

I walked back to Eury, cradled her head in my lap and stayed awake, scanning the desert for art cars with drunk drivers or men too high on drugs to know when to stop.

The Text

I woke up again, wiped the dust off my face. A blue glow spread up from the mountains, washing the purple out of the sky. Eury was snoring like a handsaw and I stroked her head when a hard bulge in her purse buzzed.

"Well, if you can read my journals," I said and opened it, saw her cell phone, "now, let's see who you are." But there was nothing, no photos, no call log, no list of names, just one text that she had sent. I pressed the button to open it and read, "I'll meet you in the desert, my love."

My head spun and I blinked. Roma sent me this text. I erased it and thought of it as a hallucination. But here it was at the exact time and date, here it was. I looked down at Eury who was awake and staring at me.

"What the fuck is this?" I yelled.

She got up, grabbed the phone, her coat and began to walk away, her legs like scissors cutting, cutting through the desert. I grabbed her wrist, her arms, she twisted out.

"Who the fuck are you?" I screamed in rage, in fear, in absolute confusion as Eury ran to the city.

Exodus

"What the hell's going on?" I shouted as my campmates rolled up tents, packed food, lowered the parachute canopy like a dying jelly fish.

"Dirty bombs exploded in New York, Washington D.C. and L.A., Iran sent a fucking message," Tim said as he hauled a box of can soup into the car trunk. "We are leaving now."

Along the whole street, tents deflated and fell, carpets were being rolled up as panicked people crammed their lives back into their cars.

"There's a meeting at Center Camp where they have a projector set up to get feed from news channels," Tim panted, lifted a box and turned to me. "Some Burners believe this is the Mayan 2012 prophecy come true about the End of the World. They're going to stay in the desert and await the revelation."

"No," I covered my face, "please don't tell me they're falling for that shit."

"Coming?" Tim asked, eyes lit with survival calculations. "You can stay with me in Oakland as long as you need." Between us lay an unspoken loyalty and the fear of losing each other in the chaos rising in the world. "I'll see you there," I said, "there's someone I have to find before I go."

We shook hands, I jumped on my bike and rode the dusty streets of the collapsing city, saw the large whipping flags of Center Camp, locked the bike and dashed inside, weaving between groups of people, their faces in spasm as they yelled terror-filled questions at each other.

On stage I saw Reverend Billy, the New York activist in an all-white televangelist suit, debating a tall lanky Daniel Pinchbeck. They circled each other as the audience turned its face from one to the other.

"This could be the beginning of the cosmic alignment that destroys the old world and brings in a final stage of humanity," Pinchbeck was like a tall flagpole, his hands bouncing back and forth in front of him as if his words were rocks being placed in the air for people to step on.

"Daniel, Daniel," Reverend Billy cut in, "we can't give an otherworldly vision right now. We have to care for this world and retreating into the desert isn't going to help anyone. It's going to separate us from the world. We need a duet of activism and ideals that brings us together."

Pinchbeck twitched his dark glasses and kept pushing, "This is the prophecy come true and to tell us to go back into this world is to send us to our deaths. The rational mechanistic system is falling apart and we can be the ones who begin a New World."

They bantered back and forth, clashing on each other's rhetoric like knights jousting with words. And the audience was one big open face made of hundreds of terrified people searching for some direction, their eyes were like boiling eggs.

"WHO DO YOU LOVE?" I shouted as if to everyone I have ever known. "WHO DO YOU LOVE? WHO DO YOU LOVE? WHO DO YOU LOVE?"

The massive wave of faces turned to me and my body lit up as if being sucked in a tornado. "THINK," I yelled and put a finger to my head, stepping over a couple to a clear space in front of the stage. "THINK," I held their faces in a large open stare and said again, "THINK, who do you know, outside in the world who is scared, who this war will turn into a murderer or a victim? THINK, who will die or lose everything they have to this war?" I pushed the words into them, "FEEL THEM inside you."

Faces blinked, I saw their eyes being filled with the people they knew, "GO TO THEM! GET THEM IN THE STREETS AND STOP THE WAR!"

Their faces shook as if an alarm just woke them. The spell had been snapped. "Go occupy the city halls. Occupy police stations and the Senate and the army bases," I pointed to the rapt, focused listeners in the audience as if my voice was a hammer that could break the hold of Pinchbeck's prophecy. "When you do and the cameras are on you across the Atlantic," I shaped each word like a fist, "the Iranians will join you because they love their children too." In the back, I saw

Eury slipping between the nooks in the crowd and shot her a look.

I stepped down and people rose to talk to me as Pinchbeck tried to talk again but the audience crumbled. Reverend Billy waded through his fans throwing their voices like nets over him. We hugged and he sighed with relief, "That was close."

"Do you think a lot of people will stay with him in the desert?" I asked.

"Some," Reverend Billy pulled on his chin, "but the spell was broken and not just here but everywhere," he glanced over my shoulder. I turned and saw cameras on tripods and knew in minutes our clash over stopping the war would be uploaded on the internet. A sigh left me too.

From behind me, arms encircled my chest and I smelled Eury, felt her press herself against me. Her chin rested on my neck and she said, "I'm sorry that I didn't tell you."

Reverend Billy patted my shoulder and was turning away when I held him, looked at Eury and said, "We've known each other a long time, haven't we?"

"Forever," she smiled.

"Forever." I sighed and squeezed the Reverend's arm, "Are you licensed to perform marriages?"

"Right now?" he asked.

"Right now," Eury said and pointed beyond the circle of people waiting to talk to Reverend Billy and through the bustling crowd that filled the Center Camp and to the deep playa, "Let's take it to church."

"Hey, hey everyone," a man in a rabbit outfit yelled over our heads, "someone set The Man on fire!"

Like a dam breaking, we gushed out of Center Camp to see, in the distance, flames like an orange flower engulfing The Man who was a black figure half collapsed in fire.

"It's Thursday, he's not supposed to burn for another two days," the Rabbit Man said, "this is out of control."

The Marriage of Heaven and Hell

"If the doors of perception were cleansed," Reverend Billy intoned as he laid a fatherly hand on us, "everything would appear to man as it is, infinite."

He wrapped twine around Eury's arm, encircling it and our joined hands.

"Do you take Eury as your lawfully wedded wife?"

"I do."

"And Eury, do you take…"

"I do," she leaned over and kissed me. Reverend Billy laughed and said, "Well, I know pronounce you husband and wife." Burners cheered and lifted us on their shoulders, rum splashed on our mouths as we swigged the bottle and tossed it to the people. A nude older woman with blinking gloves lifted her turquoise scarf and put it on Eury as they hugged.

Behind us, The Man had fallen into a raging inferno, flames twisted up to the sky. Eury and I jumped down, ran around the fire, hands in a knot as we dashed in and out of the circling people, eyeing the near white blaze that singed our faces as she yelled, "That's our past! That's our past!"

As we spun around the heat, I saw my friend Tim waving me to come and leave with him. I saw Reverend Billy smiling at us and I saw the dreadlocked Satyr from the night before and countless faces screaming at a fire that was not planned or controlled but that was eating away our world.

The Turquoise Scarf

"Eury?"

I rubbed my face and sat up. Her jacket was in my arms as if she had slipped out of it as we slept. My head ached. Looking up and around, I saw it was a bright morning on the playa and that Burning Man was nearly empty. Sparse tents dotted the desert. A lone truck sped by kicking up white spiral clouds of dust.

"Eury?"

In the distance, I saw a blue scarf tumbling along the playa, being picked up by a breeze and floating then falling again. I rose and jogged to it, sprinting to catch up and snagged it. Holding it against my face, I smelled her perfume. The dust whispered in from the outer desert where the scarf had blown in from.

Endless

The desert was whiteness, endless whiteness. "EURY," I yelled over and over across the playa. Panic rose in me. My hands shook as I cupped my mouth and screamed louder, "EURY!"

Did she get drunk and fall out somewhere? Maybe she's at the medical tent? Maybe she's waiting for me at my camp? Maybe, maybe, maybe.

A dark shape was at the very edge of the horizon. I ran to it and it solidified into a person on the ground. "EURY," I sprinted to her but it was the dreadlocked Satyr, his face clawed to ribbons, one eye gouged out.

Ahead was Eury, her dress torn and scorpions crawling over her. Cradling her, I checked her pulse, nothing, checked her breathing, nothing, checked her skin and saw puffy mounds and blue sting marks. Her head flopped in my hands and I lowered my mouth to hers and forced air into her lungs. I pounded her chest and nothing, I straddled her, breathed into her and squeezed her heart to send the blood through her body, to light up her brain, to awaken her face. Nothing.

The Underworld

Night came. The moon was like a lamp above the desert. I cradled her head and said over and over, "Why? Why? Why? Why? Why? Why? Why? Why? Why? Why? Why? Why? Why? Why? Why? Why? Why? Why? Why? Why? Why? Why? Why? Why? Why? Why? Why? Why?"

Kissing her eyes, kissing her lips, kissing her cheeks, kissing her hair, kissing her hands, I felt her body become lighter and her skin drier until she crumbled into sand. There was nothing left of her. I leaned down and wept into her dust, asking her to come back, asking God to bring her back, asking every dimension that existed to unfold itself and reveal where she was so I could be with her again.

Leaning away, I took fistfuls of her dust and wiped it on my face and howled like a dog. Next to me, the Satyr floated by like a man made of white mist caught on wind, drifting into the nighttime desert. Someone else floated by and then another. Looking up and around the moonlit flatland, thousands or even millions of fog-like people were blowing toward the horizon. None had shadows or voices but they flew over the cracked earth almost like human smoke but with faces and bodies as they disappeared into the dark.

The Trials

I got up, legs shaking and saw Eury floating away, far off in the distance.

They all were. Catching my breath, I followed them and walked as they drifted by, some wore hijabs, some U.S. military uniforms, some wore Israeli and Iranian uniforms but many were children.

"Who are you?" I reached out to them but they passed through my hands leaving sweet-tasting water on my fingers, "Are you the dead? Did the war start?"

No one answered but they were carried by the breeze to a glow in the distance. I followed them. When sore, I massaged my feet. When thirsty, I held out my hands and sucked the dew they left in my palms.

Eury looked like a white flag tossed by wind. I thought she'd stop but she never looked back. Blindly stumbling forward, I heard a splash, then another. I was in a black lake, ripples widened around my feet. Wading knee high, I felt something cold slithering by, looked in the waves and saw faces from New Orleans staring at me. They reached up, bumping against the water's surface as if hitting glass. When I bent over, their hands gripped me. Bubbles streamed from their mouths. They were drowning but not dying, just endlessly drowning.

I grabbed their arms but when I pulled up, only water dripped from my fingers. I drove my arms in deeper and knotted my hands in their hands, again I pulled up but only moonlight flashed in my empty palms. Looking into the lake, I saw hundreds swimming toward me, each one thrashing underwater as the air bubbled from their mouths. Covering my eyes, I walked across the lake as the dead swam around me like a school of fish.

"I'm sorry. I'm sorry," I said to them and collapsed on the shore. Eury was gone. The distant glow she and the others were blown toward remained. I brushed the sand from my legs, got up and began again.

Breathing with swollen lips, I ached. Walking on wobbly knees, I ached. Straining to see Eury and finding only night, I grieved. But then I heard a woman's voice.

"Eury," I called out and as I jogged, it became screaming. As I sprinted, it became shrieking. I ran and the dark shapes became round mud huts with U. N. cloth roofs. A burnt army tank sat like a squashed beetle in the sand. I heard her scream from a hut, crawled inside but it was empty. Now I heard men laughing, and gunshots. I ducked and turned and crawled to the next room. Again, empty. Now she was pleading with them to stop. Again, I dashed to the next hut yelling for her but it was bare.

Staggering out, I turned to follow her shrieks but knew I was creating my own Hell. Backing away from the refugee camp, I grabbed sand and stuffed it into my ears until I couldn't hear her anymore. And I ran, ran, ran until my chest burned and legs collapsed under me.

"I can't do this anymore, Eury," I said, "I can't." The glow on the horizon rose as fog-like spirits passed silently by. "Eury, why did you leave?" I asked out loud. "You didn't look back. In your whole zigzag life, have you ever once turned and took in who you left behind?"

Lying on the sand, I closed my eyes, "Are you even there in the last horizon? Are you worth it? We only knew each other for a few hours and I was so willing to give you my whole life. Maybe it was not you, really, but my loneliness that forced me to see you as some salvation."

The faces in the fog changed. The war in the world must have grown. More than soldiers in Iranian, U.S. or Israeli uniforms now, thousands of families floated by. And it was an endless streaming of souls that made walking in between them blind guesswork. But then I saw my mother, my aunt, my uncles and cousins pass by in front of me.

"No," I said, "No. No. No. No." Running, I grabbed at them and yelled their names but they flew ahead to the glow in the distance. "Wait," I screamed, "wait!"

The war, the fucking war was consuming the planet. I chased them across the desert into the glowing phosphorescent vortex where the souls whipped around. The earth cracked like a giant puzzle being broken apart. Huge chunks teetered and dropped into a black void that seemed endless.

Gripping slick stone, I clambered down. For a moment, I stood up and saw the misty faces cascade down like Niagara Falls, a giant whispering roar filled me. Below me, a vast black hole drained hope, drained thought, and drained life. It had no bottom.

Around it swirled a whirlpool of light as soldiers, U.S., Iranian, Israeli, fell in. Whole families fell in. Everyone I saw floating by me in the desert circled around it and was ripped apart. It was the infinite hole between worlds. I saw Eury holding on to a boulder that was crumbling. She looked at me as her face dissolved in the light. Leaping down, I reached out and lost her to the black hole. And then I jumped.

Why are you here?

To bring you back.

There's no me anymore. No one is here, here is waiting to go in. Why are you still you?

I came for you. I found a way out, come with me. The gravity will bring us home. It begins again on the other side, we are new there. You can come with me, we can be us forever, no death, no words, just endless light, come with me.

There's no me, there's only oneness, can you bring us? Your face, it holds a voice. You are heavy. You own the way in and out but only for yourself, it was always for you alone. You lied to keep the invisible moving away. How can we live not being us when names are so heavy? Do you know we are falling to the origin and no one is there to welcome us? It is emptiness within emptiness but every breath can fill you.

If this is the only way, in and through, I am going with you.

How are you still you? You're too heavy for the passing over. Why are you falling with us?

We fell.

The me who was only me opened and inside they were all there, they were always there and within them many more and we had no words, no way of closing, our voices are oceans, we are, we are, we are, we are this oneness asking a name but there is no closing here, only endless opening.

Epilogue

We sat on the shore of an endless sea. She and I naked, our feet washed by the tides. Her face was transparent like a glass mask and within it I saw her whole life in one gaze, I knew every word, every touch that had shaped her. And she, staring at me, knew mine.

I felt a hand on my shoulder. I looked up and saw my Uncle, and his face, like hers, was as glass and I saw in him, his father and the terror he caused in my Uncle and every hurt crossing his life like a shadow, every rage buried and burning in him, every joy in hurting others, including me. He saw in me the child who can never close his eyes for fear of being violated. He knew that I saw him in every person who touched me.

It was all there and we hugged, weeping, letting go and then my Uncle turned to his father who had just hugged his abandoned mother. And my mother came who was just held by her mother who herself was rocked gently by her father. And my former lover who I hurt reached out to me as her sister let go of her and stroked her father who wept in the arms of his wife.

And across the vast beach, everyone I knew and loved or failed to love walked in the dark moist sand or splashed in the water to meet who they had loved or failed to love. White waves rolled in and out. I saw trillions of people crisscrossing the shore, reaching out to each other, forgiving, knowing, and loving. Someone began singing and the song spread. We let all the sacredness of our lives out into the open. This is it how it was when everyone awakened, when everyone sang.